Originally published in two separate volumes as:

Working Mom's Fast & Easy Kid-Friendly Meals © 1998 by Elise M. Griffith
Working Mom's Fast & Easy One-Pot Cooking © 1998 by Jeanne Besser

This 2003 edition is published by Gramercy Books, an imprint of Random House Value Publishing, a division of Random House, Inc., New York, by arrangement with Prima Publishing.

Gramercy is a registered trademark and the colophon is a trademark of Random House, Inc.

Products mentioned in this book are trademarks of their respective companies.

Random House
New York • Toronto • London • Sydney • Auckland
www.randomhouse.com

Printed and bound in the United States of America.

Library of Congress Cataloging-in-Publication Data

Griffith, Elise M.
    Working mom's fast & easy family cookbook : nearly 300 delicious recipes that will have your whole family begging for more / Elise Griffith and Jeanne Besser.
        p. cm.
    Reprint. Originally published: Rocklin, CA : Prima Pub., 1998.
    Includes bibliographical references and index.
    ISBN 0-517-22259-0
        1. Quick and easy cookery. I. Besser, Jeanne. II. Title.

TX833.5.G745 2003
641.5'55—dc21

2003049107

10 9 8 7 6 5 4 3

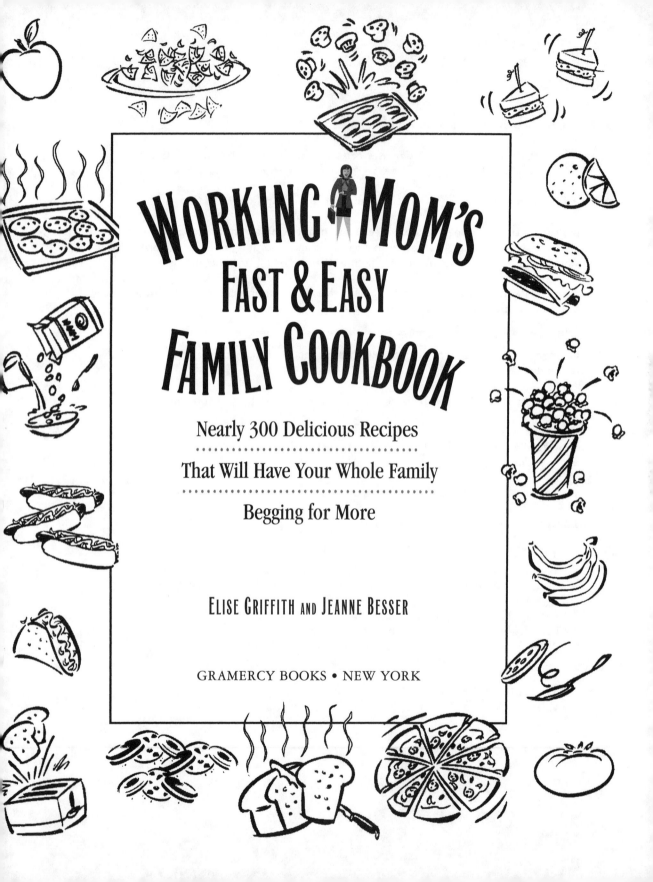

WORKING MOM'S
FAST & EASY
FAMILY COOKBOOK

Nearly 300 Delicious Recipes

That Will Have Your Whole Family

Begging for More

ELISE GRIFFITH AND JEANNE BESSER

GRAMERCY BOOKS • NEW YORK

Contents

· · · · · · · · · · · · · ·

BOOK 1:

WORKING MOM'S FAST & EASY KID-FRIENDLY MEALS

This book is dedicated to my sons,
Bobby and Zachary,
who challenge me to
tickle their tastebuds every day.

Acknowledgments

This cookbook would not have been possible without my husband, Steven Griffith, whose computer expertise and nimble fingers saved the day when I lost a month's worth of work to a technological glitch. Thank you, honey, for your patience, support, encouragement, and willing palate throughout the years.

Special thanks to the many generous folks who tested recipes and cheered me on, including: Pam Branch, Luella Bouchard, Michelle Bouchard-Schmiderer, Betty Hedegus, David Morris, Leon Morris, Joyce Palm, and Audrey Parker. I appreciate each and every one of you more than you know.

Thanks to John and Lisa Meyer for farm fresh eggs throughout the development of this cookbook; they were delicious!

Finally, thanks to Susan Silva and the entire Prima staff for their dedication to providing resources for busy families everywhere.

Contents

3 · Lunch-Box Winners   31

4 • Cook Once, Eat Three Times   49

Contents

5 · Dinner   75

6 · Vegetarian   103

Contents

Better Beans for Picky Kids

7 · Side Dishes   123

Canned Food Wonders (recipes for spruced up staples that kids love—plus seasoning and sauce tips)

Sensational Salads in Seconds

Ready in Minutes Rice and Pasta

8 · Baking   145

9 • Snacks   173

10 · Guest-Pleasing Gourmet   189

11 · Culinary Kids   211

Introduction: Fast, Healthful Meals Are Today's Specialty

They're called "improv-moms," and they're everywhere. Chances are good that if you bought or borrowed this book, you're a whiz at improvisation. You know how to juggle the demands of family and job, multitask with the best of them, and seek out anything that makes your busy life a little easier. You enjoy some old-fashioned values and activities, but you don't have the time your mother or grandmother had available to focus on homemaking. Chances are, instead of spending hours at the ironing board, you send work clothes out to be cleaned and pressed, or you've invested in an easy-care wardrobe. Rather than spending hours in the kitchen creating everything from scratch, you're making use of a new trend in grocery stores nationwide. Welcome to the age of partially prepared foods and fast, easy "sit-down" meals!

More and more busy parents are buying meats, produce, and side-dish items that are ready to go when the dinner hour rolls around. From preroasted chickens and precooked frozen beef strips, to packaged salad greens and microwavable pastas, these convenience foods are giving restaurants a run for their money. Why? Although we're busier than ever before—an estimated 75 percent of us live in dual-income families, and the average American adult works forty-five or more hours per week—we refuse to sacrifice family meal time. It's important to us to gather our children at the table several times a week and reconnect with each other. The partially prepared foods may cost more than "from scratch" recipes, but they're still a lot less expensive than dinner for four at a traditional restaurant. By using all of the products available for today's families, we save both time and money.

One big concern is whether or not these convenience foods enhance the growing focus on healthier eating. Are we sacrificing nutrition in order to cut time in the kitchen? That depends. Federal regulations require all packaged foods to contain nutritional labeling, including the total fat, carbohydrates, and calories for each serving. By learning to read labels (if you are not already doing so), you can all make smart choices for yourself and your family. Additionally, many of the new convenience foods are available in lower-fat and fat-free varieties.

Other trends in today's kitchens include cooking only once or twice a week—which I call "marathon meal preparation"—and assembly-line foods, such as specialty pizzas, tacos, or enchiladas. More and more parents are bringing the kids into the kitchen at mealtime; virtually all of the parenting magazines include articles geared toward grooming junior chefs. It's easy to see that improv-meals help to simplify even the busiest family's life. Yet what if you have the world's pickiest eaters under your roof?

Together in the Kitchen and at the Table

Some well-organized people plan meals a week or more in advance. They coordinate grocery store advertised specials with the menu, only buy what they need, and never, ever "wing it." However many of us are grateful to plan a meal a day or two ahead, and thrilled when it doesn't require another trip to the store. What's a busy, working mom to do? Involve the entire family.

Kids of all ages are fickle creatures. One day they love chicken, and the next day they won't touch it. Perhaps your little baseball pro begs for hot dogs, but your miniature musician demands vegetarian fare. On top of all of that, your teen discovered that his slacks either shrunk two sizes in the wash or his waistline is expanding, and he wants to trim down for an upcoming beach trip. By involving all of your children in meal planning, you can satisfy everyone's tastes (and needs) without opening up a short-order counter. Sounds impossible? What about fat-free chili dogs one night, a hearty veggie pizza the next evening, and Southwestern burgers with nachos at the end of the week? The big plus with each of these entrées is that your children can either pitch in or take over in the kitchen (depending on their ages); you merely supervise the process.

Of course, if you turned over all meal planning and preparation to the younger members of your household, you'd eat nothing but hot dogs, pizzas, and burgers for the next decade. Most kids know little—and care even less—about proper nutrition. You're concerned that they get adequate fruits, vegetables, grains, protein, calcium, iron, and other essential elements in their diet, but they're much more interested in taste. Regardless of how nutritious a meal might be, it needs to be appealing and delicious.

Many of the recipes in this book are geared not only to be simple and healthful, but to tempt the pickiest eater. Several involve more "assembly" than actual cooking, and are low fat to boot! A number of the recipes provide sneaky ways to get essential vegetables and fruits into tiny tyrants; the vegetarian section has tempting entrées that can fool the most dedicated beef eater. Do you sometimes find yourself entertaining unexpected company? You can feed a crowd with some of the recipes, and you'll still spend less than half an hour in the kitchen. Cleanup is also a snap, as all of the items are easy to prepare. Are you a dessert lover, but don't have time to bake and want to cut the fat in your favorite recipes? Then you'll want to whip up some of the no-bake, low-fat, tempting treats in chapter 8.

I believe that mealtime should be enjoyable, and even the busiest families should try to gather at the table as often as possible. No matter how hectic our schedule becomes, we try to sit down together at least five times a week for dinner. It may not always be "gourmet," but it's fast and wholesome. You really can have it all—simple, healthy, kid-pleasing meals in about twenty minutes.

1
GEARING UP

Be prepared—it's a time-honored motto that, implemented in many areas of our lives, helps us achieve greater success. This doesn't mean that we'll never burn a dinner, but if the kitchen is well equipped and the pantry is stocked with basics, we'll be always be ready to rumba when mealtime rolls around. As you read through this chapter, you'll uncover ways to make time in the kitchen more enjoyable . . . and more productive.

Gadgets and Gizmos for Busy Chefs

It used to be that a good set of pots, pans, and bakeware, a mixer, and some basic utensils were enough for an efficient kitchen. Those remain the staple items, but today's busy chef can benefit from several other useful, time-saving tools. Is it worth the investment? I think so. You can save over 100 hours per year in the kitchen with some of the gadgets and gizmos available on the market today. The price tag of new equipment is dropping as more and more cooks across the country look for ways to carve more time for fun and family. And if you're fortunate enough to have a resale shop nearby, you may be able to buy them for less than half their original price.

Pots and Pans

- Look for durable nonstick pots and pans that are both sturdy and heavy. Although most families don't require professional quality equipment, the lowest price point isn't necessarily the best value. Thin aluminum pans with a light Teflon coating will become warped and scratched inside of a year. If you plan to spend a lot of time in the kitchen cooking gourmet meals, and you have about $500 lying around, you can get top-of-the-line cookware that will last a lifetime. Fortunately, a set of new, good-quality cookware should only cost about $100. Farberware, Regal "Club," and T-Fal are brands that have all earned high ratings with reviewers and professional cooks. Purchase pieces one at a time if the cost of a full set doesn't fit your budget.
- Useful pots and pans include: 1-quart, 2-quart, and 5-quart pots with lids; 8-inch and 10- or 11-inch frying pans; and nonstick square griddles—ideal for weekend breakfasts and grilled cheese sandwiches.
- Nonstick bakeware is also essential for healthy, low-fat cooking. An added bonus is that clean-up is easier. You'll

need one or two cookie sheets, round and rectangular cake pans, and a twelve-cup muffin pan. You might also wish to purchase two loaf pans, a square cake pan, and a pizza pan. Chicago Metallic, Ekco, and Revere Ware offer affordable, durable, nonstick sets and individual pieces. Prices range from $5 to $15 per piece, or $20 to $60 per set.

Plug-Ins

- The aroma of freshly baked bread is almost universally comforting. Yet how many busy, working moms have the time to mix, knead, wait for the dough to rise, knead again, shape, wait for a second rise, and then bake for almost an hour? Perhaps a few times a year we'll pull out our favorite recipes, call the kids into the kitchen, and prepare home-made loaves. With a bread machine, your family can enjoy fresh bread any time. For an investment of about $50 to $75 (new) or $25 to $40 (used), you can get a durable, low-noise, basic model that's capable of baking regular and large-sized white, wheat, and sweet breads. For $20 to $30 more, you can get a machine that has dessert options. If you prefer traditional-looking loaves, expect to pay in the neighborhood of $100 for a new machine, or $70 for a quality used machine through a reseller. Brands that have done well in consumer tests include Black and Decker, Oster, Toastmaster, and West Bend.

- No busy kitchen would be complete without a slow cooker, such as a Crock-Pot. If you never thought slow cooking could produce fast healthy meals, you'll want to try a few of the recipes in chapter 5. When shopping for a slow cooker to meet your needs, look for brands and models that offer removable stoneware crocks that can be safely washed in your dishwasher. Prices range from $25 to $40, depending on size and brand. In consumer tests, Proctor Silex, Rival, and West Bend models earned the highest marks.

- Do you remember the harvest gold and avocado electric stand mixers of the 1970s? Chances are, there was one nestled under the cabinet in the kitchen of your childhood home. Today's electric mixers have come a long way, but basic models still whip up tasty batters. If you do a lot of baking from scratch, a stand mixer is a good investment. However, if you're more inclined to pull a packaged mix from the pantry, and your counter space is limited, you'll find a hand-mixer more useful. Unfortunately, hand-mixers have an outdated reputation for being much less powerful than their larger, pricier relatives. Farberware sells a very powerful, five-speed model that includes regular beaters, wire beaters, and dough hooks for about $35. Other models that can take a lot of beating include Black and Decker, Braun, and KitchenAid. Expect to pay a modest $20 to $40 for any 200-watt model.

- For fast preparation of fresh produce, along with other useful tasks, a food processor saves today's busy cook hours of time. If you already own one, you know that you can chop, dice, shred, slice, juice, blend, and mix a multitude of ingredients with this relatively small appliance. Sizes range from 1½-cup-capacity choppers to 11-cup professional models, and prices range from $20 to $200 (or more) for new machines. When you're feeding a family of four or five, a basic 6-cup model with slicing, shredding, and chopping attachments should be adequate, and will cost about $50. For gourmet cooks who prepare many meals and treats from scratch, an investment of $130 will buy a multifunction processor that also includes a dough hook, cream attachment, and citrus juicer. Durable, affordable brands include Black and Decker, Braun, Cuisinart, and KitchenAid.

- Many homes and apartments now come fully equipped with a built-in microwave oven. If you've been using one for a while, try to imagine cooking for one day without it. Today's families use microwave ovens for everything from warming coffee and leftovers to popping popcorn and roasting meat. These time-saving appliances seem "priceless" for the busy cook. You can expect to pay anywhere from $100 to $200 for a basic 1-cubic-foot-capacity model or larger (a larger model can accommodate full meals for a family of four). It's worth the investment. Look for a microwave oven that includes multiple power settings, a defrost option, one-touch keys for common tasks, and a child lock. Most experts recommend 1,000 watts of power; and many new models have shower-wave or double-emission wave systems that are believed to be safer than earlier microwave ovens. Sanyo, Sharp, and Whirlpool are all reputable brands with good consumer reviews.

• A steamer/rice cooker is also a wonderful, inexpensive appliance that affords healthier cooking and eating. Steamed fresh vegetables retain all of their original nutrients, and are ready in minutes with one of these gadgets. Cooks can also expect perfect rice (white, brown, or long grain) every time when using a steamer/rice cooker. What you may not have known is that you can also cook low-fat meats, dumplings, and other foods using your electric steamer. Black and Decker, Farberware, Salton, and Sunbeam earn the highest ratings with nutritionists and busy cooks. Model sizes range from 8-cup to 8-quart capacities, and sell for between $25 and $55.

Those are the basic appliances for today's well-equipped kitchen. Depending on your needs, tastes, time, available space, and interests, you might also consider an electric rotisserie, electric ice cream freezer, clay baker, food grinder, pasta maker, toaster oven, waffle iron, or any of the other dozens of gizmos available on the market. Some cooks can't live without a heavy-duty blender. Others insist that fondue pots will never go out of style. It seemed like every newly married couple in the 1980s received an electric wok as a gift, and not all of them were unloaded through garage sales. Choose the appliances that will do the most work for you, and don't forget to scour resale shops for bargain prices.

Stocking Up on Basic Ingredients

A well-stocked pantry is every working parent's dream, yet many of us dash in and out of the grocery store several times a week for a bag full of items because larger shopping trips are difficult to squeeze into a busy schedule. Avoid long lines at the checkout by planning early-morning grocery trips on the weekends, or pop in after 10 P.M. on week nights. The following grocery list includes all of the basics for fast, family meals:

Nonperishable Items

- cooking spray
- light canola or olive oil
- fat-free mayonnaise and salad dressings
- individual serving cups of applesauce (these are ½-cup servings, perfect for baking)
- sweet potatoes (or 4-ounce jars of strained sweet potato baby food)
- corn flakes
- bread crumbs
- instant mashed potatoes
- instant rice
- thin spaghetti
- vegetable pastas
- quick-cooking oats
- reduced-fat granola-type cereals
- marshmallows
- canned kidney, pinto, white, and black beans
- canned diced tomatoes

- canned vegetable broth and reduced-fat creamed soups
- granulated, powdered, and brown sugars
- whole wheat flour
- all-purpose flour
- packaged biscuit mix
- packaged corn muffin mix
- Rapid Rise (or bread machine) yeast
- baking powder
- cornstarch
- fat-free instant pudding
- powdered milk (premeasured envelopes are the most convenient)
- spices and seasonings
- frozen vegetables and vegetable/pasta mixtures
- frozen apple and orange juice

From the Dairy Section

- nonfat sour cream
- nonfat yogurt (plain and flavored)
- nonfat cream cheese
- fresh eggs (and/or egg substitute)
- 2%-fat milk
- reduced-fat shredded cheeses
- refrigerated canned dough (biscuits, crescent rolls, pizza dough, and so on)
- reduced-fat margarine

Fresh and Frozen Meats

- extra-lean cuts of beef
- extra-lean cuts of pork
- boneless, skinless chicken breasts (or thighs)
- ground turkey
- fresh or frozen seafood

- frozen (cooked) diced chicken or beef
- frozen meatballs

Produce

- packaged salad greens
- packaged sliced mushrooms
- onions
- green and red peppers
- assorted fruits (in season)
- assorted vegetables (in season)

Time-Saving Items

- frozen diced green peppers
- frozen diced onions
- minced garlic in a jar
- roasted red peppers in a jar
- dried herbs
- precooked, roasted whole chicken (from the deli section)
- thick-sliced deli meats (cut into strips for recipes)
- boil-in-bag pastas and rice
- reduced-fat or fat-free salad dressings (for marinades and sauces)
- reduced-fat or fat-free frozen whipped topping
- prepared pizza crusts (such as Boboli brand)
- prepared graham cracker pie shells
- heavy-duty aluminum foil
- freezer bags
- disposable foil pans

Shelf Life and Storage Tips

Can't remember what's in that plastic container in the back of the freezer? Or how long it's been nestled there? Do you have boxes of dry goods that have sat in the cupboard for months? Television news reports warn us about the dangers of tainted foods, but how many of us really know how "safe" our food is? One way you can be sure the foods you're eating are untainted is to store them properly and keep track of expiration dates.

Dry Goods and Canned Foods

- Virtually all packaged foods have an expiration date printed or stamped on the label or box. This date is the last day the store can sell the items; packages that are approaching the expiration are often sold at reduced prices. If you'd like to take advantage of the sale prices, you'll need to use the foods immediately or freeze, if possible.
- Cake mixes, flour, cereals, and other dry goods can be stored in a cool, dry pantry or cupboard for several months. As the expiration date approaches, the same items can be stored in airtight containers in the freezer for up to three months. Be sure to label the freezer bags or containers carefully, noting on the label the date you placed them in the freezer. Items containing yeast (such as packaged bread mixes) should not be frozen in their dry state; it's better to prepare the dough, allow it to rise, punch it down, shape, and then freeze, ready to bake.
- If you live in a warm or humid area, store even your freshest dry goods in airtight containers in the pantry or cupboard. This prevents bacterial and insect contamination, as well as the growth of molds. Be sure your containers are clean and dry before placing any food in them, and seal them tightly. For the safest possible storage, attach labels on the containers, noting the expiration dates from the original packaging. Place an open box of baking soda in the pantry or cupboard as well. Not only will the baking soda

absorb odors, it will help to absorb some of the moisture from the air.

- Canned foods have a long shelf life—as long as the can is not dented, swollen, or showing signs of rust. Again, it's important to check the label dates. You can drain and freeze some canned goods if the expiration date is approaching and you know you won't have the chance to use them quickly. Keep in mind that tomatoes and beans do not freeze well (once thawed, they turn to mush).

Frozen Meats

- Careful handling and thawing of meat is essential, as even the tiniest bit of bacteria causes serious illness in small children. When you've brought the groceries in, wash your hands thoroughly with soap and water before opening, handling, and freezing meats of any kind.
- Label freezer bags carefully, and use the frozen meats within a month or two. Although some meats are considered "safely frozen" beyond the two-month mark, they'll have less chance of contamination (and will taste better) when used quickly.
- Always thaw frozen meats slowly in the refrigerator or quickly in a microwave oven, rather than on a countertop.

Frozen Fruits and Vegetables

- Frozen vegetables and fruits have a long freezer life. Unopened packages can keep safely for six months or more in a storage freezer, or up to six months in the freezer section of your refrigerator.
- Freezer burn can be a problem if the temperature in your freezer is above 32 degrees, or if you live in a humid area. There's nothing worse than planning dinner and discovering that the vegetables are inedible.

- Once opened, reseal freezer packages tightly and use the items as soon as possible.

Perishable Foods

- We've all dealt with soggy lettuce and sprouted potatoes. I sometimes refer to the "vegetable crisper" as the "vegetable rotter." One reason refrigerated produce items become too ripe or moldy is that the drawer contains fungus spores. Be sure to clean out the drawer at least once a month with an antibacterial cleanser or lemon juice. Set the humidity gauge at "low" if your refrigerator has one. Keep a fresh box of opened baking soda on a refrigerator shelf, and a few tablespoons of baking soda in small, open containers in the drawers to reduce odors and humidity.
- Have you ever noticed that fruit baskets containing bananas tend to ripen very quickly? Bananas produce a gas that ripens surrounding fruit at an accelerated pace. So unless you plan to eat all of the fruit quickly, store your bananas in a separate area (away from other produce).
- Apples, peaches, pears, nectarines, and other fresh fruits will keep on the counter for a week, and in the refrigerator for two weeks or more with care.
- Keep potatoes and other root vegetables in dark, cool, dry storage (not in the refrigerator). Most varieties of potatoes will remain fresh for two weeks or more if kept away from light and humidity. Before cooking, remove any green patches or sprouts.
- Consume dairy products such as milk, eggs, and yogurt as soon as possible after purchase. Many cheeses can be stored in the refrigerator for a few weeks safely; remove and discard any mold from hard cheeses before storing or serving. Once opened, use packaged shredded cheese within a week or two for safety. If you buy farm-fresh eggs that have not been treated with chemicals or antibiotics,

use them within one week of purchase and cook them thoroughly.

- Baked goods can be stored in airtight packages in the freezer for several weeks or months. This includes breads, cakes, biscuits, cookies, and other products. The colder your freezer, the longer they'll remain fresh. Label items with the date that they were placed in the freezer, and thaw them in the refrigerator for best results.

Tips for Special Diets

- If allergies are a problem in your family, you might find that the suggested list of pantry and refrigerator items won't work for you. Many people today are on a restricted diet of some kind, which can complicate mealtime for a busy parent. Fortunately, there are wonderful products on the market for just about every dietary problem or concern.

- People with diabetes and ADD require low-sugar diets. Try substituting granulated Equal Measure (a sugar substitute) for the granulated sugar in favorite recipes. Other alternatives include frozen fruit juice concentrates (thawed), or pureed fruits and sweet vegetables. Purchase sugar-free puddings, gelatin, cereals, and other products that have been developed for sugar-restricted menus. Read labels carefully; many canned foods and other packaged items contain sugars. Ground cinnamon, ginger, and nutmeg add sweetness to homemade cookies, muffins, and cakes— without the sugar.

- Low-sodium diets can also restrict food choices. Did you know that the average can of condensed soup has a day's worth of sodium in each serving? Or that the sodium content of many packaged mixes is considered too high for most heart patients? Even reduced-sodium products can contain too much salt for severely restricted diets. Try sodium-free chips, crackers, snacks, and canned foods.

Frozen vegetables without seasonings or sauces are also good choices. Rely on herbs, onions, garlic, diced green peppers, and lemon juice to season meats, poultry, and seafood.

- Children and adults with lactose intolerance might be surprised to discover milk and milk by-products in cold cuts, but it's true: Many varieties of salami contain milk, whey, or sodium casienate (milk protein). Margarine is another hidden source of dairy; buy 100 percent vegetable oil varieties. Canned spaghetti sauce often contains milk products, as do many brands of crackers, snacks, and breads. Careful label reading can help you avoid the hidden milk in many processed foods. Many soy-based substitutes are available in the dairy section of your grocery store. If soy is also a problem in your home, consider goat milk and cheeses for cooking and baking. Many farmers have refined the diet of their animals so that the goat milk tastes nearly the same as cow's milk, but the proteins and sugars in goat milk are often more easily digested (reducing the chance of discomfort or allergic reaction).

Preparing Recipes vs. Assembling Meals

When it comes to meal preparation, many of us are not following grandma's all-day-in-the-kitchen example. That's good news for today's food industry, and it's better news for busy parents everywhere. We've never had more choices when it comes to shopping for quick and easy-to-prepare foods.

The fastest-growing sections in grocery stores today cater to meal assembly. We want "home-cooked" quality without the fuss, and it's available—at a price. A deli-roasted chicken, for example, sells at a 50 percent higher price than an uncooked chicken of comparable size. If time is money, however, then it may be worth the extra expense to dash in and out of the grocery store with dinner in the bag. In less than ten minutes, you can grab everything you need for a delicious, satisfying meal that you'll have on the table before the kids start to bicker. Tonight's menu might look like this:

grilled beef ribs from the deli
foil-wrapped baked potatoes from the deli
fresh, hot rolls from the bakery
packaged salad greens
diced and packaged assorted fresh vegetables
frozen yogurt pops

You'll probably spend between $15 and $17 for the meal; but depending on the size of your family, that will include your brown bag lunch for tomorrow and a snack or two. It's called improvisational cooking, and it usually includes nothing more than quickly warming the food in your oven before serving. According to the food industry and national marketing gurus, this is how we'll be cooking in the twenty-first century.

If you enjoy getting your hands dirty in the kitchen like I do, the recipes in this book are for you. Instead of shopping for ready-to-go meals, you can shop for items that require some cooking time but with less hassle than from-scratch recipes. If you take a quick stroll past the refrigerated butcher section in your local supermarket, you'll discover marinated uncooked meats, assembled uncooked meatballs, cellophane-wrapped packages of roast and vegetables, breaded pork chops, diced and formed potato products, and more. You can find seasoned, uncooked strips of chicken, beef, or pork, and fresh sausages. In the frozen food aisle, you'll find frozen mashed potatoes that can be ready in minutes, and sliced garlic bread that just needs heating.

Even cooking from scratch has taken on a new meaning with faster, easier recipes. If it takes more than an hour or requires more than a dozen ingredients, we probably won't try it. We love the taste of food prepared with love, we just want to accomplish our goal quickly and simply. Sometimes we tackle more elaborate meals, and sometimes we go all out, but most of our recipes have been pared down and streamlined. When our budgets or diets don't allow for prepared and partially prepared foods, cooking from scratch is essential. Did you know that you can prepare two or three days' worth of meals during one session in the kitchen?

Whether you buy a precooked dinner or prepare it from scratch, you can set and maintain a goal of sitting down together for a family meal at least five times a week. If you have picky eaters in your home, don't worry. Here are some menu suggestions based on all three options of meal-making (you'll find the recipes in this book):

Sunday: Specially Seasoned Sirloin and Vegetables, Hearty Oat Bread, tossed salad, and Fast and Low-Fat Pumpkin Pie

Monday: Last-Minute Beef Stew over rice, tossed salad, and Chewy Oatmeal Bars (also great for school lunches)

Tuesday: Chili con Corny, warm flour tortillas, and Rainbow Melon Wedges

Wednesday: Last-Minute Beefy Barbecue Wraps (using leftover chili and tortillas), Creamy Coleslaw, and Frozen Yogurt Pops

Thursday: Deli-roasted chicken (purchased), pasta salad (purchased), Simple Spinach and Broccoli, rolls (purchased), and Easiest Boston Cream Pie

Friday: Elementary Fajita Pitas (using leftover chicken), tossed salad, and Fruit and Easy Mousse

Saturday: Spaghetti and Spicy Meatballs, Easy Italian Pasta Salad, garlic bread, and Almost-Homemade Apple Pie

This cookbook contains ideas to help you make the most of your grocery store, household budget, and time in the kitchen. All of the recipes are quick, easy, and kid-tested for appeal. Since many of the recipes involve assembly, your children can pitch in with the preparation. Who knows? Mealtime might become the most relaxing part of everyone's day . . . the way it used to be.

2
BREAKFASTS

Cranberry-Orange Bars
Out-the-Door Breakfast
Citrus Breakfast Shake
Breakfast Plum-Style "Pudding"
Make-Ahead Carrot-Bran Muffins
Breakfast Brown Rice Pudding
Best Breakfast Turnovers
Sweet Potato Pancakes
All-in-One Cheese Omelet
Bed and Breakfast Quiche
Easy, Cheesy Breakfast Cobbler
Morning Sunrise Cornbread

Breakfast is often the most overlooked (and rushed) meal of the day. It's so simple to grab a processed cereal bar as we dash out the door, or pour a quick bowl of sugar-sweetened puffs before the children's bus arrives. For many years we've been reading that eating a good breakfast helps us perform at our best, but few of us feel we have the necessary time to begin each day with a balanced, healthy meal.

This chapter provides recipes for make-ahead breakfast treats that are portable and healthy. If you have a little more time, there are recipes for quick, easy alternatives to family favorites. Would you like to prepare a special family meal on a weekend morning? You'll find recipes for those, too. And when friends or relatives are visiting, you'll want to try some of the fit-for-a-crowd recipes that are worthy of your own "Bed and Breakfast" kitchen.

Here's a hint—involve your children in the preparation, and you may find that morning rush hour is a lot less stressful.

Cranberry-Orange Bars

These fast, fruity bars are ideal for days when it's your turn to taxi the carpool gang, or when you hit the snooze button one too many times.

2 tablespoons reduced-fat margarine
2 tablespoons orange marmalade
3 cups miniature marshmallows
1 box (13 ounces) cranberry almond crunch cereal
cooking oil spray

Estimated preparation time: 10 minutes
Makes 12 generous bars

1. Place margarine, marmalade, and marshmallows in a large glass mixing bowl.
2. Microwave on high for 2 minutes. Stir. If marshmallows are not completely melted, microwave on high for 1 additional minute.
3. Stir in cereal until well combined and completely coated with marshmallow creme.
4. Lightly coat a 9 × 13-inch baking dish with cooking oil spray. Spread cereal mixture evenly over the bottom. Using a sheet of waxed paper or plastic wrap, gently press cereal mixture tightly and evenly into the pan. Refrigerate until ready to serve.

Out-the-Door Breakfast

1 small banana
¾ cup skim milk
1 container (8 ounces) nonfat
    vanilla yogurt
¼ cup orange juice
2 tablespoons wheat germ

Why spend the money for canned breakfast drinks when this delicious, fruity "shake" is ready in minutes?

Estimated preparation time: 5 minutes
Makes about 2 cups

1. Place all ingredients in blender and pulse until smooth.

Citrus Breakfast Shake

If your children love those frothy orange drinks at the mall, they'll love to start the day with this fruit smoothie!

1 cup drained canned
    mandarin oranges
¾ cup skim milk
1 container (8 ounces) nonfat
    lemon yogurt
¼ cup orange juice
2 tablespoons wheat germ

Estimated preparation time: 5 minutes
Makes about 2 cups

1. Place all ingredients in blender and pulse until smooth.

Breakfast Plum-Style "Pudding"

1 package (0.3 ounces) sugar-
    free cherry gelatin
3 cups low-fat granola with
    raisins
1 teaspoon cinnamon
1 teaspoon nutmeg

Dessert for breakfast? Your children will think that's what they're eating when they try this rich, creamy "pudding."

Estimated preparation time: 8 minutes
Estimated refrigerated time: overnight
Makes 8 servings

1. Mix gelatin as directed on box and pour into sealable storage bowl. Add remaining ingredients and refrigerate overnight.
2. Spoon into small bowls or mugs for a quick, tasty breakfast or snack.

Make-Ahead Carrot-Bran Muffins

These "bakery-style" muffins provide a healthy, hearty, and portable breakfast, and they also make a delicious snack!

2 cups bran cereal
2 cups boiling water
1 package (5 or 6 ounces)
    carrot quick-bread mix
2 teaspoons baking soda
2 containers (4 ounces each)
    egg substitute, thawed
2 cups skim milk
1 cup raisins
½ cup chopped pecans
cooking oil spray (optional)

Estimated preparation time: 15 minutes
Estimated baking time: 15 minutes
Makes 2 dozen bakery-style muffins

1. Preheat oven to 375 degrees.
2. Place bran cereal in a small bowl, pour in boiling water, and let stand until softened.
3. Combine carrot bread mix, baking soda, egg substitute, and milk in a large bowl, then add softened bran mix and stir until blended. Fold raisins and pecans into batter until just moistened.
4. Line nonstick muffin tins with a light coating of cooking oil spray or cupcake papers. Pour in batter.
5. Bake for 15 minutes, or until muffins spring back when lightly touched.

Breakfast Brown Rice Pudding

2 cups cooked brown rice
1 cup nonfat milk
2 teaspoons sugar
⅓ cup raisins
1 container (4 ounces) egg
      substitute, thawed
¼ teaspoon ground cinnamon

On cold, wintry mornings, this breakfast pudding is sure to be a hit—and it's nutritious!

Estimated preparation time: 2 minutes
Estimated cooking time: 17 minutes, including time to set
Makes 4 servings

1. Place rice, milk, and sugar in a medium nonstick pot. Cook over medium-low heat for 10 minutes, stirring occasionally.
2. Add raisins and cook for an additional 2 minutes, then remove from heat.
3. Slowly stir in egg substitute, sprinkle with cinnamon, cover, and let sit for 5 minutes.

Best Breakfast Turnovers

To cut down on preparation time in the morning, prepare the dried fruits for these turnovers ahead of time and store them in a zip-top bag until ready to use.

½ cup dried apricots, chopped
½ cup dried apples, chopped
½ cup raisins
¼ cup shredded coconut
    (optional)
2 tablespoons orange juice
2 cans (8 ounces each)
    refrigerated reduced-
    fat crescent rolls
cooking oil spray
2 or 3 tablespoons nonfat milk
    (optional)

Estimated preparation time: 5 minutes
Estimated baking time: 12 minutes
Makes 8 turnovers

1. Preheat oven to 375 degrees.
2. Combine fruit, coconut, and juice in small mixing bowl.
3. Unroll sheets of crescent roll dough and separate into 16 individual triangles.
4. Place 1 or 2 tablespoons of the fruit mixture in the middle of 8 of the triangles. Carefully arrange each of the remaining triangles on top of the fruited ones. Using a fork, press all edges together tightly.
5. Lightly coat a cookie sheet with cooking oil spray. Place the turnovers on the cookie sheet and brush tops of turnovers with nonfat milk if desired. Bake for about 12 minutes, or until golden brown.

Sweet Potato Pancakes

1 can (16 ounces) sweet
     potatoes, drained
1 egg
⅔ cup nonfat milk
1 cup flour
½ teaspoon salt
1 teaspoon baking powder

What could be better than pancakes on a weekend morning? These are sweet, nutritious, low in fat, and sure to please your gang.

Estimated preparation time: 5 minutes
Estimated cooking time: 4 to 6 minutes each
Makes 8 4-inch pancakes

1. Preheat nonstick griddle or skillet over medium heat.
2. Place sweet potatoes, egg, and milk in blender and puree. Add flour, salt, and baking powder and whip until creamy-smooth.
3. Pour batter onto hot griddle to make 4-inch circles. Cook 2 to 3 minutes on each side, turning carefully. Serve with a light syrup or powdered sugar and cinnamon.

All-in-One Cheese Omelet

Even if you've never made an omelet, you'll get raves for this easy recipe.

Estimated preparation time: 5 minutes
Estimated cooking time: 5 to 7 minutes
Makes 4 servings

1. Preheat medium nonstick skillet over medium-low heat.
2. Place eggs, cottage cheese, and milk in blender and pulse until well blended.
3. Lightly spray hot skillet with cooking oil spray and immediately add egg mixture. Reduce heat to low, sprinkle on pepper and shredded cheese, cover, and cook for 5 minutes.
4. Remove to plate or platter, slice, and serve.

4 eggs, or 2 containers (4 ounces each) egg substitute, thawed
1 cup low-fat cottage cheese
½ cup nonfat milk
cooking oil spray
¼ teaspoon coarsely ground pepper
⅓ cup reduced-fat shredded cheddar cheese

Bed and Breakfast Quiche

2 cartons (4 ounces each) egg
  substitute, thawed
¾ cup nonfat sour cream
1 cup shredded fat-free
  cheddar cheese
2 green onions, finely diced
½ cup leftover chopped
  broccoli, or fresh,
  steamed broccoli that
  has cooled
¼ cup reduced-fat imitation
  bacon bits (optional)
1 purchased prepared frozen
  pie shell, thawed

Your family and guests will feel special when you serve this delicious, low-fat quiche.

Estimated preparation time: 5 minutes
Estimated baking time: 25 minutes, including time to set
Makes 8 servings

1. Preheat oven to 400 degrees.
2. Place egg substitute, sour cream, and shredded cheese in blender; pulse until smooth and well combined. Add onions, broccoli, and imitation bacon bits. Pulse twice to chop—be careful not to pulverize the vegetables.
3. Pour egg mixture into thawed, uncooked pie shell. Cover pie crust edges with thin strips of aluminum foil to protect them from burning.
4. Bake for approximately 20 minutes, or until the top of quiche is golden brown.
5. Remove from oven and allow to cool for 5 minutes before slicing and serving. Quiche should be soft-firm when cut.

Easy, Cheesy Breakfast Cobbler

Try this recipe when you're celebrating a special event or holiday with your family and friends—it makes a wonderful addition to an informal brunch menu.

Estimated preparation time: 5 minutes
Estimated baking time: 15 minutes
Makes 8 to 10 servings

cooking oil spray
1 can (5 ounces) refrigerated reduced-fat biscuits
2 cups fresh, frozen, or canned peaches, diced
1 cup fresh or frozen berries (blueberries or raspberries work best)
1 tablespoon cornstarch
1 cup shredded fat-free cheddar cheese

1. Preheat oven to 375 degrees.
2. Lightly coat a 9 × 13-inch baking pan with cooking oil spray.
3. Arrange biscuits in bottom of baking dish.
4. Place fruit on top of biscuits, and sprinkle with corn-starch. Sprinkle shredded cheese over fruit.
5. Bake for 15 minutes, or until biscuits have puffed and cheese has melted.

Morning Sunrise Cornbread

1 package (7.5 ounces) corn
    muffin mix
1 can (15 ounces) cream-style
    corn
½ cup low-fat cottage cheese
¼ cup water
cooking oil spray
fresh berries or fruit for
    garnish (optional)

This cornbread is an all-day favorite in my home—for breakfast, dinner, or dessert.

Estimated preparation time: 5 minutes
Estimated baking time: 15 to 17 minutes
Makes 6 servings

1. Preheat oven to 400 degrees.
2. Place corn muffin mix, corn, cottage cheese, and water in a medium bowl and stir until well combined. Batter will be lumpy.
3. Lightly coat a 9 × 9-inch baking dish with cooking oil spray and pour in batter.
4. Bake for 15 to 17 minutes or until a toothpick inserted in the center comes out clean.
5. Remove from oven and allow to cool slightly. Serve warm with fresh berries or fruit garnish, if desired.

3
LUNCH-BOX
WINNERS

Freezer Meat-and-Cheese Rolls
Freezer Creamy Vegetable Rolls
Freezer Hero Sandwich Rolls
Hearty Thermos Meaty Stew
Savory Thermos Rice Medley
Toddler-Sized Meaty Biscuit Bites
Preschool Peanut Butter-and-Fruity Roll-Ups
Elementary Fajita Pitas
Easy Cheese Pizza Sandwiches
Triple-Decker Turkey Sandwich
"Oh Bologna" Sandwiches
Turkey-Berry Sandwich Treats
Chicken Confetti Pitas
Cool, Creamy Ham and Fettuccini Salad
Happy Burgers and Fries
Nothing But Nachos

On busy mornings, it can be nearly impossible to get everyone dressed, fed, and out of the door on time; preparing lunches for everyone only adds to the frenzy. That's why food manufacturers came up with packaged lunches that can be slipped into a lunch pail. But those items aren't necessarily healthy or nutritious. Although school lunches are more affordable than restaurant or fast-food meals, my budget can't accommodate hot lunches every day . . . or can it?

This chapter will cover make-ahead recipes using leftovers and staple pantry items to ease morning rush-hour stress. For the sandwich lovers in your home, you'll find recipes listed according to age and taste—including recipes for budding connoisseurs. You don't have to give up fast-food lunches, and you don't have to pay fast-food prices; there are also recipes for healthy alternatives to family favorites. Each of the recipes listed in this chapter have been developed to take the worry out of feeding your lunch crew quickly, nutritiously, and affordably!

Freezer Meat-and-Cheese Rolls

Your children will love to help you assemble these delicious sandwiches, and it's a good way to use up leftover dinner meats.

1 pound frozen bread dough, thawed
2 cups diced cooked ham, chicken, turkey, or beef
1 cup reduced-fat shredded cheddar cheese

Estimated preparation time: 10 minutes
Estimated baking time: 15 to 20 minutes
Makes: 4 servings

1. Divide bread dough into 4 equal portions, and roll each portion into an 8-inch circle.
2. Place ½ cup diced meat and ¼ cup shredded cheese in the center of each dough circle. Fold tightly burrito-style, and place seam-side down on a nonstick cookie sheet.
3. Slide the cookie sheet onto the center rack of a cold oven and set the temperature to 375 degrees. Bake for 15 to 20 minutes, or until golden brown.
4. Remove from oven and allow to cool.
5. Place rolls in sandwich-sized freezer bags and freeze for up to 3 weeks. Place individual rolls in lunch boxes in the morning, and they will thaw by lunchtime.

Note: For "power baking," prepare this plus the following two recipes (at the same time), and you'll have plenty of last-minute sandwiches.

Freezer Creamy Vegetable Rolls

1 pound frozen bread dough,
    thawed
4 tablespoons garden
    vegetable-style cream
    cheese spread
2 cups packaged broccoli slaw

If you think vegetarian sandwiches are less hearty than those with meat, these will surprise you!

Estimated preparation time: 10 minutes
Estimated baking time: 15 to 20 minutes
Makes 4 servings

1. Divide bread dough into 4 equal portions. Roll each portion into an 8-inch circle.
2. Spread 1 tablespoon cream cheese in the center of each dough circle; spoon ½ cup shredded vegetables on top of cream cheese. Fold tightly burrito-style and place seam-side down on nonstick cookie sheet.
3. Slide the cookie sheet onto the center rack of a cold oven and set the temperature to 375 degrees. Bake for 15 to 20 minutes, or until golden brown.
4. Remove from oven and allow to cool.
5. Place in sandwich-sized freezer bags and freeze for up to 3 weeks. Place individual rolls in lunch boxes in the morning, and they will thaw by lunchtime.

Freezer Hero Sandwich Rolls

My guys love Italian-style foods, and these sandwiches are lunchbox favorites—add fresh fruit or salad, and your gang will enjoy a delicious, balanced meal.

1 pound frozen bread dough, thawed
4 teaspoons fat-free Italian dressing
4 slices turkey or beef salami
2 1-ounce slices reduced-fat cheese (any kind), cut in half

Estimated preparation time: 10 minutes
Estimated baking time: 15 to 20 minutes
Makes 4 servings

1. Divide bread dough into 4 equal portions and roll each portion into an 8-inch circle.
2. Spread 1 teaspoon Italian dressing in the center of each dough circle. Top with 1 slice salami and ½ slice cheese. Fold tightly burrito-style and place seam-side down on a nonstick cookie sheet.
3. Slide the cookie sheet onto the center rack of a cold oven and set the temperature to 375 degrees. Bake for 15 to 20 minutes, or until golden brown.
4. Remove from oven and allow to cool.
5. Place in sandwich-sized freezer bags and freeze for up to 3 weeks. Place individual rolls in lunch boxes in the morning, and they will thaw by lunchtime.

Hearty Thermos Meaty Stew

1 cup prepared mashed
    potatoes
⅓ cup water
1 teaspoon beef or chicken
    bouillon (depending on
    meat used)
¼ teaspoon coarsely ground
    pepper
2 cups diced cooked chicken,
    turkey, pork, or beef
2 cups cooked vegetables
    (leftovers work well)

This lunchtime entrée can warm up even the coldest day, and it's lower in fat than canned stew.

Estimated preparation time: 7 minutes
Estimated cooking time: 13 minutes, including reheating
Makes 4 servings

1. Place mashed potatoes, water, bouillon, and pepper in a medium nonstick pot.
2. Cook uncovered over medium-low heat, stirring occasionally, until mixture begins to bubble and bouillon has dissolved, about 4 minutes.
3. Add diced meat and vegetables, and stir.
4. Reduce heat to low, cover, and simmer for an additional 3 minutes.
5. Remove from heat and let cool. Transfer to airtight storage container and refrigerate or freeze. If refrigerated, serve within 4 days; store up to 3 weeks in the freezer.
6. To serve: Reheat refrigerated stew in a microwave oven on high for 6 minutes, stirring once after 3 minutes. Thaw frozen stew in your microwave, then heat as above. Spoon into lunch box thermos containers.

Savory Thermos Rice Medley

If you want to spice up your midday meal, this recipe is sure to please!

2 cups cooked rice
1 can (15 ounces) diced tomatoes
¼ teaspoon curry seasoning
1½ cups diced cooked chicken, turkey, beef, or pork
1 cup cooked vegetables (leftovers work well)

Estimated preparation time: 7 minutes
Estimated cooking time: 13 minutes, including reheating
Makes 4 servings

1. Place rice, tomatoes, and their liquid in a medium nonstick pot. Stir in curry seasoning.
2. Cook uncovered over medium-low heat for 4 minutes, stirring occasionally. Add diced meat and vegetables, stir, reduce heat to low, and simmer uncovered for an additional 3 minutes.
3. Remove from heat and let cool. Transfer to an airtight storage container and refrigerate up to 4 days.
4. To serve: Reheat stew in a microwave oven on high for 6 minutes, stirring once after 3 minutes. Spoon into lunch box thermos containers.

Toddler-Sized Meaty Biscuit Bites

1 cup diced cooked chicken,
   turkey, or beef
½ cup cooked vegetables
   (leftovers work well)
2 tablespoons mayonnaise or
   salad dressing
8 prepared biscuits

These child-sized treats are a great way to sneak vegetables into your toddler's diet.

Estimated preparation time: 10 minutes
Makes 4 servings

1. Place meat, vegetables, and mayonnaise in food processor and pulse until creamy.
2. Split biscuits in half. Fill with about 1 tablespoon plus 1 teaspoon meat mixture.
3. Place 2 filled biscuits in each of 4 sandwich-sized sealable bags. Refrigerate for up to 4 days, or freeze up to 3 weeks for a quick lunch-box treat.

Preschool Peanut Butter-
and-Fruity Roll-Ups

Your young child can help you make these easy, nutritious, and delicious snacks, and they're a healthy alternative to peanut butter and jelly sandwiches.

Estimated preparation time: 10 minutes
Makes 2 servings

3 tablespoons chunky peanut
   butter
½ ripe banana, mashed
¼ cup chopped dried fruit
   (such as raisins,
   apricots, or dates)
2 regular or whole wheat flour
   tortillas

1. Place peanut butter and mashed banana in a small bowl and stir until well combined.
2. Spread half the mixture evenly over each tortilla, sprinkle with fruit, and roll tightly. Place in sealable sandwich bags.

Elementary Fajita Pitas

2 tablespoons reduced-fat or
    regular mayonnaise
2 tablespoons mild salsa
1 cup diced cooked chicken,
    turkey, beef, or pork
2 lettuce leaves
1 whole wheat or regular pita,
    cut in half

Your elementary-school-aged child can make this fun to eat and healthy lunch—and she'll be the envy of the lunchroom.

Estimated preparation time: 10 minutes
Makes 2 child-sized sandwiches, or 1 adult serving

1. Place mayonnaise and salsa in a small bowl and stir until blended. Stir in diced meat.
2. Place 1 lettuce leaf in each pita pocket, and spoon equal portions of meat mixture into each. Carefully slide pitas into sealable sandwich bags.

Easy Cheese Pizza Sandwiches

Nearly everyone loves pizza, and your elementary-school-aged child can make these very quickly.

2 teaspoons Italian dressing
2 English muffins, split
2 thin slices tomato
2 slices (1 ounce each)
      part-skim mozzarella
      cheese

Estimated preparation time: 8 minutes
Makes 2 child-sized sandwiches, or 1 adult serving

1. Spread 1 teaspoon Italian dressing on each of 2 English muffin halves.
2. Place 1 slice of tomato and 1 slice of cheese over dressing, and top with remaining muffin halves. Carefully wrap sandwiches in plastic wrap or aluminum foil.

Triple-Decker Turkey Sandwich

2 teaspoons reduced-fat
   mayonnaise
3 slices whole wheat bread
2 thin slices cooked turkey,
   chicken, or beef
2 thin slices tomato
1 fresh spinach leaf

*Older children have larger appetites; your fourth-
or fifth-grade child will love making this extra-
special sandwich.*

Estimated preparation time: 10 minutes
Makes 1 hearty, low-fat sandwich

1. Spread 1 teaspoon of mayonnaise on top of each of 2 slices of bread.
2. Layer the ingredients: 1 slice bread, 1 slice meat, 1 slice tomato, 1 slice bread, 1 slice meat, 1 slice tomato, spinach leaf, 1 slice bread (without mayonnaise).
3. Slice sandwich in half diagonally, secure with toothpicks, and place in a sealable or fold-over sandwich bag.

"Oh Bologna" Sandwiches

An alternative to "plain" sandwiches or burgers, your preteen will enjoy eating this sandwich with homemade tortilla chips and fruit.

2 hamburger-style buns
4 teaspoons Dijonnaise brand
     creamy mustard
4 slices reduced-fat bologna
2 slices 2%-fat American
     cheese
2 thin slices tomato
2 small lettuce leaves

Estimated preparation time: 5 minutes
Makes 2 sandwiches

1. Spread each half of both buns with 1 teaspoon Dijonnaise.
2. Layer each bottom half as follows: 1 slice bologna, 1 slice cheese, 1 slice bologna, 1 slice tomato, 1 lettuce leaf, and bun top. Secure with toothpicks and slide into sealable or fold-over sandwich bags.

Turkey-Berry Sandwich Treats

4 slices (¼ inch each)
    purchased reduced-fat
    pound cake, toasted
2 tablespoons reduced-fat
    cream cheese spread
2 slices cooked turkey or deli
    turkey lunchmeat
2 tablespoons cranberry sauce

Healthy, hearty, and delicious, this unusual sandwich is great for using up Thanksgiving leftovers. Try it for a special, post-holiday treat!

Estimated preparation time: 10 minutes
Makes 2 sandwiches

1. Spread each of 2 toasted pound cake slices with 1 tablespoon cream cheese spread.
2. Place 1 slice turkey and 1 tablespoon cranberry sauce on each, and top with remaining slices of poundcake. Wrap and pack in lunch box.

Chicken Confetti Pitas

Go from boring to "boss" with this sandwich alternative. For extra nutrition, purchase whole wheat pita breads.

2 cups shredded cooked
    chicken
1 cup packaged coleslaw
½ cup reduced-fat shredded
    cheddar cheese
2 teaspoons Thousand Island
    dressing
2 pita breads, cut in half

Estimated preparation time: 8 minutes
Makes 4 pitas, or 2 adult-sized servings

1. Place chicken, vegetables, and cheese in a medium bowl and combine. Drizzle with dressing and toss gently.
2. Spoon mixture into each pita half. Wrap individually, or store in airtight plastic containers.

Cool, Creamy
Ham and Fettuccini Salad

1 tablespoon reduced-fat
    mayonnaise
¼ cup honey-mustard dressing
4 cups cooked fettuccini
    noodles, rinsed and
    drained
¼ cup diced green onions
3 thin slices cooked ham, cut
    into thin strips
1 cup frozen peas and carrots,
    thawed

On warm days, or when a microwave is not easily available, this creamy salad will win rave reviews from your gang.

Estimated preparation time: 15 minutes
Estimated refrigeration time: overnight
Makes 4 to 5 servings

1. In a medium bowl, whisk together mayonnaise and honey–mustard dressing. Add remaining ingredients and toss until well combined. Chill overnight.
2. Divide recipe evenly into 4 or 5 one-pint airtight containers. Salad can be safely refrigerated for up to 5 days.

Happy Burgers and Fries

Would you like to give your child a special lunch without the extra fat or expense? This recipe will help you make him feel like a lunchtime king!

Estimated preparation time: 10 minutes
Estimated baking time: 15 minutes
Makes 4 servings

1. Preheat oven to 400 degrees.
2. Lightly coat a nonstick cookie sheet with cooking oil spray. Place vegetarian burgers at each of the four corners of the cookie sheet.
3. Drop frozen shoestring potatoes in a large paper bag, sprinkle with cornstarch and seasoned salt, fold the top of the bag, and shake vigorously. Spread coated potatoes on cookie sheet and mist lightly with cooking oil spray.
4. Slide the cookie sheet onto the center rack of the oven and bake for 15 minutes, or until potatoes are slightly golden.
5. Remove cookie sheet from oven. Assemble sandwiches (hot vegetarian burgers, cheese, and condiments) on whole wheat buns. Serve with slightly cooled fries.

....

Note: Consider saving small, inexpensive stickers or toy items throughout the year to include with your Happy Burger meals.

....

cooking oil spray
4 preformed frozen vegetarian burgers (traditional-style)
1 bag (16 ounces) frozen shoestring potatoes
2 tablespoons cornstarch
1 tablespoon seasoned salt
4 slices 2%-fat American cheese
pickles, mustard, ketchup, to taste
4 whole wheat hamburger-type buns

Nothing But Nachos

½ pound purchased baked
    tortilla chips
1 can (14 ounces) nonfat
    refried beans
1 can (15 ounces) diced
    tomatoes and chilies,
    drained
1 cup reduced-fat shredded
    cheddar cheese

Nachos are fast, fun, and yummy snacks, but this recipe also makes a balanced, nutritious meal. Your children will want to help you whip it up and gobble it down!

Estimated preparation time: 10 minutes
Estimated baking time: 10 minutes
Makes 6 to 8 servings

1. Preheat oven to 350 degrees.
2. Arrange tortilla chips along the sides of a large, oven-safe platter. Spoon refried beans into center, and top with tomatoes and cheese. Place the platter on the center rack of the hot oven and bake for 10 minutes, or until cheese melts.
3. Remove from oven, place on hot pad in the center of table, and enjoy.

4
COOK ONCE, EAT THREE TIMES

Specially Seasoned Sirloin and Vegetables

Last-Minute Beef Stew

Steak and Tomato Baked Bruschetta

Marvelous Microwave Meatloaf

Cheesy Meatloaf Burgers

Zesty Meatloaf Salad

Honey-Mustard Roasted Chicken Breasts

Easy Chicken Tacos

Fuss-Free Chicken Potpie Casserole

Almond Chicken Cups

Grilled Dilled Salmon Steaks

Scrambled Egg and Salmon Frittata

Orange-Baked Catfish

Saucy Seafood Burgers

Oven-Fried Cod

South of the Border Pork Roast

Zesty Pork and Tortilla Soup

Easy Pork Enchiladas

Pork Chops with Blackberry Mustard Sauce

Hawaiian Pork Buns

Almost-Traditional Turkey Dinner

Turkey-and-Stuffing Custard Cups with Cranberry Sauce

Spicy Ground-Turkey Meatballs

Spaghetti and Spicy Meatballs

Today's weekdays and nights are filled with activities and commitments. When you want to make the most of your time in the kitchen, prepare basic dishes that can become the foundation for several evening meals. You can also plan a marathon cooking session on Saturday or Sunday and prepare a week's worth of dinners in a few hours.

This chapter includes simple beginnings and fast encores—the recipe for each main dish is be followed by at least two ideas for the leftovers. Consider cooking two or three main dishes at one time and freezing the items you won't be consuming in a few days. To make even better use of your time, cook one of the main course recipes for Crock-Pots in chapter 5 while you're preparing one or more of these.

Beginning with recipes for beef, you'll find enough ideas for several weeks' worth of menus. Don't forget that many grocery stores today sell partially-prepared items like meatballs and chicken or pork strips, and those foods can be substituted according to your time, budget, and tastes.

One note: Cooked fish doesn't always refreeze well, so the recipes for seafood leftovers have been developed to keep (with care) for a day or two. For safety purposes, no pork recipes call for cold, cooked pork, and all recipes have been designed for well-done main course meats.

Specially Seasoned Sirloin and Vegetables

By taking advantage of extra lean cuts of meat, this beefy recipe is less fatty than traditional pot roast and vegetables, without sacrificing taste. Serve this roast with a tossed green salad and dinner rolls.

Estimated preparation time: 10 minutes
Estimated baking time: 2 to 3 hours
Makes 8 to 10 servings

1. Preheat oven to 325 degrees.
2. Place sirloin in medium to large roasting pan. Spread steak sauce on top, and sprinkle with pepper and basil. Arrange vegetables along sides of meat.
3. Cover tightly with aluminum foil, place in oven, and bake for 2 to 3 hours (about 40 minutes per pound of meat), or until well done.

1 lean sirloin roast (3 to 4 pounds)
2 tablespoons A-1 Bold and Spicy steak sauce
½ teaspoon coarsely ground pepper
2 tablespoons chopped fresh sweet basil
12 small red potatoes, unpeeled
1 package (16 ounces) peeled baby carrots
1 jar (8 ounces) pearl onions, drained

Last-Minute Beef Stew

2 cups chopped cooked sirloin
from Specially
Seasoned Sirloin and
Vegetables (recipe,
page 51)
1 cup ready-made reduced-fat
beef gravy
remaining potatoes from
Specially Seasoned
Sirloin and Vegetables
(recipe, page 51),
quartered
remaining carrots from
Specially Seasoned
Sirloin and Vegetables
(recipe, page 51), cut
in half
1½ cups frozen peas, thawed

This is an ideal recipe for a satisfying, last-minute meal from leftovers; it's also great with frozen meatballs in place of the beef (and is no less quick to prepare). When you've made one meal of Specially Seasoned Sirloin and Vegetables, chop 2 cups of leftover meat, make the following recipe, and freeze it for another meal. Serve with sliced French bread or garlic bread.

Estimated preparation time: 15 minutes
Estimated cooking time: 10 minutes
Makes 4 servings

1. Place all ingredients in medium nonstick pot and stir.
2. Cover and cook over medium heat until gravy begins to boil, stirring occasionally.

Steak and Tomato Baked Bruschetta

Looking for a lighter alternative to a steak and vegetable dinner? This is it! Serve with a tossed salad or sliced fruit, and enjoy the compliments.

Estimated preparation time: 15 minutes
Estimated baking time: 10 minutes
Makes 4 to 5 servings

1. Preheat oven to 400 degrees.
2. Arrange bread slices side by side on nonstick cookie sheet. Brush bread with Italian dressing, sprinkle with chopped sirloin, and add tomato quarters and Parmesan cheese.
3. Bake for 10 minutes and serve immediately.

1 loaf (12 ounces) fresh Italian bread, cut diagonally into 1-inch-thick slices
3 tablespoons fat-free Italian dressing
1½ cups finely diced cooked sirloin from Specially Seasoned Sirloin and Vegetables (recipe, page 51)
½ pint cherry tomatoes, quartered
¼ cup finely shredded Parmesan cheese

Marvelous Microwave Meatloaf

2 pounds extra-lean ground
     beef
1 egg
1 cup bread crumbs
1 package (1.25 ounces)
     teriyaki seasoning mix
cooking oil spray

Many of us consider meatloaf a "comfort" food; but few of us have time to prepare it—this recipe whittles your time in the kitchen by half.

Estimated preparation time: 10 minutes
Estimated cooking time: 32 minutes, including cooling
    time
Makes 8 servings

1. Preheat oven to 375 degrees.
2. Place all ingredients in large mixing bowl, folding and stirring until well combined.
3. Lightly coat 9 × 4¾-inch glass loaf pan with cooking oil spray. Form meat mixture into loaf shape and place in pan.
4. Microwave meatloaf on high for 12 minutes. Transfer to preheated oven and bake for 15 minutes. Remove from oven and allow to cool for 5 minutes before slicing.

· · · · · · · · · · · · · · · ·

Note: Serve this favorite with mashed potatoes, steamed vegetables, and rolls.

· · · · · · · · · · · · · · · ·

Cheesy Meatloaf Burgers

What is meatloaf if not hamburger? Try this burger recipe for a quick, lazy-day dinner or lunch on the run.

Estimated preparation time: 10 minutes
Estimated baking time: 10 to 15 minutes
Makes 4 servings

1. Preheat oven to 325 degrees.
2. Wrap burger buns in foil. Lay meatloaf slices flat on a large piece of foil and wrap.
3. Warm buns and meatloaf in oven for 10 to 15 minutes.
4. Remove buns and meatloaf from oven and assemble burgers. Serve with baked potato chips and fresh fruit.

4 whole wheat burger buns
4 slices leftover meatloaf (from Marvelous Microwave Meatloaf recipe, page 54)
4 slices (1 ounce each) 2%-fat American cheese
4 slices tomato
4 leaves lettuce
ketchup, mustard, pickles, or other condiments, to taste

Zesty Meatloaf Salad

1 tablespoon oil
dash chile oil
2 slices leftover meatloaf
(from Marvelous
Microwave Meatloaf
recipe, page 54)
1 package (12 ounces) salad
greens
1 small red onion, sliced into
thin rings
1 small green pepper, cut into
thin strips
½ pint cherry tomatoes,
quartered

Your family will be surprised by the taste and texture of this delicious entrée. Serve this unusual salad with the dressing of your choice and plenty of fresh bread.

Estimated preparation time: 15 minutes
Estimated cooking time: 4 minutes
Makes 6 servings

1. Preheat a medium nonstick skillet over medium heat, and add the oils.
2. Sauté the meatloaf slices for 2 minutes on each side. Remove and dice into cubes.
3. Place salad greens in large serving bowl, top with vegetables, and sprinkle with cubed meatloaf.

Honey-Mustard Roasted Chicken Breasts

Serve this delicious chicken with steamed rice and vegetables. My picky five-year-old gave this recipe two thumbs up—your children will love it, too!

cooking oil spray
8 boneless, skinless chicken breasts
1 small red onion, sliced into thin rings
1 teaspoon garlic powder
1 bottle (12 ounces) reduced-fat honey-mustard dressing

Estimated preparation time: 10 minutes
Estimated baking time: ½ hour
Makes 8 servings, or 4 servings if you reserve half the meat

1. Preheat oven to 375 degrees.
2. Lightly coat a 9 × 13-inch baking dish with cooking oil spray. Arrange chicken breasts in the bottom, spread onion slices over chicken, and sprinkle with garlic powder. Pour the entire bottle of dressing over all.
3. Cover baking dish with foil and bake for ½ hour, removing foil during last 10 minutes.

• • • • • • • • • • • • • • •

Note: Here's a time-saving tip: When the cooked chicken has cooled enough to be handled, dice or slice half the total yield for use in other recipes—it will keep in the refrigerator for up to 3 days in an airtight container.

• • • • • • • • • • • • • • •

Easy Chicken Tacos

2 cups diced chicken meat
    from leftovers
1 can (15¼ ounces)
    Del Monte Fiesta corn
1 cup salsa
12 packaged taco shells
1 cup reduced-fat shredded
    cheddar cheese

This tasty, colorful alternative to fast-food tacos is as fun to make as it is to eat.

Estimated preparation time: 10 minutes
Estimated cooking time: 10 minutes
Makes 6 servings

1. Place chicken, corn, and salsa in medium pot and heat over low heat, stirring occasionally, until hot.
2. Spoon the heated filling into prepared taco shells, sprinkle with cheese, and serve.

Fuss-Free Chicken Potpie Casserole

At the end of a long, tiring day nothing could be simpler than this low-fat recipe using leftover chicken.

Estimated preparation time: 15 minutes
Estimated baking time: 20 minutes
Makes 8 servings

1. Preheat oven to 375 degrees.
2. Place the chicken, mixed vegetables, soup, and cheese in a large mixing bowl and stir until well combined.
3. Lightly coat a 9 × 13-inch baking dish with cooking oil spray. Open 1 can crescent rolls, unroll dough sheet (do *not* separate the rolls), and press into bottom of baking dish. Spoon meat and vegetable mixture onto the dough and spread evenly.
4. Open remaining can of dough, unroll, place on top of meat and vegetable mixture, and press. Pinch edges of dough to seal.
5. Bake for 20 minutes, or until dough is cooked and filling is bubbly.

1½ cups diced cooked chicken breast
1 can (15 ounces) mixed vegetables, drained
1 can (10¾ ounces) reduced-fat cream of mushroom soup
½ cup fat-free shredded cheddar cheese
cooking oil spray
2 cans reduced-fat crescent rolls

Almond Chicken Cups

½ cup chopped red bell
    pepper
½ cup chopped onion
2 cups chopped cooked
    chicken (leftovers
    work well)
⅔ cup bottled sweet and sour
    sauce
½ cup whole almonds
6 flour tortillas (6 inch)

These attractive, tasty "cups" will win over anyone who normally turns down "leftovers."

Estimated preparation time: 10 minutes
Estimated baking time: 12 to 15 minutes, including cooling time
Makes 12 chicken cups

1. Preheat oven to 400 degrees.
2. Place pepper, onion, chicken, sweet and sour sauce, and almonds in a medium bowl. Toss gently to combine.
3. Cover tortillas with a damp paper towel and microwave on high for 30 seconds to soften.
4. Cut each tortilla in half. Place each half in a paper-lined muffin tin. Fill each tortilla with ¼ cup chicken mixture.
5. Bake for 8 to 10 minutes, until chicken mixture is hot. Remove from oven and allow to cool for 5 minutes before serving.

Grilled Dilled Salmon Steaks

This salmon is great with a simple side dish of steamed rice and vegetables. If you have any left-over salmon, flake it and use it to make the Scrambled Egg and Salmon Frittata that follows.

4 small salmon steaks
    (¼ pound each)
2 tablespoons olive oil
2 tablespoons freshly
    squeezed lemon juice
2 teaspoons chopped fresh dill
    weed

Estimated preparation time: 5 minutes
Estimated cooking time: 10 to 14 minutes
Makes 4 servings

1. Preheat the broiler or grill.
2. Rinse salmon steaks and pat dry.
3. Mix oil, lemon juice, and dill in a small bowl and stir briskly to combine. Brush over steaks.
4. Grill or broil salmon, turning once, until cooked through (about 5 to 7 minutes a side). Serve immediately.

Scrambled Egg and Salmon Frittata

2 tablespoons light canola oil
3 cups frozen hash brown
    potatoes, thawed
8 eggs, or 4 containers egg
    substitute, thawed
¾ cup nonfat sour cream
2 teaspoons chopped chives
1 cup flaked, cooked salmon
    (from Grilled Dilled
    Salmon Steaks recipe,
    page 61)

Simple to prepare and ready in twenty minutes or less, this dinner is a lifesaver on busy nights.

Estimated preparation time: 10 minutes
Estimated cooking time: 7 to 10 minutes
Makes 8 servings

1. Preheat large nonstick skillet over medium heat. Add canola oil, and spread hash brown potatoes evenly over bottom of pan.
2. Place eggs, sour cream, and chives in medium bowl and whisk together. Stir in flaked salmon.
3. Pour egg mixture over potatoes, cover, reduce heat to low, and simmer for 7 to 10 minutes.
4. Slide frittata onto a serving dish, cut into wedges, and serve.

Orange-Baked Catfish

Tender, tangy, and low in fat, this dish proves that fish doesn't need to be fried in order to be delicious. Serve it with wild rice and salad for a truly special treat your family will love.

¼ cup frozen orange juice
    concentrate, thawed
1 tablespoon light canola oil
2 tablespoons lemon juice
1 teaspoon minced garlic
⅛ teaspoon coarsely ground
    pepper
4 to 6 catfish fillets

Estimated preparation time: 5 minutes
Estimated baking time: 12 to 15 minutes
Makes 4 to 6 servings

1. Preheat oven to 400 degrees.
2. Place orange juice, oil, lemon juice, garlic, and pepper in small bowl. Stir to combine.
3. Arrange fish fillets in the bottom of nonstick 9 × 13-inch baking pan and pour sauce over fish.
4. Place fish on the center rack of the oven and bake for 12 to 15 minutes.

Saucy Seafood Burgers

2 cups leftover cooked
    seafood, flaked
2 green onions, chopped fine
1 egg
¾ cup dried bread crumbs
1 tablespoon prepared
    mustard
½ teaspoon prepared
    horseradish
4 whole wheat hamburger-
    style buns

Leftover fish doesn't need to be thrown away. Try these burgers with oven "fries" and fresh fruit.

Estimated preparation time: 10 minutes
Estimated baking time: 12 minutes
Makes 4 servings

1. Preheat oven to 400 degrees.
2. In medium bowl, blend seafood, onion, egg, bread crumbs, mustard, and horseradish until well combined. Shape into 4 equal patties.
3. Place patties on a nonstick cookie sheet and bake for 12 minutes. Remove from oven, place on burger buns, and garnish to taste.

Oven-Fried Cod

As a child, I looked forward to the all-you-can-eat fish fry at Fass Brothers restaurant. I can achieve the same results today with much less fat, and you can, too.

2 tablespoons reduced-fat mayonnaise
2 tablespoons fat-free honey-mustard dressing
1 teaspoon lemon juice
⅔ cup dried bread crumbs
⅓ cup finely crushed corn flakes
6 cod fillets, thawed if frozen

Estimated preparation time: 15 minutes
Estimated baking time: 10 to 12 minutes
Makes 6 servings

1. Preheat the oven to 425 degrees.
2. Thoroughly combine mayonnaise, dressing, and lemon juice in a pie tin. Combine bread crumbs and crushed corn flakes in a second pie tin.
3. Dredge cod fillets first in wet ingredients, and then in dry ingredients. Be sure to coat fillets completely with each dredge.
4. Place on nonstick baking sheet and bake for 10 to 12 minutes.

Note: Serve these fillets with oven fries and coleslaw.

South of the Border Pork Roast

1 lean pork roast (3 to 4
     pounds)
⅓ cup dry red wine
¼ cup fat-free Italian dressing
1 teaspoon minced garlic
2 tablespoons chili powder
¼ teaspoon ground cumin

No one will believe that this spicy, savory roast was prepared using only five ingredients!

Estimated preparation time: 5 minutes
Estimated baking time: 2 to 3 hours
Makes 8 to 10 servings

1. Preheat oven to 350 degrees.
2. Place pork in medium roasting pan.
3. Whisk together the remaining ingredients in a small bowl and pour over the meat.
4. Bake for 2 to 3 hours, or until well done.

Note: Serve this flavorful roast with rice, beans, and a tossed salad.

Zesty Pork and Tortilla Soup

Would you like a "South of the Border," balanced dinner that's ready to serve before the evening news ends? Then you'll love this one-pot meal!

1 can (15 ounces) diced tomatoes
1 can (8 ounces) tomato sauce
1 can (4 ounces) diced green chilies
¼ cup chopped cilantro
2 cups shredded cooked pork (from South of the Border Pork Roast recipe, page 66)
3 cups water
6 corn tortillas (6 inch), cut into strips

Estimated preparation time: 10 minutes
Estimated cooking time: 10 minutes
Makes 6 servings

1. Place all ingredients except tortilla strips into medium nonstick pot and bring to a low boil.
2. Reduce heat to low, stir in tortilla strips, and simmer for 2 to 3 minutes.

Easy Pork Enchiladas

2 cups shredded cooked pork
2 green onions, diced
½ cup picante sauce
cooking oil spray
6 corn tortillas (6 inch)
1 cup reduced-fat shredded
    cheddar cheese

Picky eaters will gobble up these enchiladas with glee; serve them with rice, nonfat refried beans, and a tossed salad.

Estimated preparation time: 15 minutes
Estimated baking time: 10 minutes
Makes 6 servings

1. Preheat oven to 350 degrees.
2. Place pork, onions, and ¼ cup picante sauce in small bowl and combine.
3. Lightly coat both sides of each corn tortilla with cooking oil spray. Layer between paper towels and microwave for 30 seconds.
4. Spoon meat mixture into center of each tortilla, roll enchilada-style, and place seam-side down in nonstick 9 × 13-inch baking dish. Spoon remaining picante sauce over enchiladas and top with shredded cheddar cheese.
5. Bake for 10 minutes.

Pork Chops with Blackberry Mustard Sauce

These sweet and tangy pork chops can be used in a variety of unusual recipes. Shred leftover meat and serve on burger buns with sliced, golden tomatoes, and your family will feel they're being treated to gourmet fare!

6 lean pork sirloin or loin chops
1 cup fresh blackberries
¼ cup Dijon mustard
3 tablespoons honey
1 tablespoon red wine vinegar
1 teaspoon thyme
¼ teaspoon salt
¼ teaspoon pepper

Estimated preparation time: 5 minutes
Estimated baking time: 45 minutes
Makes 6 servings

1. Preheat oven to 400 degrees.
2. Arrange pork chops in the bottom of 9 × 13-inch baking pan.
3. Place the remaining ingredients in blender and pulse until smooth. Pour over meat.
4. Cover baking dish with foil and bake for 45 minutes.

Hawaiian Pork Buns

1 can (15 ounces) refrigerated
    pizza dough
2 cup diced cooked pork
¼ cup frozen orange juice
    concentrate, thawed
¼ cup crushed pineapple
1 tablespoon minced cilantro

Use the leftover meat from the Pork Chops with Blackberry Mustard Sauce recipe (page 69) for extra zing in this quick, easy dish.

Estimated preparation time: 10 minutes
Estimated baking time: 20 minutes
Makes 6 servings

1. Preheat oven to 375 degrees.
2. Unroll refrigerated pizza dough. Slice in half lengthwise and in thirds horizontally to form 6 squares. Press each square of dough to flatten.
3. Combine remaining ingredients in small bowl, tossing to coat pork thoroughly.
4. Using a slotted spoon, drop one-sixth of the meat mixture into the center of each square, fold up corners, and pinch to seal.
5. Place buns on a nonstick baking sheet and bake for 20 minutes or until golden brown.

Almost-Traditional Turkey Dinner

Turkey dinners remind us of hearth and home but are time consuming and messy to prepare. This is a faster, simpler alternative with all the flavor your family expects.

Estimated preparation time: 15 minutes
Estimated baking time: 25 minutes
Makes 6 servings

2 tablespoons light canola oil
6 fresh turkey breast slices
1 package (6.9 ounces) chicken flavor rice mix (such as Rice-A-Roni brand)
3 cups cornbread cubes for stuffing
3 cups hot water
1 cup dried cranberries
4 leaves fresh spinach, chopped fine, or 1 cup frozen chopped spinach, thawed and patted dry
1 jar (16 ounces) reduced-fat turkey gravy

1. Preheat the oven to 350 degrees.
2. Heat medium nonstick skillet over medium heat. Add oil, and quickly brown both sides of each turkey slice. Set aside.
3. Place chicken flavored rice mix, cornbread cubes, and hot water in large mixing bowl. Toss to combine, and allow to sit for 2 minutes. Add the dried cranberries and chopped spinach, and toss. Spread mixture evenly in the bottom of nonstick 9 × 13-inch baking dish. Arrange browned turkey slices over stuffing, and the pour entire jar of gravy over all.
4. Bake for 25 minutes, until heated through.

....

Note: A double-leftover bonanza: Serve this leftover turkey-day meal with salad and rolls. Then use the left-overs from this meal to make Turkey-and-Stuffing Custard Cups with Cranberry Sauce (page 72).

....

Turkey-and-Stuffing Custard Cups
with Cranberry Sauce

2 cups diced cooked turkey
    breast
2 cups leftover stuffing,
    slightly warmed (not
    hot)
1 container (4 ounces) egg
    substitute, thawed, or
    two eggs, beaten
cooking oil spray
1 cup canned jellied cranberry
    sauce
6 large lettuce leaves

These meal-in-a-muffin custard cups are portable, packable, and ideal for last minute dinners or picnics. Although small, they're very rich—they can also be individually wrapped and frozen for quick lunchtime fare.

Estimated preparation time: 10 minutes
Estimated baking time: 12 minutes
Makes 6 servings

1. Preheat the oven to 400 degrees.
2. Combine turkey, stuffing, and eggs or egg substitute in medium bowl.
3. Lightly coat muffin tin with cooking oil spray. Spoon turkey and stuffing mixture into prepared muffin cups. Place on center rack of the oven and bake for 12 minutes.
4. Place the jellied cranberry sauce in glass measuring cup and microwave on high for 1 minute. Stir, and microwave for an additional 30 seconds (the sauce will be very hot).
5. Arrange lettuce leaves on each dinner plate. Place 2 turkey-and-stuffing custard cups on each leaf, and drizzle with cranberry sauce.

Spicy Ground-Turkey Meatballs

You can purchase prepared meatballs in the freezer section of your grocery store, yet budget-conscious cooks will appreciate the savings these lower-fat meatballs provide.

1 pound ground turkey
¼ cup diced green pepper (fresh or frozen)
¼ cup diced onions (fresh or frozen)
¼ teaspoon chili powder
1 egg
¾ cup Italian-seasoned bread crumbs
2 tablespoons light canola oil
1 cup water

Estimated preparation time: 5 minutes
Estimated cooking time: 15 minutes
Makes approximately 24 meatballs

1. Preheat large nonstick skillet over medium-low heat.
2. Place ground turkey, green pepper, and onions in medium bowl, and combine. Sprinkle with chili powder, add egg and seasoned bread crumbs, and mix well. Form into 1-inch balls.
3. Add oil to skillet and brown meatballs over medium-low heat, turning carefully. When meatballs have browned, add water and simmer until all liquid has evaporated (about 10 minutes).

. . . .

Note: When these meatballs have cooled slightly, place them in zip-top freezer bags and freeze for up to 2 months. Use them in other recipes, such as Spaghetti and Spicy Meatballs (page 74).

. . . .

Spaghetti and Spicy Meatballs

1 pound spaghetti, cooked
1 jar (28 ounces) chunky
    spaghetti sauce
12 Spicy Ground-Turkey
    Meatballs (recipe,
    page 73)

The microwave oven makes this classic even easier, and you can add fresh herbs, mushrooms, or other favorites according to your family's tastes.

Estimated preparation time: 5 minutes
Estimated cooking time: 10 minutes
Makes 6 generous servings

1. Place the spaghetti noodles in a large, microwavable serving bowl. Pour the spaghetti sauce over the pasta and arrange the meatballs on top.
2. Cover with plastic wrap and microwave on medium-high for 10 minutes.

Note: Serve with tossed salad and garlic bread.

5
DINNER

If you regularly put in long hours at work, battle rush-hour traffic, or act as taxi driver for multiple weekday-evening events, you know how important it is to have a collection of "ready when you are" dinner recipes on hand. That's what this chapter is all about—providing you with a little kitchen magic.

Each of the soup recipes listed can be assembled in the morning and heated quickly in the evening. The Crock-Pot entrées go together in minutes and simmer happily while you're busy with the rest of your life. Or, when the pantry is almost bare, grab a few supermarket ingredients on your way home to make a meal in minutes.

If you love freshly baked breads but don't feel you have the time to make them, you'll love the simple bread machine recipes—and they can be served with most of the dinners in this cookbook. With all of the ideas on the following pages, you'll be ready to unwind and enjoy a waiting meal at the end of your busy day.

Simply Creamy
Chicken-Vegetable Soup

A handful of ingredients, one pot, three minutes of preparation time, and ten minutes to serve. What could be easier?

Estimated preparation time: 3 minutes
Estimated cooking time: 10 minutes
Makes 8 servings

2 cups diced cooked chicken
(leftovers work well)
1 cup cooked rice (leftovers
work well)
1 can (15 ounces) mixed
vegetables, drained
1 can (15 ounces) cream-style
corn
1 cup water
salt and pepper, to taste

1. Place all ingredients in medium nonstick pot. Cook over medium heat, stirring occasionally.
2. When soup begins to bubble, remove from heat and serve.

....

Note: Serve this soup with fresh bread or reduced-fat biscuits.

....

Two-Step Pepperoni Minestrone

1 can (15 ounces) Italian-style
    diced tomatoes
1 can (8 ounces) tomato sauce
1 can (16 ounces) red kidney
    beans, drained
2 cups packaged coleslaw
1 package (3.5 ounces)
    pepperoni slices,
    halved
4 cups water
½ cup uncooked bow-tie pasta

Pepperoni soup? It's simple, zesty, and sure to please the pickiest eaters.

Estimated preparation time: 10 minutes
Estimated cooking time: 10 minutes
Makes 6 servings

1. Combine canned tomatoes, tomato sauce, and kidney beans in medium nonstick pot. Stir. Add vegetables and pepperoni, and stir again. Add water and pasta.
2. Bring soup to low boil over medium heat, reduce heat to low, cover, and simmer for 5 minutes.

Note: Serve with garlic toast and fresh fruit.

Easy Corn Bisque

For everyone who loves traditional corn chowder (but doesn't want the traditional fat and calories), this bisque is a delicious surprise.

Estimated preparation time: 5 minutes
Estimated cooking time: 12 minutes, including setting time
Makes 6 servings

1 can (16 ounces) sweet potatoes, drained
2 cans (15 ounces each) cream-style corn
½ cup diced onion (fresh or frozen)
1 teaspoon minced garlic
½ teaspoon coriander
½ teaspoon sage
1 cup nonfat sour cream

1. Place sweet potatoes, corn, onion, garlic, coriander, and sage into blender and pulse until smooth. Continue, or refrigerate until ready to use.
2. Pour pureed corn mixture into a medium nonstick pot. Heat on low until mixture begins to bubble, stirring occasionally. Remove from heat and cool for 2 minutes.
3. Stir in sour cream and serve.

Really Easy Roast Beef

1 lean beef roast (2 or 3
   pounds), frozen or
   partially frozen (any
   cut, shaped to fit your
   Crock-Pot)
1 pound small, unpeeled red
   potatoes
1 package (16 ounces) peeled
   fresh baby carrots
½ pound fresh snap peas in
   pods (if available)
1 can (15 ounces) French
   onion soup
½ cup water

Five minutes preparation in the morning is all it takes for this "down home" recipe that's ready when you are. Serve with fresh bread and salad if desired.

Estimated preparation time: 5 minutes
Estimated cooking time: 8 to 10 hours
Makes 8 servings

1. Place roast in the bottom of Crock-Pot and arrange potatoes, carrots, and peas around meat. Pour the can of soup and water over meat and vegetables.
2. Cover and cook on low for 8 to 10 hours.

Three-Star Chuck Roast

Sometimes the simpler the recipe, the better the meal; such is the case with this family favorite. You don't need fancy seasonings to get stellar reviews at dinner time.

1 boneless chuck roast
    (3 pounds)
½ teaspoon salt
½ teaspoon coarsely ground
    pepper
¼ teaspoon garlic powder
½ cup chopped onion (fresh
    or frozen)

Estimated preparation time: 3 minutes
Estimated cooking time: 7 to 8 hours
Makes 8 servings

1. Place roast in Crock-Pot and sprinkle with salt, pepper, garlic powder, and onion.
2. Cover and cook on low for 7 to 8 hours.

Really Simple Roasted Chicken

1 roasting chicken (4 to 5
    pounds)
½ teaspoon salt
½ teaspoon coarsely ground
    pepper
½ teaspoon dried thyme
¼ teaspoon garlic powder

Chicken can be prepared safely in a slow cooker. Be sure to drain and discard the drippings, and store any leftover chicken in a clean container in the refrigerator.

Estimated preparation time: 5 minutes
Estimated cooking time: 7 to 8 hours
Makes 4½ cups cooked chicken, or serves 8

1. Remove giblets from chicken. Reserve for later use (boil giblets in a small amount of water until cooked, and freeze or refrigerate) or discard.
2. Rinse chicken in cold water, drain, and place breast side up in the Crock-Pot. Sprinkle with salt, pepper, thyme, and garlic powder.
3. Cover and cook on low for 7 to 8 hours.

Caribbean One-Pot Chicken

For chicken with a little more zing, prepare this recipe for your gang. Use any leftovers in a simple, savory salad.

Estimated preparation time: 5 minutes
Estimated cooking time: 5 to 8 hours
Makes 6 servings

6 boneless, skinless chicken breasts
1 can (15 ounces) mandarin oranges, drained
1 red onion, thinly sliced
1 cup orange juice
¼ teaspoon garlic powder
½ teaspoon ground ginger

1. Arrange chicken breasts in the bottom of Crock-Pot and top with oranges and onion slices. Pour orange juice over all, and sprinkle with garlic powder and ginger.
2. Cover and cook on low for 5 to 8 hours.

Year-Round BBQ Chicken

2 pounds frozen chicken
thighs (to reduce fat,
purchase boneless,
skinless variety)
½ cup Kentucky Bourbon
½ cup A-1 Bold and Spicy
steak sauce
¼ teaspoon Chinese hot
mustard
1 tablespoon vinegar
2 tablespoons honey
½ cup warm water
3 bell peppers (1 each red,
yellow, and green)
sliced (optional)

Summer months aren't the only time of year you can enjoy barbecued chicken. This recipe also works well with beef or pork ribs.

Estimated preparation time: 5 minutes
Estimated cooking time: 6 to 8 hours
Makes 6 servings

1. Allow chicken thighs to partially thaw, and arrange in the bottom of a Crock-Pot.
2. Place remaining ingredients except peppers in large glass measuring cup or small glass bowl. Whisk together until well blended, then pour over the chicken.
3. Cover and cook on low for 6 to 8 hours. If desired, add peppers during the last hour of cooking.

Note: Serve with rice, salad, and rolls.

Favorite Braised Lamb Chops

If you think lamb dishes are too complicated to tackle in your kitchen, you'll be surprised at how easy this is to prepare.

Estimated preparation time: 7 minutes
Estimated cooking time: 6 to 8 hours
Makes 6 to 8 servings

1. Arrange the lamb chops in the bottom of a Crock-Pot and cover with the onion slices.
2. Place remaining ingredients except potatoes in a small bowl and whisk until well blended. Pour over meat and onions.
3. Cover and cook on low for 6 to 8 hours. If desired, add potatoes during the last hour of cooking, increasing setting temperature to high.

. . . .

Note: Serve with salad and fresh bread.

. . . .

2 to 3 pounds lean lamb chops
1 small sweet onion, thinly
　　　sliced
½ cup Heinz 57 sauce
¼ cup reduced-sodium soy
　　　sauce
2 teaspoons chopped fresh
　　　rosemary (if using the
　　　dry variety, reduce to 1
　　　teaspoon and crush to
　　　release flavor)
½ teaspoon minced garlic
½ cup warm water
8 small, unpeeled red potatoes
　　　(optional)

Power-Dinner Pork Roast

1 boneless pork roast or
    tenderloin (3 to 4
    pounds)
⅔ cup fat-free Italian dressing
½ teaspoon dried rosemary

Three ingredients and three minutes' preparation time make one powerful meal for busy cooks everywhere.

Estimated preparation time: 3 minutes
Estimated cooking time: 7 to 8 hours
Makes 8 servings

1. Place pork roast in Crock-Pot. Pour Italian dressing over meat, and sprinkle with rosemary.
2. Cover and cook on low for 7 to 8 hours.

Hearty Ham and Apples

This recipe has won rave reviews with my family and friends—try it and take your own bows.

1 turkey ham (3 pounds)
1 can (16 ounces) light apple
    pie filling
¼ teaspoon ground ginger
¼ teaspoon cinnamon

Estimated preparation time: 5 minutes
Estimated cooking time: 5 to 8 hours
Makes 6 to 8 servings

1. Place ham in Crock-Pot. Pour apple pie filling over ham, and sprinkle with ginger and cinnamon.
2. Cover and cook on low for 5 to 8 hours.

Crowd-Pleasing Bratwurst

12 fresh bratwurst (about 3
     pounds)
1 medium sweet onion,
     quartered
1 medium red onion,
     quartered
1 red, 1, green, and 1 yellow
     bell pepper, cored,
     seeded, and sliced into
     strips
1 can (12 ounces) beer
½ cup water
12 hamburger-style buns

Looking for the perfect recipe for your tailgate picnic? This is it!

Estimated preparation time: 10 minutes
Estimated cooking time: 6 to 8 hours
Makes 10 to 12 servings

1. Arrange bratwurst and vegetables in bottom of Crock-Pot, and cover with beer and water.
2. Cover and simmer on low for 6 to 8 hours. Discard broth.
3. Serve on hamburger buns.

. . . .

Note: Accompany this dish with creamy potato salad and salad greens.

. . . .

Shrimp and Veggie Empanadas

Supermarket staples make this recipe a mom's best friend, and the kids love it, too!

Estimated preparation time: 5 minutes
Estimated baking time: 20 minutes
Makes 4 servings (2 large empanadas)

1. Preheat oven to 400 degrees.
2. Combine rice, sour cream, and cheese in a large mixing bowl. Gently stir in tomato, broccoli, and shrimp.
3. Spoon half the rice mixture onto the center of each pie crust. Gently fold crust to form half-moon shape, then press with a fork to seal edges.
4. Place empanadas on a nonstick cookie sheet, and bake for 20 minutes, or until golden brown. Cut in half and serve.

2 cups cooked rice (leftovers work well)
½ cup nonfat sour cream
½ cup shredded reduced-fat cheddar cheese
1 medium tomato, diced fine
1 cup cooked chopped broccoli (leftovers work well)
1 package (6 ounces) frozen cooked shrimp, partially thawed
1 package (15 ounces) refrigerated unbaked pie crust (2 crusts)

In-a-Flash Chicken Empanadas

2 cups diced cooked chicken
(leftovers or packaged,
frozen)
1 can (15 ounces) whole-
kernel corn, drained
¼ cup diced green pepper
(fresh or frozen)
¾ cup chunky salsa
1 package (15 ounces)
refrigerated unbaked
pie crust (2 crusts)
1 cup shredded reduced-fat
cheddar cheese

Because you just can't have too many empanada recipes . . .

Estimated preparation time: 5 minutes
Estimated baking time: 20 minutes
Makes 4 servings (2 large empanadas)

1. Preheat oven to 400 degrees.
2. Combine chicken, corn, pepper, and salsa in a large mixing bowl.
3. Spoon half the mixture onto each pie crust, and sprinkle half the cheese over the mixture. Gently fold crust to form half-moon shape, then press with a fork to seal edges.
4. Place empanadas on an ungreased cookie sheet and bake for 20 minutes, or until golden brown. Cut in half and serve.

Winning Beef and Vegetables

My youngest is suspicious of most entrées that contain a lot of vegetables, but he eats this without complaint.

Estimated preparation time: 5 minutes
Estimated cooking time: 15 minutes
Makes 6 servings

1 tablespoon canola oil
½ cup chopped onion (fresh or frozen)
2 cups chopped cooked beef (from leftovers)
1 can (15 ounces) diced tomatoes
1 can (15 ounces) mixed vegetables, drained

1. Preheat nonstick skillet over medium heat.
2. Add oil and sauté onions, stirring frequently. Add beef, tomatoes, and vegetables and stir.
3. Reduce heat to low and simmer for 10 minutes.

. . . .

Note: Serve over cooked pasta or rice for success with your picky eaters.

. . . .

Creamy Beef Stroganoff

2 cups diced cooked beef
    (from leftovers)
1 can (10.75 ounces) reduced-
    fat cream of
    mushroom soup
1 can (15 ounces) mixed peas
    and carrots, drained
1 cup sliced fresh mushrooms
1 package (16 ounces) egg
    noodles, cooked and
    drained

Beef Stroganoff used to take hours to prepare, but not any more!

Estimated preparation time: 5 minutes
Estimated cooking time: 7 to 8 minutes
Makes 6 to 8 servings

1. Place beef, soup, peas and carrots, and mushrooms in microwavable casserole dish.
2. Microwave for 5 minutes on high, then stir. Microwave for an additional 2 to 3 minutes on high, and stir again.
3. Serve over noodles.

Creamy Ham and Vegetables

This is a great way to use up leftover ham. Serve over cooked rice or biscuits.

Estimated preparation time: 4 minutes
Estimated cooking time: 7 minutes
Makes 6 servings

2 cups diced cooked ham
    (leftovers work well)
1 can (10.75 ounces)
    condensed cream of
    celery soup
⅓ cup skim milk
1 can (15-ounces) mixed
    vegetables, drained
¼ teaspoon coarsely ground
    pepper

1. Place all ingredients in microwavable casserole dish.
2. Microwave on high for 3 minutes, then stir. Microwave for an additional 3 to 4 minutes on high, and stir again.

Golden Ham and Pasta Salad

1 package (12 ounces) spiral
    pasta, cooked and
    drained
2 cups diced cooked ham
    (leftovers work well)
1 can (8 ounces) French-style
    green beans, drained
1 can (8 ounces) sliced
    carrots, drained
½ cup fat-free honey-mustard
    salad dressing
¼ cup golden raisins

Your children will love the sweet, tangy flavor and golden raisins in this special salad.

Estimated preparation time: 5 minutes
Estimated cooking time: 8 minutes (pasta)
Estimated refrigeration time: 20 minutes
Makes 6 servings

1. Place all ingredients in large salad bowl and toss to combine. Chill before serving.

Ham and Cheese Burritos

Try these for breakfast, brunch, lunch, dinner, or snacks . . . they're so easy and yummy, it's hard to limit them to one meal.

1½ cups diced cooked ham
　　(leftovers work well)
1 cup reduced-fat shredded
　　cheddar cheese
2 green onions, finely
　　chopped
6 flour tortillas (8 inch)

Estimated preparation time: 5 minutes
Estimated baking time: 10 minutes
Makes 6 servings

1. Preheat oven to 350 degrees.
2. Place diced ham, cheese, and onions in medium bowl and toss to combine.
3. Spoon mixture into center of tortillas and fold burrito style.
4. Arrange burritos on nonstick cookie sheet and bake for 10 minutes, until cheese is melted.

Basic Bread Machine Mix

3 cups flour
2 tablespoons sugar
1 tablespoon powdered skim
    milk
1½ teaspoons salt
2¼ teaspoons bread machine
    yeast

> *I adore my bread machine, but can't always afford the prices of fancy bread mixes. This basic recipe can be adapted many, many ways, as you'll see in the recipes that follow.*

Estimated preparation time: 5 minutes
Makes 3 cups bread mix, enough for 1 loaf (1½ pounds)

1. Combine all ingredients.
2. Store in an airtight container and refrigerate for up to 3 weeks.

Savory Herbed Bread

I prefer to use fresh herbs whenever possible, but slightly crushed dried herbs work well in this recipe.

Estimated preparation time: 5 minutes
Estimated baking time: varies according to bread machine
Makes 12 slices (1½-pound loaf)

1 cup warm water
Basic Bread Machine Mix (recipe, page 96)
1 tablespoon reduced-fat margarine
1 tablespoon fat-free grated Parmesan cheese
½ teaspoon thyme
½ teaspoon oregano

1. Pour warm water into bread machine. Add bread mix and remaining ingredients.
2. Select basic/white cycle on machine and press start.
3. Remove bread from pan while still warm. Allow to cool, then slice and serve.

Spicy Pepper Bread

1 cup warm water
Basic Bread Machine Mix
    (recipe, page 96)
2 tablespoons canola oil
2 tablespoons diced red
    pepper (fresh, frozen,
    or canned)
1 teaspoon lemon pepper
    seasoning

My recipe testers raved about this adaptation for the basic bread mix recipe; it'll be a hit in your home, too.

Estimated preparation time: 5 minutes
Estimated baking time: varies according to bread
   machine
Makes 12 slices (1½ pound loaf)

1. Pour warm water into bread machine. Add bread mix and remaining ingredients.
2. Select basic/white cycle on machine and press start.
3. Remove bread from pan while still warm. Allow to cool, then slice and serve.

Sour Cream and Chives Bread

Even if you never thought of sour cream and chives in a bread recipe before, you'll be convinced that this combination works when you try it.

Estimated preparation time: 5 minutes
Estimated baking time: varies according to bread
    machine
Makes 12 slices (1½-pound loaf)

1 cup warm water
Basic Bread Machine Mix
    (recipe, page 96)
¼ cup instant mashed potato
    flakes
⅓ cup fat-free sour cream
1 tablespoon chopped fresh
    chives

1. Pour warm water into bread machine. Add bread mix and remaining ingredients.
2. Select basic/white cycle on machine and press start.
3. Remove bread from pan while still warm. Allow to cool, then slice and serve.

Breakfast Bread

1 cup warm water
¼ cup frozen orange juice
    concentrate, thawed
Basic Bread Machine Mix
    (recipe, page 96)
¾ cup fat-free granola
2 tablespoons nonfat plain
    yogurt

I have baked this many times by setting the bread machine timer to have warm bread ready when the alarm clock interrupts my slumber—it's delicious!

Estimated preparation time: 5 minutes
Estimated baking time: varies according to bread machine
Makes 12 slices (1½-pound loaf)

1. Pour warm water into bread machine.
2. Pour thawed frozen orange juice concentrate into glass measuring cup. Microwave on medium for 20 seconds.
3. Add warm orange juice to the water in the bread machine. Add bread mix and remaining ingredients.
4. Select sweet cycle on machine and press start.
5. Remove bread from pan while still warm. Allow to cool, then slice and serve.

Hearty Oat Bread

Oats add body and texture to this special winter adaptation (but you can enjoy it any time of year).

Estimated preparation time: 5 minutes

Estimated baking time: varies according to bread machine

Makes 12 slices (1½-pound loaf)

1¼ cups warm water
Basic Bread Machine Mix (recipe, page 96)
½ cup old fashioned oats
2 tablespoons dark brown sugar
2 tablespoons nonfat plain yogurt

1. Pour warm water into bread machine. Add bread mix and remaining ingredients.
2. Select sweet cycle on machine and press start.
3. Remove bread from pan while still warm. Allow to cool, then slice and serve.

6

VEGETARIAN

Vegetable Pizza Calzones
Easy Italian Pasta Salad
Lemon-Pepper Pasta and Black Bean Salad
Simple Summer Salad
Terrific Tortellini Salad
Berry Delicious "Chicken" Salad
Surprising Taco Pizza
Simply Surprising Family-Sized Calzone
Smooth and Creamy Chili-Mac
Farm Vegetable Ragout in Crust
Creamy Coleslaw
Colorful Bean Salad
Classic Spinach Salad
Tomato and Spinach Salad
Full-Meal Salad
Cilantro Black Beans and Rice
Kid-Pleasing Tomato Cups
Chili con Corny

Whether you're a full-fledged vegetarian, or you're just trying to eat healthier, today's grocery products help to make meatless eating more delicious and enjoyable. Some of the recipes in this chapter may be familiar to you, and others may surprise you; but all require a minimum of ingredients, preparation, cooking, and clean-up time.

Many busy cooks rely heavily on make-ahead meals, so you'll find several recipes for days when time is at a premium. You'll also find several recipes that utilize partially prepared or frozen meat substitutes . . . and if you don't tell your family, they'll probably never notice. When a festive dinner is in order, try a few of the gourmet-style recipes (they're easier than you think to whip up). And for those households—like mine—where beans aren't a popular entrée, you'll discover spruced-up recipes that your kids will eat.

Vegetable Pizza Calzones

These rolled-up-pizzas have been a hit with dozens of folks, and are sure to bring compliments to the chef.

Estimated preparation time: 10 minutes
Estimated baking time: 9 to 13 minutes
Makes 6 calzones

1. Preheat the oven to 425 degrees.
2. Lightly coat cookie sheet with cooking oil spray. Unroll pizza dough onto cookie sheet, and cut into six equal rectangles.
3. Place tomatoes, onions, peppers, and cheese in large bowl and mix to combine.
4. Divide vegetable and cheese mixture into six even portions. Put one portions on each rectangle and spread slightly. Starting at the longest side of each rectangle, fold dough over and fold to form a turnover-shaped packet. Pinch to seal edges. When done, they should resemble the commercial "hot pockets."
5. Bake for 9 to 13 minutes, or until tops of calzones are golden brown.

cooking oil spray
1 can (10 ounces) refrigerated pizza crust dough
1 can (15 ounce) diced tomatoes, drained
⅓ cup chopped onions (fresh or frozen)
⅓ cup diced green peppers (fresh or frozen)
1¼ cups shredded Italian-seasoned mozzarella cheese

Easy Italian Pasta Salad

1 package (12 ounces) roasted
    garlic and red bell
    pepper rotelle pasta
3 cups chopped fresh broccoli
4 large carrots, thinly sliced
1 can (19 ounces) chick-peas,
    drained and rinsed
1 cup fat-free Italian salad
    dressing
¼ cup fat-free grated
    Parmesan cheese
    (optional)

You can use this salad as a hearty main dish, or a savory side dish at potluck dinners and picnics.

Estimated preparation time: 10 minutes
Estimated cooking time: 8 minutes
Estimated refrigeration time: 20 minutes
Makes 8 servings

1. Bring a large pot of water to a rolling boil. Add pasta, reduce heat to medium, and simmer, stirring occasionally, until pasta is tender. Drain and rinse with cold water.
2. Place cooked pasta, broccoli, carrots, and chick-peas in large bowl, and toss lightly. Drizzle salad dressing over pasta and vegetables and toss again.
3. Cover salad with plastic wrap and refrigerate for at least 20 minutes. Sprinkle with Parmesan cheese before serving, if desired.

Lemon-Pepper Pasta and Black Bean Salad

This winning pasta salad was the result of grabbing a handful of items from the pantry and improvising—it's best chilled, but can be served warm.

Estimated preparation time: 10 minutes
Estimated cooking time: 8 minutes
Estimated refrigeration time: 20 minutes
Makes 8 servings

1 package (12 ounces) lemon-pepper penne rigate pasta
1 can (16 ounces) black beans, drained and rinsed
1 medium tomato, diced
1 cup frozen peas, thawed
¼ cup freshly squeezed or bottled lemon juice
¼ cup honey

1. Bring a large pot of water to a rolling boil. Add pasta, reduce heat to medium, and simmer, stirring occasionally, until pasta is tender. Drain and rinse with cold water.
2. Place cooked pasta, black beans, tomato, and peas in large bowl, and toss gently.
3. Place lemon juice and honey in small bowl and stir until honey has dissolved. Drizzle lemon and honey mixture over pasta and vegetables, then toss to coat.
4. Cover salad with plastic wrap and refrigerate for at least 20 minutes before serving.

Simple Summer Salad

1 package (12 ounces) elbow
    macaroni, uncooked
1 can (15 ounces) whole-
    kernel corn, drained
    and rinsed
2 cups diced zucchini
1 cup chopped dried apricots
2 tablespoons diced green
    onion
¾ cup fat-free honey-mustard
    salad dressing
2 honeydew melons,
    quartered, seeds
    scooped out (optional)

For steamy evenings when it's just too hot to cook, toss this salad together and serve with fresh bread or rolls.

Estimated preparation time: 10 minutes
Estimated cooking time: 8 minutes
Estimated refrigeration time: 20 minutes
Makes 8 servings

1. Bring a large pot of water to a rolling boil. Add pasta, reduce heat to medium, and simmer, stirring occasionally, until pasta is tender. Drain and rinse with cold water.
2. Place cooked pasta, corn, zucchini, apricots, and onion in large bowl, and toss gently. Drizzle salad dressing over pasta, vegetables, and fruit, and toss again.
3. Cover salad with plastic wrap and refrigerate for at least 20 minutes. Serve in quartered honeydew melons, if desired.

Vegetarian

Terrific Tortellini Salad

Young children especially love this tasty treat, and it's satisfying enough to handle big appetites.

Estimated preparation time: 5 minutes
Estimated cooking time: 10 minutes
Makes 6 servings

2 packages (9 ounces each) refrigerated cheese-filled tortellini
1 pound asparagus, sliced into 1-inch inch pieces
1 pound cherry tomatoes, halved
2 tablespoons chopped fresh basil
⅔ cup fat-free Caesar salad dressing

1. Bring a large pot of water to a rolling boil. Add tortellini, reduce heat to medium, and simmer, stirring occasionally, until pasta is tender. Add asparagus pieces during last 2 minutes of cooking. Drain and rinse with cold water.
2. Place tortellini and asparagus in large bowl, add tomato and basil, and toss gently. Drizzle pasta and vegetables with salad dressing, and toss again. Serve immediately.

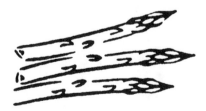

Berry Delicious "Chicken" Salad

1 can (16 ounces) diced
    peaches in juice,
    drained, juice reserved
2 tablespoons rice vinegar
1 tablespoon honey
1 package (16 ounces) salad
    greens
2 cups canned imitation diced
    chicken ("vegetable
    protein," available in
    the health food section
    of most grocery stores)
2 cups fresh raspberries
½ cup sliced celery

Although no animal meat is used in this recipe, your family (or guests) will never know, and the sweet, tangy dressing makes the salad special.

Estimated preparation time: 10 minutes
Makes 6 to 8 servings

1. Put reserved juice from peaches in small bowl, add rice vinegar and honey, and stir until dissolved.
2. Place salad greens, peaches, imitation chicken, raspberries, and celery in large bowl, and toss gently. Drizzle dressing over salad, and toss again.
3. Serve immediately, or refrigerate until ready to serve.

Surprising Taco Pizza

My guys love this pizza, and it's far healthier than anything that can be delivered. Better yet, it's ready in a flash!

Estimated preparation time: 3 minutes
Estimated baking time: 15 minutes
Makes 12 square slices of pizza

cooking oil spray
1 can (10 ounces) refrigerated
    pizza crust dough
½ cup picante sauce
1½ cups Harvest Burgers For
    Recipes (meat
    substitute)
1 cup shredded fat-free
    cheddar cheese

1. Preheat oven to 400 degrees.
2. Lightly coat a cookie sheet with cooking oil spray. Press canned pizza dough evenly onto the cookie sheet and spread picante sauce over dough. Sprinkle with meat substitute, then with cheese.
3. Bake for about 15 minutes, or until cheese begins to bubble.

Simply Surprising
Family-Sized Calzone

2 cups Harvest Burgers For
    Recipes (meat
    substitute)
1 cup shredded reduced-fat
    Italian cheese mixture
1 medium tomato, diced
2 green onions, finely diced
½ teaspoon Italian seasoning
½ teaspoon garlic powder
1 can (10 ounces) refrigerated
    pizza crust dough

When your gang is gathered 'round the television watching the big game, pop this in the oven and prepare for enthusiastic praise!

Estimated preparation time: 5 minutes
Estimated baking time: 20 minutes
Makes 6 servings

1. Preheat oven to 400 degrees.
2. Place meat substitute, shredded cheese, tomato, and green onions in medium mixing bowl. Add Italian seasoning and garlic powder and toss lightly to mix.
3. Unroll pizza crust dough on a clean, flat surface. Spoon filling into the center of the dough (lengthwise). Carefully pull up the sides of the dough and pinch together in a seam down the center; roll and pinch ends to seal.
4. Bake for about 20 minutes, or until golden brown. Allow to cool slightly before slicing and serving.

Vegetarian

Smooth and Creamy Chili-Mac

> *If hearty appetites demand a hot, filling meal, serve up this chili with rolls or cornbread.*

Estimated preparation time: 3 minutes
Estimated cooking time: 12 minutes
Makes 8 hearty servings

1. Place all ingredients except sour cream in medium nonstick pot. Heat over medium-low heat until mixture begins to bubble, stirring occasionally.
2. Reduce heat to low, cover, and continue cooking for 5 to 7 minutes, or until macaroni is cooked thoroughly.
3. Serve in individual bowls. Top with a dollop of nonfat sour cream if desired.

1 can (15 ounces) diced tomatoes
1 can (10 ounces) tomato soup
1½ cups water
1 can (16 ounces) red kidney beans, drained and rinsed
1 box (7.25 ounces) macaroni and cheese
½ teaspoon chili powder
nonfat sour cream (optional)

Farm Vegetable Ragout in Crust

1 package (16 ounces) frozen
    Midwest-style
    vegetables (broccoli,
    carrots, cauliflower,
    peas), thawed
1 can (16 ounces) red kidney
    beans, drained and
    rinsed
1 medium tomato, diced
¼ cup reduced-fat honey-
    mustard salad dressing
2 cans (8 ounces each)
    reduced-fat crescent
    roll dough

Would you like a power-packed dinner with a zesty, sweet twist? This recipe will meet the challenge.

Estimated preparation time: 10 minutes
Estimated baking time: 8 minutes
Makes 4 generous servings

1. Preheat oven to 375 degrees.
2. Combine vegetables, beans, and diced tomato in medium mixing bowl. Drizzle salad dressing over mixture and toss lightly.
3. Spoon seasoned vegetable mixture into 4 small (1¾-cups) casserole dishes or ovenproof bowls.
4. Divide crescent roll dough into 4 rectangles, carefully pressing perforations together to seal. Using a pizza cutter or knife, slice each rectangle into 6 strips (lengthwise). Assemble the strips in a lattice pattern over each casserole, pressing ends to seal.
5. Bake for 8 minutes, or until golden brown.

Creamy Coleslaw

I've made many gallons of coleslaw over the past twenty years, and this is the indisputable favorite.

Estimated preparation time: 5 minutes
Makes 6 servings

1. Place mayonnaise, lemon juice, vinegar, sugar, and flax seeds in large bowl and whisk together.
2. Add coleslaw mix and watercress, and toss gently to coat.

2 tablespoons mayonnaise
2 tablespoons lemon juice
2 tablespoons white balsamic vinegar or white vinegar
1 tablespoon sugar
2 teaspoons flax seeds (available at health food stores)
1 package (16 ounces) coleslaw mix
½ bunch watercress (about ¼ pound)

Colorful Bean Salad

1 package (10 ounces) frozen
    green beans, thawed
1 can (16 ounces) white
    kidney beans, drained
    and rinsed
1 can (16 ounces) red kidney
    beans, drained and
    rinsed
1 red onion, chopped
½ cup fat-free Italian dressing
¼ cup chopped fresh cilantro
large lettuce leaves (optional)

Three-bean salad has always been a staple dish during summertime picnics, but you can serve this adaptation any time of year.

Estimated preparation time: 5 minutes
Makes 4 servings

1. Combine all ingredients except lettuce in large bowl, tossing to mix well.
2. If desired, use a large lettuce leaf as a serving bowl.

Vegetarian

Classic Spinach Salad

Some classic recipes are hard to improve on. This salad is lower in fat—and it's meatless—but it's just as tasty as the original version.

Estimated preparation time: 5 minutes
Makes 4 servings

1. Place spinach, mushrooms, tomatoes, and bacon bits in medium-sized bowl and toss to combine.
2. Combine vinegar, water, oil, and brown sugar in small glass bowl or large glass measuring cup. Whisk until well combined.
3. Drizzle dressing over salad and toss gently. Serve immediately.

2 cups chopped fresh spinach leaves
1 cup sliced mushrooms
1 pint cherry tomatoes, quartered
2 tablespoons imitation bacon bits
2 tablespoons cider vinegar
¼ cup water
¼ cup canola oil
1 tablespoon light brown sugar

Tomato and Spinach Salad

¼ cup spicy tomato juice
2 teaspoons lemon juice
2 tablespoons vegetable oil
2 teaspoons minced fresh
    thyme
⅛ teaspoon salt
⅛ teaspoon coarsely ground
    pepper or cracked
    black pepper
⅛ teaspoon ground cumin
1 bag (10 ounces) fresh
    spinach
1 small red onion, finely sliced
1 pint cherry tomatoes,
    quartered

Here's a spicy, robust salad that becomes a meal in a bowl when served with fresh bread or rolls.

Estimated preparation time: 5 minutes
Makes 4 servings

1. Whisk together juices, oil, and spices in large bowl.
2. Add remaining ingredients and toss to coat evenly.

Full-Meal Salad

When you're feeding a crowd, this salad will provide ample servings. Add a decorative platter of wheat crackers, and enjoy the satisfied smiles after dinner.

Estimated preparation time: 15 minutes
Makes 8 servings

1. Layer lettuce, tomatoes, mushrooms, peas, cheese, and onions in large serving bowl.
2. Spread salad dressing over onions to edge of bowl, then cover. Refrigerate several hours or overnight. Garnish with chives and parsley.

6 cups shredded iceberg lettuce
2 cups chopped tomatoes
2 cups sliced mushrooms
1 package (10 ounces) frozen peas, thawed and drained
4 ounces fat-free cheddar cheese, cubed
½ medium red onion, sliced into rings (about 1 cup rings)
2 cups light salad dressing
1 tablespoon chopped chives, for garnish
1 small bunch fresh parsley sprigs, for garnish

Vegetarian

119

Cilantro Black Beans and Rice

1 can (13¼ ounces) vegetable
    broth
½ cup raw white rice
1 can (16 ounces) black
    beans, drained and
    rinsed
½ teaspoon grated lemon peel
½ cup loosely packed cilantro
    leaves

Simple and mild, this dish is ideal for kids who turn their noses up at spicier southwestern fare.

Estimated preparation time: 5 minutes
Estimated cooking time: 15 minutes
Makes 4 servings

1. Bring broth to a boil in medium saucepan. Add rice and reduce heat to low. Cover and let simmer for 15 minutes.
2. Stir in black beans and lemon peel, and continue cooking until rice is tender and liquid is completely absorbed (about 5 minutes).
3. Top with cilantro leaves and serve.

Kid-Pleasing Tomato Cups

Kids will have fun assembling—and eating—these colorful treats.

Estimated preparation time: 10 minutes
Makes 6 servings

1. Place quinoa, peas, parsley, onion, oil, and orange peel in medium bowl, and toss to combine well. Season to taste with salt and pepper.
2. Fill tomatoes with quinoa mixture and serve.

2 cups cooked quinoa
1 cup frozen green peas, thawed
¼ cup chopped fresh parsley
½ small red onion, minced
1 teaspoon canola oil
1 teaspoon grated orange peel
salt and pepper
6 tomatoes, hollowed out

Chili con Corny

1 can (15 ounces) diced
    tomatoes
1 can (16 ounces) hot chili
    beans
1 can (16 ounces) black
    beans, drained
1 can (15 ounces) whole-
    kernel corn
1 cup water

Who'd think that pouring four cans of vegetables and beans into a pot could bring about such an appealing bowl of chili? You will when you assemble this recipe in five easy minutes.

Estimated preparation time: 5 minutes
Estimated cooking time: 10 to 12 minutes
Makes 6 to 8 servings

1. Place all ingredients in medium nonstick pot and stir. Bring to a low boil over medium-low heat, stirring occasionally, until hot, about 10 minutes.
2. Remove from heat and serve.

Vegetarian

7
SIDE DISHES

Saucy Green Beans
Sweetly Seasoned Beets
Bay-Watcher Carrots
Creamy Herbed Corn
Two Peas and Dill Surprise
Simple Spinach and Broccoli
Last-Minute Salad
Fast Herbed Salad
Fast Oriental-Style Salad
Red, White, and Greens
   Salad

Side-Dish Fettuccini
Creamy Shells and Cheese
Lemon-Dill Tortellini
Speedy Almond Rice
Brown Rice Pilaf
Cheesy Mashed Potatoes
Beefy Mashed Potatoes
Fast Potato Pancakes
Easy Au Gratin Potatoes
Low-Sugar Sweet Potatoes

Pulling the main dish together for dinner can be challenging enough—why tackle complicated side dishes? You'll be amazed at how fast, easy, and delicious the following recipes are. The secret lies on grocery store shelves. Did you know that canned vegetables are no less nutritious than frozen ones, or that quick-cooking rice and pasta can be spruced up and ready to serve in the time it takes to set the table?

You'll enjoy recipes that are as basic as opening a few cans and adding a pinch of seasoning. You'll have winning salads in a snap using packaged salad greens and a few other ingredients. Rice and pasta dishes get rave reviews with a few easy, extra touches; and if you think potatoes are boring, you're in for a big surprise! Keep your pantry and freezer stocked with a few basics (listed in chapter 1), and side dishes are simple to whip up.

Saucy Green Beans

My youngest is a green-vegetable phobe, but he loves this dish (and sometimes asks for seconds).

1 tablespoon light canola oil
½ cup chopped onion
2 cans (14.5 ounces each) French-style green beans
3 tablespoons white vinegar
1 beef bouillon cube
2 tablespoons cornstarch

Estimated preparation time: 5 minutes
Estimated cooking time: 12 minutes
Makes 6 servings

1. Preheat medium nonstick pot over medium-high heat. Add oil and onion, and stir. Pour green beans and their liquid into pot, and add vinegar and bouillon cube.
2. Cook until bouillon cube has dissolved. Reduce heat to low and stir in cornstarch. Continue stirring constantly until sauce thickens.
3. Remove from heat and serve.

Sweetly Seasoned Beets

1 can (16 ounces) sliced beets,
    drained
¼ cup orange juice
½ teaspoon chopped fresh
    savory
½ teaspoon chopped fresh
    basil

These are not bland, salad bar–style beets. Once your family has tried them, they'll become a healthy favorite.

Estimated preparation time: 5 minutes
Estimated cooking time: 10 minutes
Makes 4 servings

1. Place all ingredients in small nonstick pot. Cook over medium heat until liquid begins to boil.
2. Reduce heat to low and simmer, uncovered, for 5 minutes, stirring occasionally.

Bay-Watcher Carrots

If you're used to serving carrots seasoned with margarine, this recipe packs more flavor into every vitamin-filled bite . . . and it's much lower in fat!

1 can (15 ounces) sliced
    carrots
1 green onion, finely diced
1 beef bouillon cube
1 bay leaf

Estimated preparation time: 5 minutes
Estimated cooking time: 10 minutes
Makes 4 servings

1. Pour canned carrots and their liquid into small non-stick pot. Add remaining ingredients.
2. Cook over medium heat, stirring occasionally, until bouillon has dissolved.
3. Reduce heat to low and simmer, uncovered, for 5 minutes.

Creamy Herbed Corn

1 can (15 ounces) whole-
    kernel golden corn
1 can (15 ounces) whole-
    kernel white corn
1 can (10.75 ounces) reduced-
    fat condensed cream of
    celery soup
½ teaspoon celery seed
1 tablespoon chopped chives

Here's a new twist on an old favorite: If you have leftovers from this recipe, puree in a blender and stir into a purchased corn muffin mix (in place of liquid)

Estimated preparation time: 5 minutes
Estimated cooking time: 7 minutes
Makes 8 servings

1. Pour corn and its liquid into medium nonstick pot. Add soup, celery seed, and chives.
2. Cook over medium-low heat, stirring occasionally, until sauce is smooth and begins to bubble.

Two Peas and Dill Surprise

A colorful dish with a lot of flavor, this is almost a meal in itself. Enjoy it as a side dish; the next night, heat up a can of your favorite creamed soup, stir in the leftovers, and pour it over pasta for a quick dinner (angel hair pasta works very well).

1 can (15 ounces) tender sweet peas, drained
1 can (16 ounces) chick-peas, drained
1 tablespoon light olive oil
1 tablespoon chopped fresh dill

Estimated preparation time: 3 minutes
Estimated cooking time: 4 to 5 minutes
Makes 8 servings

1. Place all ingredients in microwavable casserole dish, toss gently, and cover.
2. Microwave on high for 4 to 5 minutes, or until the peas are heated thoroughly.

Simple Spinach and Broccoli

1 can (15 ounces) chopped
    spinach, drained
1 cup cooked broccoli (from
    leftovers)
1 tablespoon reduced-fat
    margarine
1 tablespoon lemon juice
¼ teaspoon coarsely ground
    pepper

In the mood for a quick, crustless pie? This dish is fabulous on its own, but you can stir leftovers into a batter made of 1 cup biscuit mix, 4 eggs, ½ cup nonfat sour cream, and ½ cup nonfat milk. Then pour it into a pie pan and bake at 375 degrees for 20 minutes.

Estimated preparation time: 3 minutes
Estimated cooking time: 4 to 5 minutes
Makes 6 servings

1. Place all ingredients in microwavable casserole dish, stir, and cover.
2. Microwave on high for 4 to 5 minutes, or until vegetables are heated thoroughly.

Last-Minute Salad

You're running late, you've grabbed a deli-roasted chicken on your way home, and you'd like a little something extra with your meal; this recipe couldn't be simpler.

1 package (16 ounces) salad
   greens
1 cup sliced fresh mushrooms
10 to 12 cherry tomatoes
2 tablespoons roasted shelled
   sunflower seeds or
   nuts

Estimated preparation time: 3 minutes
Makes 6 servings

1. Place salad greens in medium bowl, arrange mushrooms and tomatoes on top, and sprinkle with seeds or nuts.
2. Serve with your favorite dressings, or olive oil and vinegar.

. . . .

Note: Add drained, water-packed tuna to any remaining salad for a quick, low-fat lunch.

. . . .

Fast Herbed Salad

1 package (16 ounces) salad
    greens
1 small bunch lemon basil or
    sweet basil
2 tablespoons chopped fresh
    thyme
¼ cup fat-free Italian dressing

For a special gourmet touch to an everyday salad, add fresh herbs and take a bow.

Estimated preparation time: 5 minutes
Makes 6 servings

1. Place salad greens and herbs in medium bowl.
2. Drizzle with dressing and toss lightly.

Note: Add diced cooked beef and 1 tablespoon Parmesan cheese to any remaining salad for a quick lunch.

Fast Oriental-Style Salad

Children of all ages love this colorful, crunchy, and zesty salad—and it's ready in minutes!

Estimated preparation time: 5 minutes
Makes 8 servings

1. Place salad greens and mixed vegetables in medium bowl and toss.
2. Sprinkle with noodles and drizzle with dressing.

• • • • • • • • • • • • • • • •

Note: Add diced cooked chicken to any remaining salad for a quick lunch.

• • • • • • • • • • • • • • • •

1 package (16 ounces) salad greens
2 cups frozen Oriental-style vegetables, thawed and drained
¼ cup chow mein noodles (such as Chun King brand)
½ cup sweet and spicy type dressing (such as Kraft brand Catalina)

Red, White, and Greens Salad

1 package (16 ounces) salad greens
1 cup frozen broccoli and cauliflower mixture, thawed and drained
10 cherry tomatoes, halved
⅓ cup fat-free ranch dressing

Cool , creamy, and eye-appealing, this salad will wow your guests or potluck gang—and they'll never know you made is so quickly.

Estimated preparation time: 7 minutes
Makes 6 servings

1. Place salad greens in medium bowl.
2. Arrange other vegetables on top and drizzle with dressing.

Side-Dish Fettuccini

This side dish can also be served as a main dish on a hectic night (serve beans, nuts, or dairy products for protein). The fresh herbs add zing to many convenience foods. Try experimenting with different flavor combinations!

1 package (5.1 ounces) fettuccini Alfredo noodle mix
1 tablespoon chopped fresh basil
1 tablespoon chopped fresh oregano
¼ teaspoon garlic powder
⅓ cup plain dried bread crumbs

Estimated preparation time: 7 minutes
Estimated cooking time: 20 minutes conventional,
   8 minutes microwave
Makes 4 servings

1. Prepare pasta according to package instructions.
2. Add basil, oregano, and garlic powder and toss to combine. Sprinkle with bread crumbs and serve.

Creamy Shells and Cheese

1 package (5.1 ounces) shells
    and cheese noodle mix
    (such as Noodle-Roni
    brand)
½ cup nonfat sour cream
1 teaspoon chopped chives

Tired of plain old macaroni and cheese? You and your family will love this easy, creamy recipe!

Estimated preparation time: 7 minutes
Estimated cooking time: 20 minutes conventional,
    8 minutes microwave
Makes 4 servings

1. Prepare pasta according to package instructions.
2. Stir in sour cream, sprinkle with chives, and serve.

Lemon-Dill Tortellini

This surprising combination is delicious. If you have leftover Lemon-Dill Tortellini, toss it with 1 cup of salad greens for a quick lunch.

1 package (9 ounces) fresh
   cheese tortellini
1 tablespoon margarine,
   melted
1 tablespoon lemon juice
2 teaspoons chopped fresh dill

Estimated preparation time: 7 minutes
Estimated cooking time: 8 to 10 minutes
Makes 6 servings

1. Prepare pasta according to package directions.
2. Whisk margarine, lemon juice, and dill in small bowl.
3. Pour sauce over pasta, toss to combine, and serve.

Speedy Almond Rice

½ cup slivered almonds
2 tablespoons reduced-fat
    margarine
1 cup water
1 cup instant rice (such as
    Minute Rice brand)
¼ teaspoon cinnamon

When you don't have time to steam traditional rice, instant versions work well, but may need a little help in the flavor department; this recipe is one solution.

Estimated preparation time: 3 minutes
Estimated cooking time: 5 minutes
Makes 4 servings

1. Place all ingredients in microwavable casserole dish, cover, and microwave on high for 3 minutes. Stir.
2. Microwave uncovered for an additional 2 minutes, and stir again.

Brown Rice Pilaf

A big hit with the kids, this side dish works well with just about any beef, pork, or poultry.

Estimated preparation time: 7 minutes
Estimated cooking time: 7 to 8 minutes
Makes 4 servings

1 can (10.75 ounces) chicken
    broth
⅓ cup water
2 cups instant brown rice
    (such as Uncle Ben's
    brand)
1 green onion, finely chopped
½ cup raisins

1. Pour broth and water into medium nonstick pot and bring to boil over medium heat.
2. Stir in rice, reduce temperature to low, and simmer for 2 minutes. Remove from heat.
3. Stir in onion and raisins. Cover and let sit 2 to 3 minutes.

• • • • • • • • • • • • • •

Note: Sprinkle Brown Rice Pilaf with ⅛ teaspoon saffron and ⅛ teaspoon ginger for a Middle Eastern flavor.

• • • • • • • • • • • • • •

Cheesy Mashed Potatoes

1 ⅓ cups water
½ cup nonfat milk
1 ⅓ cups instant mashed
    potato flakes
¼ teaspoon coarsely ground
    pepper
¼ teaspoon paprika
½ cup reduced-fat shredded
    cheddar cheese

Children can't seem to get enough of this alternative "comfort food."

Estimated preparation time: 5 minutes
Estimated cooking time: 3 minutes
Makes 4 servings

1. Pour water and milk into microwavable casserole dish, add potato flakes, and stir.
2. Microwave on high, uncovered, for 3 minutes.
3. Sprinkle with pepper, paprika, and cheese, stirring until smooth.

Beefy Mashed Potatoes

Much more flavorful than ordinary mashed potatoes, this dish is a treat. Because there are no dairy products in this recipe, it's perfect for lactose-intolerant family members.

1 can (10 ounces) beef broth
½ cup water
1⅓ cups instant mashed
     potato flakes
¼ teaspoon coarsely ground
     pepper

Estimated preparation time: 5 minutes
Estimated cooking time: 3 minutes
Makes 4 servings

1. Pour broth and water into microwavable casserole dish. Stir in potato flakes and pepper.
2. Microwave on high for 3 minutes, stir, and serve.

Fast Potato Pancakes

2 cups frozen mashed
   potatoes, thawed
¼ cup flour
1 egg
1 cup nonfat sour cream
¼ cup chopped fresh chives
cooking oil spray

*With my Germanic background, I've enjoyed po-
tato pancakes all of my life; but these days I need a
streamlined, lower-fat recipe. This is it.*

Estimated preparation time: 7 minutes
Estimated cooking time: 10 to 12 minutes total
Makes 12 small pancakes, or 4 servings

1. Preheat large nonstick skillet or griddle over medium
   heat.
2. Place mashed potatoes, flour, egg, sour cream, and
   chives in medium bowl and mix until well combined.
   Batter will be thick.
3. Lightly coat hot skillet with cooking oil spray. Drop
   batter onto surface using ¼ cup measure. Cook 2 to 3
   minutes on each side.

Easy Au Gratin Potatoes

Rich and creamy—yet lower in fat than boxed varieties—these potatoes will satisfy hearty appetites.

Estimated preparation time: 7 minutes
Estimated cooking time: 14 minutes
Makes 4 servings

cooking oil spray
½ cup chopped onion (fresh or frozen)
1 can (10.75 ounces) reduced-fat condensed cream of mushroom soup
2 ounces reduced-fat cream cheese, cubed
3 cups frozen hash browns

1. Lightly coat microwavable casserole dish with cooking oil spray.
2. Place onions in bottom of dish and microwave on high for 1 minute.
3. Add undiluted soup and cream cheese, then microwave on high for 3 minutes.
4. Stir in hash browns, cover, and microwave on high for an additional 10 minutes.

• • • • • • • • • • • • • • • •

Note: Try this recipe using frozen cottage-style fries for a different look. Be sure to increase the final cooking time to 12 minutes.

• • • • • • • • • • • • • • • •

Low-Sugar Sweet Potatoes

1 can (16 ounces) sweet
    potatoes, drained and
    diced
1 can (16 ounces) crushed
    pineapple, drained
2 tablespoons reduced-fat
    margarine, cut into
    small pats
2 teaspoons sugar substitute
    for baking (such as
    Equal or Measure
    brands)

Almost everyone loves candied yams, but if you'd like a lower-sugar version that's just as tasty, try these. You can double or triple this recipe for holiday entertaining.

Estimated preparation time: 10 minutes
Estimated cooking time: 5 minutes
Makes 4 servings

1. Combine sweet potatoes and pineapple in microwavable casserole dish. Top with margarine and sugar substitute.
2. Cover, and microwave on high for 5 minutes.

8
BAKING

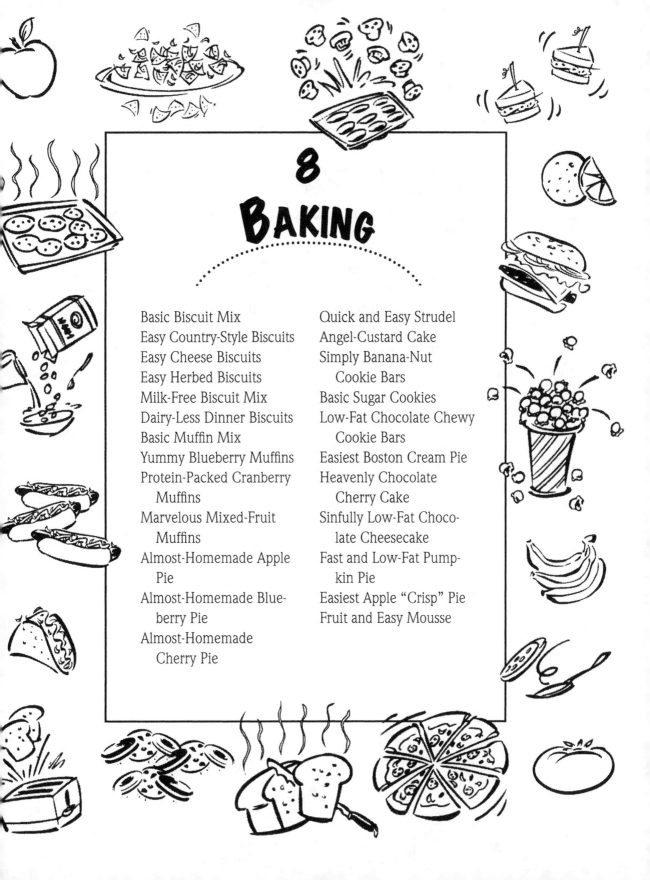

My mother and grandmother baked almost daily, and the heavenly aroma of fresh-from-the-oven treats filled their homes with love. As a new mother, I tried to live up to the examples I'd had, but soon found that the heirloom recipes were both time consuming and quite fattening. A few years ago I began developing fast, low-fat alternatives for many of my childhood favorites.

There are certainly many varieties of refrigerated or frozen products on the market, and packaged mixes in regular and reduced-fat styles; the cost of those products can be a bit steep sometimes, and "homemade" is a better budget alternative when possible. In this chapter, you'll find basic mix recipes for biscuits and muffins, with variations for each. You'll also find recipes for power baking on the weekend, quicker, healthier cookies, and no-bake miracles that get rave reviews.

Basic Biscuit Mix

This Basic Biscuit Mix is easy to prepare, stays fresh for weeks, and replaces commercial (boxed) mixes— it's also lower in fat and calories.

6 cups bread flour
1 cup dry buttermilk (available
    in the baking section
    of your grocery store)
1½ teaspoons iodized salt
¼ cup baking powder
½ cup reduced-fat margarine,
    softened

Estimated preparation time: about 5 minutes
Makes about 8 cups biscuit mix

1. Place all ingredients in food processor and pulse until well combined.
2. Store mix in airtight container and refrigerate for up to 4 weeks.

Easy Country-Style Biscuits

2 cups Basic Biscuit Mix (page
    147)
1 teaspoon sugar
⅔ cup water

Here's the perfect, last-minute mealtime batch of biscuits.

Estimated preparation time: 10 minutes
Estimated baking time: 8 to 10 minutes
Makes 12 biscuits

1. Preheat oven to 425 degrees.
2. Place all ingredients in medium bowl and stir with fork to combine.
3. Turn dough onto floured surface and knead for 2 minutes; allow to rest for 2 minutes.
4. Roll out dough ¼ inch thick and cut into rounds using cookie cutter or glass dipped in flour.
5. Arrange biscuits on nonstick cookie sheet and bake for 8 to 10 minutes.

Easy Cheese Biscuits

Great with soups, chili, or meal-sized salads, these biscuits will be gobbled up quickly.

2 cups Basic Biscuit Mix (page 147)
¼ cup reduced-fat Parmesan cheese
⅔ cup water

Estimated preparation time: 10 minutes
Estimated baking time: 8 to 10 minutes
Makes 12 biscuits

1. Preheat oven to 425 degrees.
2. Place all ingredients in medium bowl and stir with fork to combine.
3. Turn dough onto floured surface and knead for 2 minutes; allow to rest for 2 minutes.
4. Roll out dough ¼ inch thick and cut into rounds using cookie cutter or glass dipped in flour.
5. Arrange biscuits on nonstick cookie sheet and bake for 8 to 10 minutes.

Easy Herbed Biscuits

2 cups Basic Biscuit Mix (page 147)
¼ teaspoon sage
½ teaspoon thyme
⅔ cups water

Use fresh herbs and fresh herb blends for wonderfully aromatic biscuits.

Estimated preparation time: 10 minutes
Estimated baking time: 8 to 10 minutes
Makes 12 biscuits

1. Preheat oven to 425 degrees.
2. Place all ingredients in medium bowl and stir with fork to combine.
3. Turn dough onto floured surface and knead for 2 minutes; allow to rest for 2 minutes.
4. Roll out dough ¼ inch thick and cut into rounds using cookie cutter or glass dipped in flour.
5. Arrange biscuits on nonstick cookie sheet and bake for 8 to 10 minutes.

Milk-Free Biscuit Mix

Many families today grapple with allergies and follow restricted diets. This recipe is ideal for lactose-intolerant family members, but the taste is not identical to that of traditional biscuits.

6 cups bread flour
1 cup powdered low-iron soy
   formula (available near
   baby food)
1½ teaspoons iodized salt
¼ cup plus 1 teaspoon baking
   powder
½ cup reduced-fat dairy-free
   margarine, softened

Estimated preparation time: about 5 minutes
Makes about 8 cups mix

1. Place all ingredients in food processor and pulse until well combined.
2. Store mix in an airtight container and refrigerate for up to 4 weeks.

Dairy-Less Dinner Biscuits

2 cups Milk-Free Biscuit Mix
(page 151)
1 teaspoon sugar
⅛ teaspoon cumin
⅔ cup water

Although tasty on their own, you can add fresh herbs or herb blends to add zest to these easy biscuits.

Estimated preparation time: 10 minutes
Estimated baking time: 8 to 10 minutes
Makes 12 biscuits

1. Preheat oven to 425 degrees.
2. Place all ingredients in medium bowl and stir with fork to combine.
3. Turn dough onto floured surface and knead for 2 minutes; allow to rest for 2 minutes.
4. Roll out dough ¼ inch thick and cut into rounds using cookie cutter or glass dipped in flour.
5. Arrange biscuits on nonstick cookie sheet and bake for 8 to 10 minutes.

Basic Muffin Mix

Muffins are a popular breakfast or after-school treat in our home, and with this mix, I'm always ready to whip up a quick batch. Substitute powdered low-iron soy formula for dry milk if dairy is a problem in your household.

2 cups whole wheat flour
2 cups all-purpose flour
1 cup oat bran or wheat germ
2 cups nonfat dry milk
2 cups sugar
1 tablespoon plus 1 teaspoon
    baking powder
1 teaspoon baking soda
1 teaspoon salt

Estimated preparation time: 10 minutes
Makes about 9 cups mix

1. Mix all ingredients thoroughly in large bowl.
2. Store in airtight container in pantry or cupboard for up to 4 weeks, or in airtight freezer bags in the freezer for up to 4 months.

Yummy Blueberry Muffins

cooking oil spray
2 cups Basic Muffin Mix
      (page 153)
1 egg
2 tablespoon canola oil
¾ cup water
½ cup orange juice
½ pint fresh blueberries (or
      frozen and thawed)

Take advantage of seasonal specials; buy blueberries in large quantities in season, and store them in zip-top freezer bags for year 'round goodies.

Estimated preparation time: 10 minutes
Estimated baking time: 15 minutes
Makes 12 muffins

1. Preheat oven to 400 degrees.
2. Lightly coat muffin tin with cooking oil spray.
3. Combine muffin mix, egg, oil, water, and orange juice in medium bowl until just moistened. Batter will be lumpy. Fold in blueberries.
4. Spoon batter into muffin tin and bake for 15 minutes.

• • • • • • • • • • • • • • • •

Note: All baked muffins can be frozen in airtight freezer bags and microwaved for a quick breakfast or snack.

• • • • • • • • • • • • • • • •

Protein-Packed Cranberry Muffins

These muffins are an ideal source of calcium, iron, and many vitamins—they're also delicious!

Estimated preparation time: 10 minutes
Estimated baking time: 15 minutes
Makes 12 muffins

1. Preheat oven to 400 degrees.
2. Lightly coat muffin tin with cooking oil spray.
3. Combine muffin mix, egg, oil, milk, and yogurt in medium bowl until moistened. Batter will be lumpy. Fold in cranberries.
4. Spoon batter into muffin tin and bake for 15 minutes.

cooking oil spray
2 cups Basic Muffin Mix
    (page 153)
1 egg
1 tablespoon canola oil
⅔ cup nonfat milk
1 cup nonfat plain yogurt or
    sour cream
1½ cups dried cranberries

Marvelous Mixed-Fruit Muffins

cooking oil spray
2 cups Basic Muffin Mix
    (page 153)
1 egg
1 tablespoon canola oil
¾ cup water
⅓ cup unsweetened
    applesauce
1 ripe banana, mashed
1 cup raisins

Try these muffins with honey butter on a cold, dreary day, or as a breakfast surprise.

Estimated preparation time: 10 minutes
Estimated baking time: 15 minutes
Makes 12 muffins

1. Preheat oven to 400 degrees.
2. Lightly coat muffin tin with cooking oil spray.
3. Combine muffin mix, egg, oil, water, applesauce, and banana in medium bowl until moistened. Batter will be lumpy. Fold in raisins.
4. Spoon batter into muffin tin and bake for 15 minutes.

Almost-Homemade Apple Pie

When I don't have time to bake a homemade pie from scratch—but I want my home to smell like I have—I jazz up purchased, frozen pies and enjoy the compliments.

1 frozen apple pie (9 inches)
½ cup powdered sugar
½ teaspoon cinnamon
1 tablespoon water
¼ cup chopped nuts

Estimated preparation time: 10 minutes
Estimated baking time: varies according to brand of
   frozen pie
Makes 8 medium or 10 small servings

1. Bake frozen pie according to package directions. Cool.
2. Place powdered sugar, cinnamon, and water in small bowl and stir with fork until smooth.
3. Spread frosting over top of cooled pie, sprinkle with nuts, and serve.

Almost-Homemade Blueberry Pie

1 frozen blueberry pie
    (9 inches)
½ cup powdered sugar
1 tablespoon plus ½ teaspoon
    lemon juice
1 teaspoon lemon zest

Did your child volunteer you for the PTA bake sale? This last-minute solution will save your sanity and your pride.

Estimated preparation time: 10 minutes
Estimated baking time: varies according to brand of
    frozen pie
Makes 8 medium servings or 10 small servings

1. Prepare pie according to package directions. Cool.
2. Place powdered sugar and lemon juice in small bowl and stir with fork until smooth. Frosting will be thin.
3. Spread frosting over cooled pie, sprinkle with lemon zest, and serve.

Almost-Homemade Cherry Pie

Make a few of these on (or near) President's Day, and give the extras to neighbors or coworkers.

1 frozen cherry pie (9 inches)
½ cup cherry preserves
¼ cup chopped pecans

Estimated preparation time: 5 minutes
Estimated baking time: varies according to frozen pie
    brand
Makes 8 medium servings or 10 small servings

1. Prepare pie according to package directions. Cool.
2. Place preserves in small, microwavable bowl and microwave on high, uncovered, for 1 minute.
3. Stir and spread on cooled pie. Sprinkle with nuts and serve.

Quick and Easy Strudel

1 package (15 ounces) refrigerated pie crusts
1 can (16 ounces) light apple pie filling
½ cup reduced-fat biscuit mix (or Basic Biscuit Mix, page 147)
1 tub (4 ounces) nonfat cream cheese spread
¼ cup powdered sugar
¼ cup chopped nuts

My mother was mistress of strudels, and she received compliments for every one she baked—this recipe is my version. Before frosting, you can freeze one strudel in an airtight freezer bag for up to one month.

Estimated preparation time: 15 minutes
Estimated baking time: 15 minutes
Makes 8 to 10 servings

1. Preheat oven to 400 degrees.
2. Bring pie crusts to room temperature and unfold on lightly floured surface.
3. Combine pie filling and biscuit mix in medium bowl.
4. Spoon half of mixture down the center of each pie crust. Carefully fold opposite sides of crusts toward center, overlapping about 1 inch to form semi-rectangular shape. Fold up remaining edges just to touch center seams.
5. Transfer pastries to nonstick cookie sheet and bake for 15 minutes, or until golden brown. Remove from oven, cool, and transfer to serving platters.
6. Place cream cheese spread and sugar in a small bowl and combine until well blended. Spread half the mixture onto each cooled pastry.
7. Sprinkle each strudel with 2 tablespoons nuts and serve.

·················

Variations:

Cheery, Cherry Strudel: *Omit apple pie filling and substitute 1 can light cherry pie filling.*

Purely Peach Strudel: *Omit apple pie filling and substitute 1 can peach pie filling, or 3 cups sliced canned peaches, drained.*

Holiday Mincemeat Strudel: *Omit apple pie filling and substitute 2 cups reduced-fat mincemeat from jar. Omit cream cheese frosting and nuts, and substitute a sprinkling of lemon-flavored confectioner's sugar.*

·················

Angel-Custard Cake

cooking oil spray
1 ready-made angel food cake
 (10 to 12 ounces)
1 can (8 ounces) evaporated
 skim milk
2 cartons (4 ounces each) egg
 substitute, thawed, or
 4 eggs, beaten
2 tablespoons sugar
¼ teaspoon nutmeg
1 tub (8 ounces) nonfat non-
 dairy whipped topping,
 thawed (optional)
fresh fruit (optional)

This is an adaptation of my grandmother's favorite dessert recipe.

Estimated preparation time: 15 minutes
Estimated baking time: 15 minutes
Makes 12 servings

1. Preheat oven to 375 degrees.
2. Lightly coat 9 × 13-inch baking dish with cooking oil spray.
3. Cut angel food cake into bite-sized cubes and arrange in bottom of prepared baking dish, making sure that cake pieces are touching one another.
4. Place milk, egg substitute, sugar, and nutmeg in medium bowl and whisk together. Pour over cake pieces.
5. Cover baking dish with aluminum foil and bake for 15 minutes. Remove from oven, uncover, and cool. Serve with whipped topping or fresh fruit. Refrigerate leftover cake after serving, discarding any uneaten cake after 3 days.

Simply Banana-Nut Cookie Bars

This began as an accidental recipe, but received such rave reviews that it's been gobbled up dozens of times.

Estimated preparation time: 5 minutes
Estimated baking time: 20 to 25 minutes
Makes 1 dozen bar cookies

1. Preheat oven to 350 degrees.
2. Cream together margarine, sugar, and egg in medium bowl. Slowly stir in biscuit mix. Batter will be stiff. Fold in mashed bananas and chopped nuts.
3. Lightly coat 9 × 9-inch nonstick baking dish with cooking oil spray. Spread batter in dish.
4. Bake for 20 to 25 minutes, or until golden brown. Remove from oven, cool, and slice into bars.

¼ cup reduced-fat margarine, softened
¾ cup sugar
1 egg
2 cups reduced-fat biscuit mix
2 ripe bananas, mashed
½ cup chopped nuts
cooking oil spray

Basic Sugar Cookies

2 cups reduced-fat biscuit mix
⅔ cup sugar
½ cup reduced-fat margarine,
    softened
1 egg
⅓ cup nonfat milk
1 teaspoon vanilla

I keep plenty of this mix on hand whenever possible, because it's common for my sons to announce before bedtime that I'm to bake cookies for a class party the next day.

Estimated preparation time: 3 minutes
Estimated baking time: 8 to 10 minutes
Makes 3 dozen cookies

1. Preheat oven to 350 degrees.
2. Place biscuit mix and sugar in medium bowl and cut in softened margarine. Add remaining ingredients and stir vigorously with wooden spoon until well combined.
3. Drop by tablespoonsful onto an ungreased nonstick cookie sheet.
4. Bake for 8 to 10 minutes, or until golden brown. Remove cookies from oven and cool on absorbent paper or wire rack.

．．．．．．．．．．．．．．．．．

Variations:

Easy Raisin-Walnut Cookies: *Prepare Basic Sugar Cookie dough and stir in 1 cup of raisins and ½ cup chopped walnuts before baking.*

Easy Apricot-Pecan Cookies: *Prepare Basic Sugar Cookie dough and stir in 1 cup diced dried apricots and ½ cup chopped pecans before baking.*

Easy Peanut Butter Cookies: *Prepare Basic Sugar Cookie dough, substituting ½ cup creamy peanut butter for the margarine.*

．．．．．．．．．．．．．．．．．

Low-Fat Chocolate Chewy Cookie Bars

2 cups reduced-fat biscuit mix
¼ cup powdered
      unsweetened cocoa
      (for baking)
¾ cup sugar
1 jar (8 ounces) pureed prunes
1 egg
½ cup nonfat milk
cooking oil spray

Nothing beats chocolate when you have a sweet tooth, and these cookies will satisfy the cravings (with fewer calories and less fat).

Estimated preparation time: 3 minutes
Estimated baking time: 20 minutes
Makes 1 dozen cookie bars

1. Preheat oven to 350 degrees.
2. Place biscuit mix, cocoa, and sugar into medium bowl and stir to combine. Add pureed prunes, egg, and milk, and stir vigorously with wooden spoon until mixture is creamed.
3. Lightly coat 9 × 9-inch nonstick baking dish with cooking oil spray, and spread batter in dish.
4. Bake for 20 minutes. Remove from oven, cool, and slice into bars.

Easiest Boston Cream Pie

This recipe was served to nearly twenty hungry musicians who insisted it could not be low fat—it is.

Estimated preparation time: 10 minutes
Makes 8 servings

1. Slice pound cake horizontally into 3 layers. Place bottom layer on serving dish.
2. Gently beat pudding mix and milk in medium bowl until pudding begins to thicken.
3. Spoon half the pudding mixture over the bottom cake layer and top with second cake layer. Spoon remaining pudding mixture onto middle cake layer, and place final cake layer on top.
4. Place chocolate baking chips and water in 2-cup glass measuring cup. Microwave on high for 45 seconds. Whisk briskly with fork until smooth.
5. Pour melted chocolate over all three cake layers, allowing some of the chocolate to drizzle down the sides. Refrigerate until ready to serve.

1 purchased reduced-fat or nonfat pound cake
1 package (3.4 ounces) fat-free instant vanilla pudding mix
1 cup skim milk, chilled
½ cup reduced-fat semisweet chocolate baking chips
2 tablespoons water

Heavenly Chocolate Cherry Cake

1 ready-made angel food cake
    (10 to 12 inches)
1 cup nonfat whipped topping
1 package (8 ounces) nonfat
    cream cheese, softened
½ cup reduced-fat chocolate
    baking chips
2 tablespoons water
1 can (20 ounces) light cherry
    pie filling

My oldest son chose the name for this recipe as he licked his dessert plate clean.

Estimated preparation time: 15 minutes
Makes 12 servings

1. Cut cake into bite-sized pieces and place in large mixing bowl.
2. Place whipped topping and cream cheese in full-sized food processor and pulse until blended. Allow to sit while you prepare the chocolate.
3. Pour chocolate baking chips into 2-cup measuring cup, add water, and microwave on high for 45 seconds. Whisk melted chocolate with fork until smooth.
4. Immediately pour chocolate sauce over the cream cheese mixture in food processor and pulse until smooth and creamy.
5. Pour chocolate-cheese mixture over angel food cake pieces. Add cherry pie filling, and gently fold all ingredients together until well combined.
6. Spread mixture evenly in 9 × 13-inch baking dish. Refrigerate until ready to serve. Top with additional nonfat whipped topping, if desired.

Sinfully Low-Fat Chocolate Cheesecake

No one will believe that this rich, fudgy cheesecake has less than 5 grams of fat per slice—and if you don't tell them, they'll never know.

Estimated preparation time: 8 minutes
Estimated refrigeration time: 1 hour
Makes 8 to 10 servings

1. Place cream cheese, sweetened condensed milk, and whipped topping in full-sized food processor. Pulse until smooth. Slowly add pudding mix, pulsing to blend.
2. Pour cream cheese mixture into pie shell. Refrigerate for at least 1 hour before serving. Top with dollop of additional nonfat whipped topping if desired.

1 package (8 ounces) nonfat cream cheese, softened
1 can (8 ounces) nonfat sweetened condensed milk
1 cup nonfat whipped topping, thawed
1 package (3.4 ounces) nonfat instant chocolate pudding mix
1 ready-made chocolate cookie pie shell

Fast and Low-Fat Pumpkin Pie

1 package (3.4 ounces) nonfat instant vanilla pudding mix
1 cup nonfat whipped topping, thawed
½ cup skim milk
1 cup canned pumpkin
1½ teaspoons pumpkin pie spice
1 purchased reduced-fat graham cracker pie shell

Replace your standard pumpkin pie recipe with this one, and you'll free up oven space for a larger turkey.

Estimated preparation time: 5 minutes
Estimated refrigeration time: 1 hour
Makes 8 to 10 servings

1. Place pudding mix, whipped topping, milk, pumpkin, and pumpkin pie spice in medium bowl. Using an electric mixer, beat on low speed until smooth.
2. Pour pumpkin mixture into graham cracker pie shell and refrigerate for at least 1 hour before serving. Top with dollop of additional nonfat whipped topping, if desired.

Easiest Apple "Crisp" Pie

Everyone loves this super-simple pie—your family will, too.

Estimated preparation time: 15 minutes
Estimated refrigeration time: 1 hour
Makes 8 generous servings

1 can (20 ounces) light apple pie filling
½ cup water
1 envelope (2 ounces) unflavored gelatin
1 purchased reduced-fat graham cracker pie shell
¾ cup low-fat granola cereal

1. Place apple pie filling in medium glass bowl, gently stir in water, and microwave on high for 2 minutes. Stir. Microwave on high for an additional 1 to 2 minutes.
2. Sprinkle unflavored gelatin over hot apple mixture and stir until dissolved. Allow to cool slightly, then pour warm apple mixture into pie shell, spreading evenly. Sprinkle granola on top. Refrigerate for 1 to 2 hours before serving.

Fruit and Easy Mousse

1 package (8 ounces) nonfat
    cream cheese, softened
1 container (8 ounces) nonfat
    whipped topping,
    thawed
1 cup nonfat lemon flavored
    yogurt
1 package (3.4 ounces) nonfat
    instant lemon pudding
    mix
2 cups fresh berries (such as
    blueberries,
    raspberries,
    strawberries)

It tastes sweet and decadent, but this no-bake dessert is packed with nutrition.

Estimated preparation time: 10 minutes
Estimated refrigeration time: 1 hour
Makes 6 to 8 servings.

1. Place cream cheese, whipped topping, and yogurt into full-sized food processor and pulse until smooth. Slowly add pudding mix, pulsing until well blended.
2. Remove blade from food processor and gently fold in fresh berries with spatula.
3. Spoon mousse mixture into small dessert bowls. Refrigerate for at least 1 hour before serving.

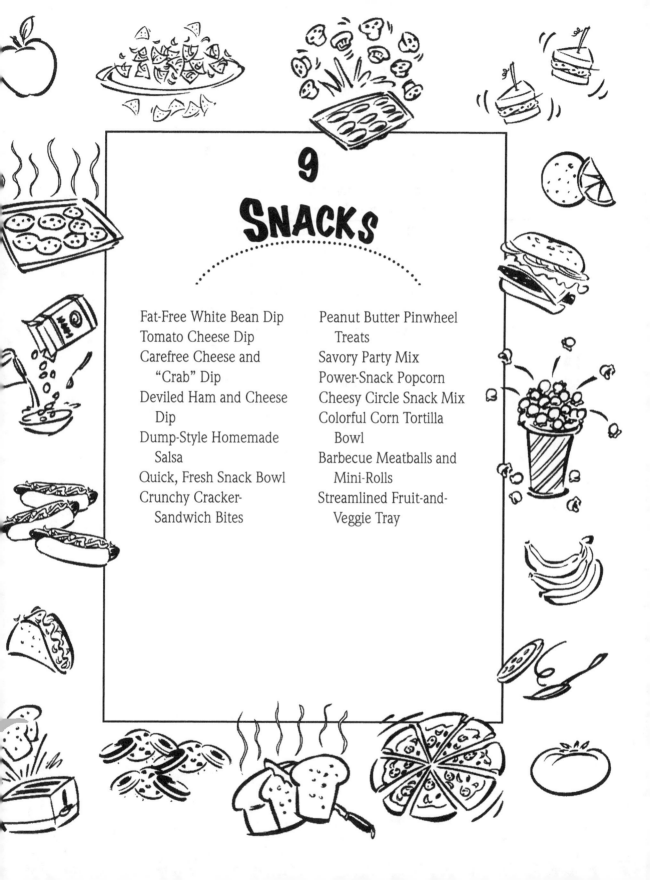

9

SNACKS

Fat-Free White Bean Dip
Tomato Cheese Dip
Carefree Cheese and
    "Crab" Dip
Deviled Ham and Cheese
    Dip
Dump-Style Homemade
    Salsa
Quick, Fresh Snack Bowl
Crunchy Cracker-
    Sandwich Bites

Peanut Butter Pinwheel
    Treats
Savory Party Mix
Power-Snack Popcorn
Cheesy Circle Snack Mix
Colorful Corn Tortilla
    Bowl
Barbecue Meatballs and
    Mini-Rolls
Streamlined Fruit-and-
    Veggie Tray

I admit . . . we don't stock a lot of potato chips, packaged snacks, or other munchies in our pantry. It wasn't always that way, but several years ago—at over 200 pounds—I realized that those tasty treats weren't doing me or my family any good. In my own efforts to lose weight and get back in shape, I didn't want my husband or children to feel deprived. So I began making healthier munchies we could all enjoy freely.

Nothing beats chips, veggies, and dips when last-minute company pops in, so you'll find recipes for delicious entertaining in this chapter. You'll also find recipes for tempting appetizers that double as healthy after-school snacks. When you want to munch on the run, you'll find ideas for quick and easy nibbles you throw together using basic pantry items, and there are even recipes for large gatherings or parties.

Fat-Free White Bean Dip

My guys love this creamy, lowfat dip, and you can use it in place of refried beans for many recipes.

Estimated preparation time: 5 minutes
Makes about 2¼ cups

1 can (19 ounces) white beans, rinsed and drained
1 medium white onion, finely chopped
1 clove garlic, minced
¼ teaspoon cumin
1 tablespoon lemon juice
salt and pepper

1. Puree beans in food processor.
2. Add onion, garlic, cumin, and lemon juice. Pulse to combine. Season with salt and pepper.
3. Serve hot or cold. Refrigerate for up to 5 days.

Tomato Cheese Dip

1 pound reduced-fat processed
    cheese spread, cubed
1 can (10 ounces) diced
    tomatoes and chilies

This is not quite as spicy, salty, or "fatty" as standard nacho dips, but it tastes great!

Estimated preparation time: 5 minutes
Makes about 2½ cups

1. Place ingredients in microwavable covered dish. Microwave on high, stirring once, until cheese melts, about 2 minutes.
2. Serve immediately. Refrigerate remainder for up to 3 days, and reheat to serve.

Carefree Cheese and "Crab" Dip

Planning a dinner party? Be sure to include this winning recipe!

Estimated preparation time: 5 minutes
Makes about 2 cups dip

1. Place all ingredients in food processor and pulse until creamy.
2. Transfer to small serving bowl, cover, and refrigerate until ready to serve. Consume within 3 days.

....

Note: You can also serve this dip in the center of a platter with baked whole wheat crackers and fresh vegetables for a cool, light summer dinner.

....

1 package (8 ounces) imitation crab meat
1 cup nonfat creamed cottage cheese
2 tablespoons nonfat plain yogurt or sour cream
1 tablespoon lemon juice
½ teaspoon garlic powder
2 sprigs fresh dill

Deviled Ham and Cheese Dip

1 can (4.5 ounces) deviled
    ham
1 container (4 ounces) nonfat
    cream cheese spread
½ cup nonfat plain yogurt
6 to 8 pimiento-stuffed olives

Holidays are a wonderful time to wow your family and friends with this simple dip.

Estimated preparation time: 5 minutes
Makes about 1½ cups

1. Place all ingredients in food processor and pulse until smooth.
2. Transfer to small serving bowl, cover, and refrigerate until ready to use. Consume within 3 days.

Note: Serve it with fresh vegetables and bread sticks for a quick, springtime snack.

Dump-Style Homemade Salsa

Not all bottled salsas meet everyone's tastes. With this less expensive, "homemade" version, you can use more or less chili powder to control heat—remember, the spice intensifies after a day or two.

1 can (15 ounces) diced tomatoes, drained
1 can (6 ounces) diced green chilies, drained
½ cup diced onion (fresh or frozen)
½ teaspoon minced garlic
½ to 1 teaspoon chili powder

Estimated preparation time: 5 minutes
Makes about 2⅔ cups

1. Place all ingredients into small bowl and toss well to combine.
2. Cover and refrigerate for up to 1 week.

Quick, Fresh Snack Bowl

1 small bunch seedless white
    or green grapes
1 small bunch seedless red
    grapes
2 medium apples, cored and
    sliced into wedges
2 oranges, seeded, peeled, and
    separated into wedges
4 ounces reduced-fat cheddar
    cheese, cut into small
    cubes
4 ounces reduced-fat
    Monterey Jack cheese,
    cut into small cubes

Assemble this nutritious mix and refrigerate for after-school snacking, or bring a double batch to your child's classroom party.

Estimated preparation time: 10 minutes
Makes 4 servings

1. Place all ingredients in medium bowl—toss together, or arrange by type—and serve.

Crunchy Cracker-Sandwich Bites

Your children can make their own cracker sandwiches using two crackers, a piece of cheese, and a vegetable round for each—try them in lunches, too.

16 whole wheat crackers
16 saltine crackers
4 slices 2%-fat American cheese, each cut into four equal pieces
1 medium zucchini or cucumber, sliced into thin rounds

Estimated preparation time: 7 minutes
Makes 4 servings

1. Arrange crackers, cheese, and zucchini or cucumber on serving platter.
2. Serve immediately, allowing people to put together their own sandwiches. If not serving immediately, cover and refrigerate until ready.

Peanut Butter Pinwheel Treats

4 flour tortillas (8 inch)
4 tablespoons chunky peanut
butter
2 tablespoons unsweetened
applesauce

Preschoolers love this easy snack.

Estimated preparation time: 10 minutes
Makes 3 to 4 servings

1. Put tortillas between damp paper towels and micro-wave on high for 20 seconds to warm.
2. Blend peanut butter and applesauce in small bowl until smooth, and spread evenly on each tortilla.
3. Layer two tortillas by placing one on top of another, peanut butter side up. Roll and refrigerate for at least 10 minutes. Slice into 1-inch segments and serve.

Note: you can store Peanut Butter Pinwheel Treats in sandwich bags in the refrigerator for a quick lunch-box surprise.

Savory Party Mix

Almost everyone loves Chex brand party mix, and this lower fat alternative is just as delicious.

4 cups shredded wheat cereal nuggets
1 cup small unsalted pretzels
1 cup popped popcorn
3 tablespoons margarine, melted
1 tablespoon Worcestershire sauce
1 teaspoon seasoned salt

Estimated preparation time: 3 minutes
Estimated cooking time: 5 to 6 minutes
Makes about 12 servings

1. Mix cereal, pretzels, and popcorn in large microwavable bowl.
2. Whisk together margarine, Worcestershire sauce, and seasoned salt in small bowl. Drizzle evenly over dry mixture, tossing to coat evenly.
3. Microwave on high for 3 minutes, and stir. Microwave for 2 to 3 minutes, or until crisp.
4. Remove from microwave and allow to cool. Store in tightly sealed container.

Power-Snack Popcorn

1 bag (3.5 ounces) regular
    microwavable popcorn
¼ teaspoon cayenne pepper
¾ teaspoon ground cumin
¾ teaspoon salt
½ teaspoon garlic powder
1½ cups peanuts, preferably
    honey-roasted
1½ cups raisins

We eat lots of popcorn in our home, but the boys get tired of the same old snack. The seasonings, peanuts, and raisins make this a favorite play-date treat.

Estimated preparation time: 15 minutes
Makes about 16 cups

1. Pop popcorn according to package directions and place in large bowl.
2. Sprinkle with cayenne, cumin, salt, and garlic powder, and toss to coat evenly. Stir in peanuts and raisins.

Cheesy Circle Snack Mix

This unusual mix was another winning "accident" on a rushed afternoon—you can substitute other unsweetened cereals with similar results.

2 cups toasted oats cereal
2 cups corn puff cereal
2 tablespoons reduced-fat
    Caesar dressing

Estimated preparation time: 3 minutes
Estimated cooking time: 2 minutes
Makes 4 cups

1. Place cereal in 1-gallon plastic storage bag. Drizzle dressing over cereal, seal, and shake vigorously.
2. Microwave sealed bag on high for 2 minutes.
3. Remove bag from oven, shake bag again, and pour seasoned mix into serving bowl.

Colorful Corn Tortilla Bowl

2 bags (12 ounces each) white
    corn tortilla chips
2 bags (12 ounces each) blue
    corn tortilla chips
Fat-Free White Bean Dip
    (recipe, page 175)
Dump-Style Homemade Salsa
    (recipe, page 179)

This is an ideal treat for informal parties, and can also act as lunch during the weekend—be sure to have plenty on hand for the big game.

Estimated preparation time: 10 minutes
Makes 12 servings

1. Combine chips in large bowl.
2. Prepare the two dips and serve.

Barbecue Meatballs and Mini-Rolls

This "snack" is more like a meal, and when your crew is hungry, they'll love it.

Estimated preparation time: 5 minutes
Estimated cooking time: 10 minutes
Makes 12 rolls

1 package (16 ounces) frozen cooked meatballs
1 cup bottled barbecue sauce (any variety)
12 French-style rolls, cut in half lengthwise

1. Place meatballs and sauce in medium nonstick pot. Cook over medium-low heat for 10 minutes, stirring occasionally.
2. Transfer to platter or serving bowl. Serve with rolls to make quick meatball sandwiches.

. . . .

Note: If you don't have French rolls on hand, use prepared biscuits to make up to 20 mini-sandwiches.

. . . .

Streamlined Fruit-and-Veggie Tray

1 pint fresh strawberries or
    raspberries
¾ pound seedless white or
    green grapes
1 pint cherry tomatoes
1 pint fresh broccoli florets
1 bag (16 ounces) baby carrots
1 cup nonfat ranch dressing

Fruit and vegetable trays are undoubtedly healthy, but cutting and dicing are a lot of work—let the grocer do your work for you, and relax.

Estimated preparation time: 5 minutes
Makes 12 servings

1. Arrange fruit and vegetables on serving platter.
2. Pour dressing into small bowl and place in center of the platter. Serve.

10
GUEST-PLEASING
GOURMET

Terrific and Easy Trifle
Two-Grocery-Bag Party
Freezer Section Party Fare
Easy Freezer Dessert
Christmas in a Hurry
Black Forest Chocolate
    Cheesecake
Amazing Easter Dinner
Amazing Blackberry Pyra-
    mid Cake
Easy New Year's Brunch
Quick and Kosher Holiday
    Dinner

Last-Minute Sweet and
    Sour Shrimp
Last-Minute Creamy
    "Crab" Roll-ups
Last-Minute Beefy Barbe-
    cue Wraps
Last-Minute Hawaiian
    Pizza
Last-Minute Baked Maca-
    roni and Cheese
Speedy Southwestern
    Dinner
Almost-Catered Chicken
    Dinner

I've been cooking for more than twenty years, so family and friends have come to expect "better than basics" food when I entertain (and I entertain as often as possible). I'm a very busy working mom. I don't always have time to prepare complicated dishes—and thanks to new supermarket items, I don't have to. Neither do you! "Gourmet" no longer has to mean you spent hours in the kitchen; it means you made something special out of basic fare.

This chapter will show you how to impress your guests with simple party recipes. You'll also find recipes for fast, full-course holiday meals. When friends pop in unexpectedly, you'll be ready to roll with last-minute magic tricks—and for large, planned celebrations you'll find entire menus for not-quite-catered success.

Terrific and Easy Trifle

Trifles are not only easy to prepare, they look fabulous—this one is sure to be a favorite with your guests.

1 package (16 ounces) vanilla
  wafers
1 quart prepared chocolate
  pudding (from grocery
  deli)
1 can (16 ounces) light cherry
  pie filling

Estimated preparation time: 7 minutes
Makes 16 to 18 servings

1. Slightly crush the cookies by removing inner bag from box, shaking vigorously, and applying gentle pressure. Place half of the crushed cookies in the bottom of a clear, large serving bowl.
2. Spoon pudding onto cookies, and add another layer of cookies on the pudding. Top with pie filling.
3. Cover and refrigerate until ready to serve.

Two-Grocery-Bag Party

cooking oil spray
8 russet potatoes, halved
    lengthwise
6 lamb rib chops
6 pork sausage links
6 marinated boneless, skinless
    chicken breasts
1 bunch fresh rosemary,
    leaves stripped from
    stems
4 to 6 portobello mushrooms,
    halved
2 packages (16 ounces each)
    salad greens
salad dressing

An entire party in two grocery bags? Absolutely! You can feed up to eighteen guests with this menu: Serve meats, potatoes, mushrooms, and salad with fresh fruit, fresh bread from the grocery bakery, and beverages of your choice. For dessert, serve Terrific and Easy Trifle, page 191.

Estimated preparation time: 15 minutes
Estimated cooking time: 24 minutes
Makes 16 to 18 servings

1. Preheat broiler. Lightly coat broiling pan and nonstick cookie sheet with cooking oil spray.
2. Place potatoes cut side up in microwave oven and microwave on high for 10 minutes. Allow to sit in microwave.
3. Arrange chops, sausages, and chicken breasts on broiler pan. Sprinkle chops with fresh rosemary leaves.
4. Arrange partially cooked potatoes cut-side down on cookie sheet. Arrange mushrooms on cookie sheet and broiler pan (so that all items can fit on 2 pans in 1 small oven).
5. Place cookie sheet on bottom rack in oven. Place broiler pan on middle rack of oven. Close oven door and broil for 7 minutes; slide middle rack out enough

Guest-Pleasing Gourmet

to turn the meats, slide back into place, and broil for an additional 5 minutes.

6. Turn oven off, remove broiler pan and cookie sheet, and arrange meats, potatoes, and mushrooms on two large platters.

7. Place salad greens in a large serving bowl and drizzle with your favorite dressing.

Freezer Section Party Fare

Sandwiches:

2 packages (9 ounces each) frozen stuffed Philly steak and cheese sandwiches (such as Lean Pockets brand)

2 packages (9 ounces each) frozen stuffed ham and cheese sandwiches (such as Lean Pockets brand)

2 packages (9 ounces each) frozen stuffed turkey and ham with cheddar sandwiches (such as Lean Pockets brand)

⅓ cup nonfat Italian dressing

Potatoes:

2 packages (16 ounces each) frozen O'Brian-style diced potatoes (with onions and peppers)

⅔ cup reduced-fat mayonnaise

¼ cup prepared mustard

Grab all of the ingredients at the supermarket, and your party will be ready any time. Serve with tossed, green salad and Easy Freezer Dessert, which follows this recipe.

Estimated preparation time: 10 minutes
Estimated cooking time: 22 minutes
Makes 12 servings

1. Preheat oven to 425 degrees.
2. Remove frozen sandwiches from wrappers and arrange on 2 nonstick cookie sheets. Brush with Italian dressing and place on center rack of hot oven. Reduce heat to 350 degrees and bake for 12 minutes. Remove from oven and allow to cool slightly.
3. Fork-puncture frozen bags of potatoes, place one at a time in microwave oven, and microwave on high for 6 minutes each.
4. Remove potatoes from bags and place in large serving bowl. Add mayonnaise and mustard and toss well.

Note: You can cut your cooking time in half by starting the potato salad while the sandwiches are baking.

Easy Freezer Dessert

This is one of the easiest desserts you'll ever make. Serve the berries that top this waffle whole, or puree them for a quick sauce.

12 frozen reduced-fat waffles
½ gallon vanilla frozen yogurt
1 package (12 ounces) frozen
    berries, thawed

Estimated preparation time: 10 minutes
Estimated cooking time: 5 to 8 minutes
Makes 12 servings

1. Lightly toast waffles (or warm in 350-degree oven for 5 minutes).
2. Top each waffle with a scoop of frozen yogurt and 1 tablespoon thawed berries; serve immediately.

Christmas in a Hurry

Make the most of this meal by asking your children to assist you in the preparation. Serve this Christmas dinner with tossed salad, fresh rolls, and Black Forest Chocolate Cheesecake (page 197).

Turkey:

1 whole smoked turkey (12 to 14 pounds)

Sweet Potatoes:

cooking oil spray
2 cans (16 ounces each) sweet potatoes, drained
2 jars (8 ounces each) pureed apricots
¼ cup brown sugar, loosely packed

Creamed Spinach:

1 package (16 ounces) frozen chopped spinach, thawed
1 can (10.75 ounces) reduced-fat condensed cream of mushroom soup
1 cup crushed cornflakes

Stuffing:

2 packages (10 ounces each) complete stovetop stuffing mix
1 cup raisins

Estimated preparation time: 30 minutes
Estimated baking time: 1 hour
Makes 12 servings

1. Preheat oven to 350 degrees.
2. Prepare the turkey: Place smoked whole turkey in large roasting pan, cover with foil, and bake at 350 degrees for 1 hour, or until thoroughly heated.
3. Prepare the sweet potatoes: Lightly coat casserole dish with cooking oil spray. Add canned sweet potatoes and apricot puree. Sprinkle brown sugar on top. Cover, add to preheated oven, and cook for 20 to 25 minutes.
4. Prepare the spinach: Lightly coat microwavable casserole dish with cooking oil spray. Add thawed spinach and condensed soup, and stir. Cover and microwave on high for 12 minutes. Stir. Sprinkle with crushed cornflakes and microwave uncovered on high for an additional 3 to 4 minutes, or until sauce begins to bubble. Remove from microwave, cover, and let sit.
5. Prepare the stuffing: Prepare mix according to package directions. Stir in raisins before serving.

Black Forest Chocolate Cheesecake

This festive recipe bakes longer than many recipes in this cookbook, but it's definitely worth it. For a larger crowd, bake two at the same time.

Estimated preparation time: 15 minutes
Estimated baking time: 45 minutes
Estimated refrigeration time: 1 hour
Makes 8 medium or 10 small servings

2 packages (8 ounces each) cream cheese, softened
1 can (14 ounces) chocolate sweetened condensed milk (not evaporated milk)
3 eggs
1 prepared chocolate cookie pie crust
1 can (21 ounces) cherry pie filling, chilled

1. Preheat oven to 350 degrees.
2. Beat the cream cheese in large bowl until fluffy. Gradually beat in sweetened condensed milk until mixture is smooth. Add eggs and mix well.
3. Pour mixture into pie crust and bake for 45 minutes, or until center is set. Allow to cool, then refrigerate at least 1 hour. Top with cherry pie filling before serving.

Amazing Easter Dinner

Ham:

1 fully cooked whole ham,
    bone in (8 to 10
    pounds)
1 can (13.25 ounces)
    pineapple chunks,
    drained
1 can (16 ounces) apricot
    halves, drained
1 cup bottled sweet and sour
    sauce

Sweet Potatoes:

2 cans (16 ounces each) sweet
    potatoes, drained
1 teaspoon cinnamon
⅔ cup nonfat milk
2 tablespoons margarine

Vegetables:

1 package (16 ounces) frozen
    specialty peas and baby
    carrots, thawed

Simplicity assures holiday success, and this Easter dinner couldn't be simpler. Serve with tossed salad, fresh bread, and Amazing Blackberry Pyramid Cake (opposite).

Estimated preparation time: 25 minutes
Estimated baking time: 1 hour
Makes 12 servings

1. Preheat oven to 350 degrees.
2. Prepare the ham: Place ham in large roasting pan, add pineapple and apricots, and pour sweet and sour sauce over all. Bake for 1 hour, or until heated thoroughly.
3. Prepare the sweet potatoes: Place sweet potatoes, cinnamon, and milk in food processor and pulse until smooth. Transfer to microwavable casserole dish, drop margarine in center, cover, and microwave on high for 10 to 12 minutes.
4. Prepare the vegetables: Place thawed peas and baby carrots in medium nonstick pot. Add ⅓ cup water, cover, and simmer over medium low heat for 15 minutes, stirring occasionally.

Amazing Blackberry Pyramid Cake

Your guests will think you baked for hours to make this special cake, and it tastes as great as it looks!

Estimated preparation time: 20 minutes
Makes 12 servings

1 package (16 ounces) frozen pound cake, thawed
1 cup plus 2 tablespoons blackberry preserves
1 cup frozen nonfat whipped topping, thawed

1. Trim the top, bottom, and sides off the pound cake to make sharp edges. (Take your time: If the cake isn't trimmed neatly, the result will be a lumpy—rather than stunning—dessert.)
2. Slice cake horizontally into quarters.
3. Spread 3 tablespoons preserves on three of the four cake layers.
4. Align the long edge of the bottom layer at the edge of a countertop. Stack layers to form a layered cake.
5. Using a long, serrated knife held at a 45-degree angle to the countertop, slice the layered cake in half (the end of the knife should extend through the cake out past the edge of the countertop—use the countertop edge as a cutting guide)—you'll have two long, triangular pieces. Place the triangular pieces "back to back" to form a long pyramid, so that the filling of the layers shows vertical.
6. Spread the remaining preserves between the two halves to form the final layer. Frost with whipped topping and refrigerate until ready to serve.

Easy New Year's Brunch

Pancake Rolls:

16 frozen buttermilk pancakes
16 precooked pork sausage
    links (or kielbasa links)
2 cups reduced-fat cottage
    cheese
½ cup light maple syrup

Potatoes:

cooking oile spray
1 package (16 ounces) fresh
    shredded potatoes (or
    frozen, thawed)
½ cup chopped onion (fresh
    or frozen)
½ cup chopped green pepper
    (fresh or frozen)
¼ cup chopped, fresh parsley,
    or 2 tablespoons dried
    parsley flakes
3 containers (4 ounces each)
    egg substitute, thawed
⅔ cup nonfat milk

Fruit Dessert:

1 can (16 ounces) light apple
    pie filling
1 can (16 ounces) light cherry
    pie filling
1½ cups dried apricots
½ cup currants
whipped cream (optional)

I often prefer a casual brunch to a fancy dinner party, and New Year's Day is the perfect time to host one. The following menu will start your year successfully.

Estimated preparation time: 20 minutes
Estimated baking time: 20 minutes
Makes 12 servings

1. Preheat oven to 350 degrees.
2. Prepare the pancakes: Place frozen pancakes between slightly damp paper towels and microwave on high for 30 seconds. Rearrange order of pancakes, return to microwave, and heat on high for an additional 30 seconds. Continue until all pancakes are warm and pliable (about 2 minutes).
3. Roll sausages in pancakes and arrange (seam-side down) in 9 × 13-inch foil baking pans. Cover with foil and set aside on counter.
4. Place cottage cheese and maple syrup in small bowl, stir to combine, cover, and refrigerate. Spoon 1 tablespoon sweetened cottage cheese onto center of each pancake roll before serving.
5. Prepare the potatoes: Lightly coat another 9 × 13-inch baking pan with cooking oil spray. Spread shredded potatoes evenly on the bottom of pan. Sprinkle onion,

green pepper, and parsley over potatoes. Place egg substitute and milk in medium bowl and whisk together. Pour over potatoes.

6. Place all three baking pans in preheated oven and bake for 20 minutes. Remove from oven, cool slightly, and slice into 12 equal portions.

7. Prepare the fruit dessert: Pour pie fillings in medium nonstick pot. Stir in dried fruits and cook over low heat for 10 to 12 minutes, stirring occasionally. When mixture begins to bubble, cover and remove from heat. Serve with whipped cream if desired.

Quick and Kosher Holiday Dinner

Beef:

1 whole beef tenderloin (5 to
 6 pounds)
2 tablespoons extra virgin
 olive oil
1 small bunch fresh rosemary
1 small bunch fresh thyme

Rice:

1 cup white rice
1 cup wild rice
½ cup dried cranberries
½ cup chopped pecans
2 cans (10.75 ounces each)
 chicken broth
½ cup orange juice
2 tablespoons honey

Salad:

2 packages (16 ounces each)
 salad greens
salad dressing

This is a fast, easy, and delicious meal for any number of holidays.

Estimated preparation time: 20 minutes
Estimated baking time: 1 hour
Makes 12 servings

1. Preheat oven to 375 degrees.
2. Prepare the beef: With very clean hands, place beef tenderloin on large sheet of heavy duty aluminum foil (shiny side up) and brush with oil. Arrange fresh herbs on top of meat. Wrap tightly in foil, place in medium roasting pan, and cover. Turn heat down to 350 degrees and bake for 1 hour. Remove from oven and allow to sit for 15 minutes before unwrapping and carving. Meat will be rare.
3. Prepare the rice: Combine rice, cranberries, pecans, broth, orange juice, and honey in a microwavable 2-quart casserole dish. Cover and microwave on high for 20 minutes, stirring and turning once during cooking.
4. Prepare the salad: Place salad greens in large bowl and drizzle with dressing of your choice.

Note: Beef tenderloin tastes best when cooked rare; exercise caution when handling raw meat.

Guest-Pleasing Gourmet

Last-Minute Sweet and Sour Shrimp

With a dash to the grocery store for items you might not have on hand, and three minutes preparation time, it's easy to entertain improvisationally. Serve this to your last-minute guests with a fresh salad.

Estimated preparation. time: 3 minutes
Estimated cooking time: 15 minutes
Makes 8 servings

1. Place all ingredients in a large, nonstick pot.
2. Cook over medium-high heat, stirring occasionally, until liquid begins to bubble.
3. Reduce heat to lowest setting, cover, and cook for an additional 10 minutes. Serve.

2 cups uncooked instant rice
1½ cups water
2 tablespoons lemon juice
1 tablespoon reduced-sodium soy sauce
2 tablespoons apricot preserves or seedless raspberry preserves
1 package (6 ounces) frozen cooked shrimp
1 package (16 ounces) frozen broccoli stir-fry vegetable mix (broccoli, carrots, onions, red peppers, celery, water chestnuts, mushrooms)

Last-Minute Creamy "Crab" Roll-ups

1 package (6 ounces) imitation crab meat, diced
1 package (8 ounces) reduced-fat cream cheese, cubed
2 scallions, finely diced
1 medium tomato, finely diced
8 flour tortillas (8 inch)
cooking oil spray
nonfat sour cream (optional)

When company drops by unexpectedly, make this fast, simple meal. Serve with canned or fresh fruit.

Estimated preparation time: 8 minutes
Estimated baking time: 12 minutes
Makes 8 servings

1. Preheat oven to 375 degrees.
2. Arrange imitation crab meat, cream cheese cubes, and vegetables evenly on each flour tortilla. Carefully roll the tortillas enchilada-style.
3. Lightly coat 9 × 13-inch baking dish with cooking oil spray. Arrange roll-ups in dish.
4. Bake for 12 minutes, or until tortillas are just beginning to turn golden brown. Top with nonfat sour cream, if desired.

Last-Minute Beefy Barbecue Wraps

This is a wonderful "company" meal when served with coleslaw and Spanish rice from your grocery deli.

Estimated preparation time: 10 minutes
Estimated baking time: 10 to 12 minutes
Makes 8 servings

2 cups chopped cooked beef
    (leftovers work well)
8 flour tortillas (8 inch)
½ cup barbecue sauce
½ cup diced green peppers
    (fresh or frozen)
1 cup reduced-fat shredded
    cheddar cheese
cooking oil spray

1. Preheat oven to 350 degrees.
2. Arrange beef in center of each tortilla. Spoon 1 tablespoon barbecue sauce over meat, then sprinkle with green peppers and cheese.
3. Lightly coat 9 × 13-inch baking pan with cooking oil spray. Roll tortillas enchilada-style and place seam-side down in baking dish.
4. Bake for 10 to 12 minutes, or until cheese melts.

Last-Minute Hawaiian Pizza

2 prepared pizza shells
    (12 inch)
2 medium tomatoes, sliced
    very thin
2 pounds cooked ham, cut
    into thin strips or deli
    sliced
2 small onions, sliced very
    thin
2 cans (6 ounces each) pine-
    apple chunks, drained
3 cups reduced-fat shredded
    mozzarella cheese

If your friends and family have hearty appetites, consider making a second pizza by spreading canned chili on a pizza shell and sprinkling with cheddar cheese—the flavors work well together.

Estimated preparation time: 10 minutes
Estimated baking time: 12 minutes
Makes 6 servings

1. Preheat oven to 400 degrees.
2. Place pizza shells on cookie sheet or pizza pan. Arrange tomato slices on pizza shells, then lay strips of ham over tomato slices. Top with onion slices, pineapple chunks, and shredded cheese.
3. Bake for 12 minutes, or until cheese bubbles.

Last-Minute
Baked Macaroni and Cheese

This is the perfect "grab it on your way home" meal for a crowd. Serve with a simple tossed salad and fresh bread.

1 package (4 to 5 pounds)
    frozen macaroni and
    cheese (party size)
1 cup plain dry bread crumbs
½ cup grated Romano cheese
¼ cup chopped fresh parsley

Estimated preparation time: 3 minutes
Estimated baking time: varies according to brand
Makes 12 generous servings

1. Bake macaroni and cheese according to package directions.
2. Combine remaining ingredients in a small bowl.
3. When the macaroni and cheese is ready, sprinkle bread crumb mixture over it and bake for another 5 minutes, or until bread crumbs turn golden brown.

Speedy Southwestern Dinner

1 package (12 ounces) frozen
 cooked beef for fajitas
1 package (12 ounces) frozen
 cooked chicken breast
 for fajitas
1 green pepper, sliced into
 thin strips
1 red pepper, sliced into thin
 strips
1 medium onion, sliced into
 thin strips and halved
½ pint cherry tomatoes,
 halved
1½ pounds prepared Spanish
 rice (from grocery deli)
2 cans (15 ounces each)
 seasoned pinto beans,
 drained
8 flour tortillas (8 inch)

This easy-to-assemble menu goes from grocery bag to dinner table in twenty-seven minutes.

Estimated preparation time: 15 minutes
Estimated cooking time: 12 minutes
Makes 8 servings.

1. Preheat oven to 375 degrees.
2. Place frozen meat, sliced peppers, and onion on a nonstick cookie sheet. Slide cookie sheet onto center rack of oven and heat for 10 minutes. Add cherry tomatoes and heat for 2 minutes longer.
3. Place rice in medium-sized microwavable bowl. Cover, and microwave on high about 3 minutes to reheat.
4. Place beans in medium microwavable bowl. Microwave on high about 4 minutes or until thoroughly heated.
5. Microwave tortillas on high about 1 minute to warm. Assemble fajitas. Serve with hot rice and beans.

. . . .

Note: If your children won't eat bell pepper strips, experiment with other vegetables, such as thinly sliced zucchini and carrots.

. . . .

Guest-Pleasing Gourmet

Almost-Catered Chicken Dinner

> *When you don't have time to cook, but don't have the budget to hire a caterer, this menu solves all of your problems.*

Estimated preparation time: 15 minutes
Estimated baking time: 20 to 25 minutes
Makes 8 to 10 servings

1. Prepare the chicken: Place chickens side by side in large roasting pan. Cover, place in cold oven, and set temperature for 375 degrees. Heat thoroughly, about 20 to 25 minutes.
2. Remove baked potatoes from their packaging, and microwave according to package directions. Transfer to cookie sheet. Drop 1 tablespoon cold soup onto each potato, place in oven with chicken, and heat until soup has melted, about __ minutes.
3. Prepare the coleslaw: Put coleslaw vegetables, raisins, and dressing in medium bowl. Toss until well combined. Sprinkle with sunflower seeds and refrigerate.
4. Heat the rolls, and serve with honey butter.

Chicken:

2 deli rotisserie chickens (3 to 4 pounds each)

Potatoes:

4 packages (10 ounces each) frozen baked potatoes (such as Twice Baked brand by Ore Ida)
1 can (10.75 ounces) reduced-fat condensed golden mushroom soup

Coleslaw:

1 package (16 ounces) broccoli coleslaw
1 cup raisins or currants
1 cup bottled coleslaw dressing
2 tablespoons roasted sunflower seeds

Rolls:

1 dozen fresh bakery rolls
1 tub (4 ounces) honey butter

Additional Ideas for Fast Dinners

....

Fabulous French Fare: *Impress your guests with heated and jazzed-up quiche from your grocery deli. Top a traditional spinach quiche with a large dollop of nonfat sour cream and a small sprig of fresh herbs.*

Nearly Take-Out Chinese: *Use frozen chicken nuggets or popcorn shrimp, bottled sweet and sour sauce, canned pineapple, and fresh or frozen vegetables over prepared instant rice. Purchase fortune cookies in the specialty section of your grocery store.*

Improvised Italian Dinner: *Look in the freezer section for stuffed manicotti, raviolis, lasagna roll-ups, and garlic bread. Add a jar of spaghetti sauce and a simple tossed salad.*

"Fast Food" Chicken Sandwiches and Fries: *Heat precooked, breaded chicken patties (or breast slices) and frozen, microwavable fries; with burger buns, lettuce, tomato, and condiments you can duplicate restaurant chain varieties.*

Savory Subs: *For no-cook success, purchase unusual loaves of bakery breads (for example, sun-dried tomato). Instead of the standard lettuce, tomato, and American cheese, try spinach leaves, fresh herbs, golden tomatoes, and crumbled feta over deli roast beef.*

....

11

CULINARY

KIDS

Cheesy Fruit Parfaits

Easy Cheesy Waffle Sandwiches

Toasted Banana-Nut Pancakes

Quick Crunchy Porridge

Turkey Club Buns

Bologna Wrap Sandwiches

Golden Tuna Bagels

Brawny Beef Sub

Fruit and Tuna Salad Boats

Stuffed-Crust Pita Pizzas

Hot Diggity Dog Pie

Ravioli Casserole

Earthquake Taco Salad

Bread Bowl Chicken Taco Salad

Frozen Yogurt Pops

Chewy Oatmeal Bars

Rainbow Melon Wedges

Red, White, and Blue Graham Towers

Pecan Cookies

Kids in the kitchen are doing more than distracting you or making a mess—they're learning about basic chemistry, physics, and nutrition. When your children are involved in the preparation of a meal, they're also developing lifelong skills. The same four year old who dumped three times the necessary amount of salad dressing into the bowl might grow up to be the next Wolfgang Puck. More important, children who have the opportunity to cook by your side (or on their own) gain a sense of pride and significance.

This chapter contains kid-friendly recipes for quick and easy breakfasts, short-order lunches, simple and tasty dinners, and fabulously fast desserts. Each recipe is designed with the elementary school–aged child in mind, and you can assist younger children who wish to join in the fun.

Cheesy Fruit Parfaits

These creamy, nutritious parfaits are fun and easy to assemble.

2 cups low-fat cottage cheese
1 can (16 ounces) light
    blueberry pie filling
1 cup low-fat granola without
    raisins

Estimated preparation time: 5 minutes
Makes 4 servings

1. Have your child spoon ½ cup cottage cheese into each of four small bowls.
2. Help your child divide the berry pie filling evenly between each of the bowls with a small slotted spoon.
3. Sprinkle ¼ cup granola on top of each parfait and serve.

. . . .

Note: Consider using shatterproof serving bowls when preparing this with a small child.

. . . .

Easy Cheesy Waffle Sandwiches

8 frozen waffles, thawed, or
 toasted and cooled
1 container (8 ounces)
 reduced-fat whipped
 cream cheese
4 tablespoons low-sugar fruit
 spread

Talk about an out-the-door breakfast! This recipe is ideal for days when your gang is in a rush.

Estimated preparation time: 5 to 7 minutes
Makes 4 servings

1. Have your child spread 4 waffles with whipped cream cheese, and each of 4 waffles with 1 tablespoon fruit spread.
2. Assemble sandwiches, cut in half, and serve.

Toasted Banana-Nut Pancakes

These pancakes aren't cooked on a hot griddle, so even preschoolers can whip them up quickly and easily.

4 frozen pancakes, toasted
2 bananas, sliced
½ cup chopped walnuts
4 teaspoons powdered sugar

Estimated preparation time: 5 to 7 minutes
Makes 4 servings

1. Have your child arrange banana slices on each pancake.
2. Sprinkle with nuts and sugar and serve.

Quick Crunchy Porridge

4 cups low-fat granola
1 cup nonfat vanilla yogurt
⅔ cup nonfat milk

This hearty breakfast cereal is warm and comforting on a chilly morning.

Estimated preparation time: 3 minutes
Estimated cooking time: 3 minutes
Makes 4 servings

1. Have your child combine all ingredients in medium microwavable bowl, stirring to coat evenly.
2. Microwave on high for 3 minutes, and stir.
3. Transfer hot cereal into individual serving bowls and serve.

. . . .

Note: Young children should be supervised when handling hot foods.

. . . .

Turkey Club Buns

Easy-to-assemble lunches are perfect for lazy week-ends, and this club sandwich is a winner.

Estimated preparation time: 5 minutes
Makes 4 sandwiches

1. Have your child open the burger buns, spread each side with dab of the mayonnaise, and sprinkle with bacon bits.
2. Ask your child to layer (on each bun bottom round) turkey, cheese, and tomato slices, place bun tops on the sandwiches, and serve.

4 whole wheat burger buns
2 tablespoons reduced-fat
    mayonnaise
2 tablespoons ready-made
    bacon bits
4 slices turkey breast
    lunchmeat
4 slices 2%-fat American
    cheese
4 thin slices tomato

Bologna Wrap Sandwiches

4 medium flour tortillas
2 tablespoons reduced-fat
    mayonnaise
4 large lettuce leaves
4 slices bologna
4 slices 2%-fat American
    cheese
4 thin slices tomato

Kids love bologna, and burrito-type sandwiches break lunchtime monotony.

Estimated preparation time: 5 minutes
Makes 4 sandwiches

1. Have your child spread each flour tortilla with a dab of mayonnaise, and layer with lettuce, bologna, cheese, and tomato slices.
2. Carefully fold sides of each tortilla to overlap on the center. Secure with toothpick and serve.

Golden Tuna Bagels

Bagels are another way to make a "boring" sandwich better, and this tuna treat is nutritious as well.

4 egg bagels, sliced in half
1 can (6 ounces) water-packed
   tuna, drained
4 slices 2%-fat American
   cheese
4 thin slices tomato

Estimated preparation time: 5 minutes
Estimated baking time: 5 minutes
Makes 4 sandwiches

1. Preheat oven to 350 degrees.
2. Help your child assemble each bagel sandwich by layering tuna, cheese, and tomato slices on bottom round, and topping with upper round.
3. Place sandwiches on nonstick cookie sheet and bake for 5 minutes.

Brawny Beef Sub

2 tablespoons reduced-fat
    mayonnaise
2 tablespoons fat-free Caesar
    salad dressing
1 loaf (8 ounces) French
    bread, cut in half
    lengthwise
½ pound thinly sliced deli
    roast beef
4 to 5 fresh spinach leaves
1 medium tomato, thinly
    sliced

Older children will love preparing this colossal sandwich for the family.

Estimated preparation time: 5 minutes
Makes 4 servings

1. Help your child mix together mayonnaise and Caesar dressing. Spread on each half of loaf.
2. Ask your child to assemble sliced beef, spinach leaves, and tomato on bottom half of loaf. Add top half of loaf, cut into 4 sections, and serve.

Fruit and Tuna Salad Boats

This eye-appealing entrée is as fun to make as it is to eat!

Estimated preparation time: 10 minutes
Makes 4 servings

1. Have your child place tuna, pineapple, and raisins in medium bowl and stir to combine.
2. Add salad dressing and toss gently.
3. Allow your child to spoon mixture into each cantaloupe quarter.

1 can (6 ounces) water-packed tuna, drained
1 can (6 ounces) crushed pineapple, drained
1 cup raisins
½ cup raspberry vinaigrette dressing
1 medium cantaloupe, quartered and seeded

Stuffed-Crust Pita Pizzas

6 whole wheat pitas
6 slices 2%-fat mozzarella
    cheese
⅓ cup tomato sauce
1 teaspoon Italian seasoning
3 slices turkey salami,
    chopped
1 cup reduced-fat shredded
    pizza blend cheese

This recipe has been a huge success in my home, and your children will love preparing and eating it, too.

Estimated preparation time: 10 minutes
Estimated baking time: 12 to 15 minutes
Makes 6 servings

1. Preheat oven to 375 degrees.
2. Help your child slice openings into the side of the pitas. Have your child slide 1 slice of mozzarella cheese into each pocket.
3. Place filled pitas on a nonstick cookie sheet. Spread 1 tablespoon tomato sauce evenly on top of each pita and sprinkle with Italian seasoning. Allow your child to arrange chopped salami on each pizza, then top with shredded cheese.
4. Bake for 12 to 15 minutes, remove, cool slightly, and serve.

....

Note: Be sure to keep young children away from the hot oven.

....

Hot Diggity Dog Pie

This surprising casserole is a tasty treat for the whole family.

1 package (7.5 ounces)
    cornbread mix
½ cup water
1 can (10 ounces) hot dog
    chili sauce
cooking oil spray
6 beef or turkey franks

Estimated preparation time: 10 minutes
Estimated baking time: 20 minutes
Makes 6 servings

1. Preheat oven to 375 degrees.
2. Have your child place contents of cornbread mix in medium bowl, add water, and stir until well combined. Help your child fold in contents of canned chili sauce.
3. Lightly coat 10-inch pie pan with cooking oil spray. Have your child spoon in the cornbread mixture, and arrange franks in fan design on top of the batter.
4. Bake for 20 minutes, remove from oven, cool, and serve.

Ravioli Casserole

cooking oil spray
2 packages (12 ounces each)
    fresh spinach ravioli
1 can (8 ounces) tomato sauce
1½ cups low-fat cottage
    cheese
1 can (15 ounces) Italian-style
    diced tomatoes
1 cup reduced-fat shredded
    mozzarella cheese

My boys love ravioli, and this dish is very easy to prepare.

Estimated preparation time: 10 minutes
Estimated baking time: 20 minutes
Makes 6 generous servings

1. Preheat oven to 375 degrees.
2. Lightly coat 9 × 13-inch baking dish with cooking oil spray. Have your child arrange ravioli from one package on the bottom of the dish.
3. Help your child make layers: Spread entire contents of tomato sauce over raviolis, followed by layer of cottage cheese. Arrange remaining raviolis on top of the cottage cheese layer. Spoon and spread entire contents of canned diced tomatoes over the second ravioli layer, and sprinkle with shredded cheese.
4. Cover baking dish with foil and bake for 20 minutes, until heated through.

Earthquake Taco Salad

Estimated preparation time: 10 minutes
Makes 6 to 8 servings

1. Have your child place the chicken, beans, tomato, olives, and salad greens in 1-gallon plastic bag. Seal tightly and shake vigorously.
2. Help your child transfer mixture to large salad bowl.
3. Sprinkle with shredded cheddar cheese and serve with dressings of your choice or over a bed of tortilla chips.

2 cups diced, cooked chicken meat
1 can (16 ounces) kidney beans, rinsed and drained
1 medium tomato, diced
1 can (2.25 ounces) sliced black olives, drained
1 package (16 ounces) salad greens
½ cup reduced-fat shredded cheddar cheese
salad dressing
1 bag (16 ounces) tortilla chips (optional)

Bread Bowl Chicken Taco Salad

1 round loaf of bread
(8 ounces), with the
center cut out to form
bowl
3 to 4 large lettuce leaves
2 cups diced cooked chicken
meat
½ cup mild salsa
½ cup reduced-fat shredded
cheddar cheese

Another tasty taco dinner, this time served in a bread bowl. This recipe works well on a night when you don't want to heat up the kitchen.

Estimated preparation time: 5 minutes
Makes 4 servings

1. Have your child line bread bowl with lettuce leaves.
2. Have your child combine diced chicken and salsa in small bowl.
3. Spoon onto lettuce, sprinkle with shredded cheese, and serve.

Frozen Yogurt Pops

This cool and fruity dessert is so simple even a toddler can put it together.

8 snack-size containers
(4 ounces each)
nonfat fruit yogurt
8 clean popsicle sticks

Estimated preparation time: 5 minutes
Estimated freezing time: 6 to 8 hours
Makes 8 yogurt pops

1. Help your child make small slits in the center of the wrapping on the top of each container.
2. Carefully slide popsicle sticks into slits and down into yogurt.
3. Freeze for 6 to 8 hours or overnight. Carefully remove frozen pops from containers before serving by rolling the sides between your palms for a moment to loosen them.

Chewy Oatmeal Bars

1 can (6 ounces) frozen
   unsweetened apple
   juice concentrate,
   thawed
2 tablespoons unflavored
   gelatin (such as Knox
   brand)
4 cups old fashioned oats
½ cup raisins

These chewy, low-fat, low-sugar bars are a healthy alternative to packaged treats.

Estimated preparation time: 10 minutes
Estimated cooking time: 3 minutes
Estimated refrigeration time: 1 hour
Makes 16 servings

1. Have your child place apple juice concentrate in medium microwavable bowl.
2. Microwave on high for 3 minutes. Remove.
3. Add unflavored gelatin and stir until dissolved. Quickly add oats and raisins, tossing well to coat evenly.
4. Have your child spread mixture into 9 × 9-inch baking dish and refrigerate for 1 to 2 hours, or until set. Cut into 16 bars.

. . . .

Note: Young children should be carefully supervised when handling hot liquids.

. . . .

Rainbow Melon Wedges

Estimated preparation time: 15 minutes
Estimated cooking time: 8 to 10 minutes
Estimated refrigeration time: 15 to 30 minutes
Makes 8 to 12 servings

1 cup unsweetened applesauce
1 package strawberry flavored gelatin (4-serving size)
1 cup nonfat plain yogurt
1 cup fresh blueberries
2 medium melons, halved, seeded, and patted dry

1. Help your child pour applesauce into a small saucepan and bring to boil over medium heat. Stir in gelatin until dissolved.
2. Refrigerate until quite thick but not set, about 15 minutes.
3. Have your child stir in yogurt, and beat at highest speed until doubled in volume. Stir in blueberries.
4. Have your child spoon whipped mixture into melon halves and chill until firm. Cut each half to serve.

. . . .

Note: Small children should be kept away from a hot stove, although older children can prepare this with adult supervision.

. . . .

Red, White, and Blue Graham Towers

1 package (8 ounces) reduced-
    fat cream cheese,
    softened
¼ cup sugar
½ teaspoon grated lime peel
½ teaspoon almond extract
1 pint strawberries, sliced
2 pints blueberries
24 graham cracker squares

Simple and patriotic, these healthy treats make great snacks, too. The creamed mixture holds most of the fruit in place, but like S'mores, the mess is half the fun of eating these.

Estimated preparation time: 10 minutes
Makes 8 servings

1. Have your child combine cream cheese, sugar, lime peel, and almond extract in medium bowl, and stir until smooth. Gently stir in ½ cup strawberries and ½ cup blueberries.
2. Spread each of 16 graham squares with 1 tablespoon cream cheese mixture. Sprinkle with about ⅔ remaining strawberries and blueberries.
3. To assemble, place one cheese-covered graham square on top of second, then top with plain graham square. Garnish with remaining fruit.

Pecan Cookies

The next time your children ask to bake cookies, try this streamlined "homemade" recipe.

Estimated preparation time: 15 minutes
Estimated baking time: 8 to 12 minutes
Makes 4 dozen cookies

1 package (1 pound 10 ounce) chocolate chip cookie mix
1 egg
1 tablespoon water
⅓ cup unsweetened applesauce
2 cups pecan halves

1. Preheat oven to 375 degrees.
2. Have your child place cookie mix into large bowl. Stir in egg, water, and applesauce until thoroughly moist, taking care to break up any large lumps.
3. Drop rounded teaspoonsful of dough onto lightly greased cookie sheet. Place pecan half in the center of each cookie.
4. Bake for 8 to 9 minutes for chewy cookies, 10 to 12 minutes for crisper cookies. Remove from oven and allow to cool for 1 minute, then remove to cooling rack.

Index

Biscuits
　　basic mix, 147, 160
　　dairy-less dinner, 152
　　easy cheese, 149
　　easy country-style, 148
　　easy herbed, 150
　　milk-free, 151
Black and Decker
　　bread machines by, 3
　　food processors by, 4
　　hand-mixers by, 4
　　steamer/rice cookers by, 5
Black Forest chocolate cheese-
　　cake, 196, 197
Bologna wrap sandwiches, 218
Boston cream pie, easiest, 167
Bratwurst, crowd-pleasing, 88
Braun
　　food processors by, 4
　　hand-mixers by, 4
Brawny beef sub, 220
Bread bowl chicken taco salad,
　　226
Bread machine, 3, 76
　　basic mix for, 96
Breads
　　basic bread machine mix,
　　　96
　　breakfast, 100
　　hearty oat, 101
　　savory herbed, 97
　　for savory subs, 209
　　sour cream and chives, 99
　　spicy pepper, 98
Breakfast bread, 100
Breakfast brown rice pudding, 24
Breakfast plum-style "pudding,"
　　22
Breakfasts, 17–30
　　all-in-one cheese omelet, 27
　　bed and breakfast quiche, 28
　　best breakfast turnovers, 25
　　breakfast bread, 100

breakfast brown rice pud-
　　ding, 24
breakfast plum-style "pud-
　　ding," 22
citrus breakfast shake, 21
cranberry-orange bars, 19
easy, cheesy breakfast cob-
　　bler, 29
easy cheesy waffle sand-
　　wiches, 214
make-ahead carrot-bran
　　muffins, 23
morning sunrise cornbread, 30
out-the-door breakfast, 20
quick crunchy porridge, 216
sweet potato pancakes, 26
Broccoli, simple spinach and,
　　130
Brown rice pilaf, 139
Bruschetta, steak and tomato
　　baked, 53
Burgers
　　happy, 47
　　saucy seafood, 64
　　speedy, cheesy meatloaf, 55
Burritos, ham and cheese, 95

C

Cake pans, 3
Cakes
　　amazing blackberry pyra-
　　　mid, 199
　　angel-custard, 162
　　heavenly chocolate cherry,
　　　168
Calzone
　　simply surprising family-
　　　sized, 112
　　vegetable pizza, 105
Canned foods, storage of, 10
Carefree cheese and "crab" dip,
　　177
Caribbean one-pot chicken, 83

Carrots, bay-watcher, 127
Casserole
　　fuss-free chicken pot pie, 59
　　hot diggity dog pie, 223
　　ravioli, 224
Catfish, orange-baked, 63
Cheery, cherry strudel, 161
Cheesecake
　　Black Forest chocolate, 196,
　　　197
　　sinfully low-fat chocolate, 169
Cheesy circle snack mix, 185
Cheesy fruit parfaits, 213
Cheesy mashed potatoes, 140
Cheesy meatloaf burgers, 55
Chewy oatmeal bars, 228
Chicago Metallic cookware, 3
Chicken breasts
　　in Caribbean one-pot
　　　chicken, 83
　　honey-mustard, 57
Chicken confetti pitas, 45
Chicken cups, almond, 60
Chicken, imitation, 110
Chicken nuggets, 209
Chicken pot pie casserole, fuss-
　　free, 59
Chicken, rotisserie, 210
Chicken tacos, easy, 58
Chicken thighs in year-round
　　BBQ chicken, 84
Children
　　involved in making breakfast
　　　treats, 18
　　recipes for. See Kid-friendly
　　　recipes
Chili con corny, 122
Chili-mac, smooth and creamy,
　　113
Christmas in a hurry, 196
Chuck roast, three-star, 81
Cilantro black beans and rice,
　　120

BOOK 2:

Working Mom's Fast & Easy One-Pot Cooking

To Rich, Alex, and Jack
for new beginnings

To Sarah
for her courage and inspiration

Acknowledgments

I'd like to thank Jamie Miller for bringing this book to life, and Andi Reese Brady and Naomi Lucks for their editorial contributions. Thanks to Linda Martin, Jodi Long, Rosemary Rossi, Sarah François Poncet, and Lorraine Phillips, for their friendship. To great testers and friends: Jolene Kriett, Pamela Racliff, Bill Perry, DeeAnne and Michael Canepa, Lauren and Derrick Cartwright, David Weinman, and Linda Coulter. To George and Jean Jackson for their generosity; Nancy Mc-Carten for her mouth-watering e-mails; and Bert Hoberman, Ruth Besser, and Howard Taras for their recipes.

And most of all, thank you to my families, the Hobermans and the Bessers.

Contents

Chapter 3 · Meat   295

30 Minutes or Less:

60 Minutes or Less:

Chapter 4 · Seafood   323

30 Minutes or Less:

Chapter 5 · Vegetarian   355

Chapter 6 • Weekend Cooking   393

Introduction

If you are like me—a working mom with a family to feed and not much time to do it in—you need a way to prepare dinner without spending the whole day in the kitchen and the whole night cleaning up. Let me share my secret for simplifying mealtime without sacrificing quality: one-pot cooking. Not the kind of one-pot recipes that eventually end up in one pot after cooking everything separately; I mean one pot, period. Just one pot to cook in and just one pot to wash.

From the hearty and comforting stews of yesteryear to the quicker and lighter fare favored today, you will find a wide assortment of easy-to-prepare, low-maintenance, nutritious one-pot stews, soups, chilis, gumbos, curries, casseroles, pastas, risottos, quiches, and more. These meals are very forgiving, with few repercussions for taking a break to referee a battle between siblings or answer an unexpected phone call from a child's teacher.

In addition to over 100 recipes, *Working Mom's Fast & Easy One-Pot Cooking* also includes helpful hints for quickly getting your food on the table, advice on how to choose equipment and ingredients, and ways to better organize your kitchen.

Whether you're looking for a casual dinner or an elegant meal for entertaining, *Working Mom's Fast & Easy One-Pot Cooking* lets you take back your life without forfeiting flavor.

Chart of Equivalents

Use this handy reference to help you know how much food to shop for.

1 cup = 8 ounces
1 pound = 16 ounces

1 cup cored and coarsely chopped apple = 4 ounces
1 cup cored and sliced apple = 5 ounces
1 cup sliced asparagus (1-inch pieces) = 5 ounces
1 cup packed basil leaves = 2 ounces
1 cup 1-inch-cubed butternut squash = 5 ounces
1 cup sliced carrots = 5 ounces
1 cup finely chopped carrots = 4 ounces
1 cup coarsely chopped celery = 4 ounces
1 cup shredded cheese = 4 ounces
1 cup coarsely chopped cucumber = 5 ounces
1 cup coarsely chopped eggplant = $2\frac{1}{2}$ ounces
1 cup sliced green beans (1-inch pieces) = 4 ounces
1 cup chopped bell peppers = 4 ounces
1 cup sliced leeks, white part only = 2 ounces
1 cup packed lettuce = 2 ounces
1 cup chopped mushrooms = 3 ounces
1 cup quartered mushrooms = 4 ounces
1 cup sliced mushrooms = $2\frac{1}{2}$ ounces
1 cup coarsely chopped onions = 5 ounces
1 cup $\frac{1}{2}$-inch-cubed potatoes = 6 ounces
1 cup thinly sliced potatoes = 5 ounces
1 cup shredded potatoes = $3\frac{1}{2}$ ounces
1 cup sliced shiitake mushrooms = 2 ounces
1 cup snow pea pods = 3 ounces
1 cup packed spinach = $1\frac{1}{2}$ ounces
1 cup chopped and seeded fresh tomatoes = $5\frac{1}{2}$ ounces
1 cup $\frac{1}{2}$-inch-cubed turnips = 4 ounces
1 cup $\frac{1}{2}$-inch-cubed zucchini = 4 ounces

1

BASICS

It often seems like cruel and inhuman punishment to have to think of, shop for, and prepare dinner after a long day at work. Yet there are many basic time-saving devices that can simplify and add enjoyment to this daily routine. With just a small amount of planning and preparation, dinnertime can be a relaxing part of our day; a way to unwind and forget the stresses and headaches we've just endured.

And that is what cooking should be: a creative and enjoyable process. As tired as we are when evening rolls around, it is important to lift ourselves out of our rut and aim for a higher ground. No matter how simple or unpretentious our intentions, as we hook our aprons around our waists, we must think of ourselves as part mechanic, part artist. Assemble meals with precision, but consider them an aesthetic collage; a marriage of colors, tastes, and textures.

We are not meant to be alone in our kitchen. The kitchen is a place for congregation and offers a wonderful opportunity to connect with our kids. The best way for our children to develop an appreciation and interest in food is to involve them. If we think of the meal as a chore, so will our children. But if we make its preparation an event, it will become exciting for all. Let them smell the spices, perform simple tasks, and choose creative decorations for the table. Even toddlers relish the tasks of food preparation. Stirring and pushing the buttons of a food processor allows them to be a part of the creative process.

Variety takes the monotony out of cooking. The more we expose children to a diversity of food, the more interested and adventurous eaters they will become. Expand their minds and their tastebuds. It is exciting to be able to travel using just our imaginations and our palate. Explore recipes from different regions of the country and from around the world and turn dinnertime into a geography lesson. While we're cooking up specialties from Mexico, Greece, Morocco, Italy, and France, we can discuss their cultures and locate them on the globe.

Let's begin our culinary journey with a guide to basic information and time-tested tips to help ensure success. As you read through the following pointers and techniques, try to take from them things that will work in your own kitchen.

Equipment:

- Buy the best quality equipment you can afford. Sturdier equipment will last longer, and higher quality, heavy cookware will prevent unnecessary scorching and overcooking.
- For simplicity, I have limited the number of pots and pans necessary. For a soup pot and pasta pot, I used an 8-quart stock pot; for a large sauté pan, I used a 13-inch skillet; for a smaller frying pan, I used a 10-inch nonstick skillet. Dutch ovens (heavy porcelain- or enamel-coated cooking vessels) are excellent for stove-to-oven use. They can be substituted for the pots and pans described above if they are of a similar

size or capacity. For oven use I recommend a 9-inch pie pan and a $13 \times 9 \times 2$-inch baking pan (this is a little big for four servings, but 8- or 9-inch square pans are too small). While nonstick cookware makes cleanup easier and cuts down on the amount of fat needed, they are not essential unless specifically noted.

- Before choosing your cookware, review the recipe and note if a cover is needed or if the pot needs to be ovenproof. Ovenproof pots must have handles that can withstand high heat. Whenever removing a pan from the oven, remember to use extreme caution: The pan will continue to hold its heat for a long time. I like to leave a pot holder or mitt on top of pots and lids removed from the oven as a reminder not to touch.

- A food processor is helpful for chopping and slicing large amounts of vegetables and for puréeing soups. It is important when chopping vegetables with a high water content, like onions or bell peppers, to only pulse small amounts at a time or the vegetables will end up a pulverized mush.

- Invest in an oven thermometer to make sure your oven is heating properly. A hanging mercury thermometer is most reliable. Check the temperature in different areas of your oven to make sure it has consistent heat. If you notice heating discrepancies, adjust your cooking time or temperature to compensate. Most utility companies will recalibrate your oven at no cost.

Ingredients:

- Always use high quality ingredients. If something doesn't taste good by itself, it won't taste better after cooking. Make sure vegetables and fruits are ripe and flavorful; dairy products, meats, poultry, and fish are fresh; and flavorings are the best available. Use fresh and fragrant herbs and spices. Store dried spices tightly covered in a cool and dry place for better and longer-lasting flavor. If spices are no longer aromatic, replace them.

- Most of these recipes call for fresh vegetables and herbs. Frozen vegetables may be substituted if necessary, but the texture and flavor may suffer. One exception to the "fresh-is-best" rule is the recommended use of canned tomatoes, because flavorful tomatoes are only in season for a short amount of time. Fresh tomatoes can be substituted for canned tomatoes when they are ripe and in season. The general rule of thumb for substituting dried herbs for fresh is to use one-third of the recommended amount. Many of these recipes use fresh herbs for their unique flavor, and a dried-for-fresh substitution would be lacking. So if fresh herbs are not available, just leave them out.

- Be flexible and cook for your own tastes. Cooking allows for a lot of adaptation. If you like your food extra hot, increase the cayenne pepper by a shake or two. If you don't like one of the ingredients in a recipe, or if a particular vegetable is unavailable, substitute one of your favorites that complements the dish. Just alter the cooking time, if necessary, to make up for added or decreased weight.

- Never cook with a wine you wouldn't enjoy drinking on its own. As wine cooks, its flavor intensifies. The wine doesn't need to be expensive, but it must be drinkable. If you wish to cook without alcohol, substitute an equal amount of compatible broth.

- Some recipes list optional ingredients or garnishes. While they will heighten the flavor and presentation of the dish, these ingredients are not essential. The finished meal won't suffer if you are missing them, but it will be enhanced by their inclusion. Recipe introductions sometimes offer complementary toppings and side suggestions. Again, you can choose whether or not to use them.

- Some manufacturers' canned items may vary from ¼ to ½ ounce from what is used in the recipe. This will not affect the outcome of the meal. Just use whatever you can find that is closest to the recommended size.
- Personalize your cookbooks to use as a guide for your future cooking. On the recipe, note if there are any additions or changes you would make for next time.

Before Starting the Recipe:

- Always read through the entire recipe to make sure all the ingredients are on hand and to see if additional preparation is needed (chopping, peeling, toasting, and so on). Measuring and prepping your ingredients before beginning to cook will eliminate any surprises halfway into the recipe and will save a lot of time and aggravation later on. Additionally, a more organized preparation makes for an easier cleanup.
- Another helpful technique is to line up the ingredients on your work space, in the order in which they are listed in the recipe, before starting the recipe. Move the ingredient aside after it has been used. This ensures nothing has been forgotten or added twice. To prevent accidental overflows, never measure ingredients over mixing bowls or over the cooking pan.
- Most ingredients in this book are measured by standard measurers (cups, teaspoons, tablespoons). I feel this means is the most practical for home cooks for two reasons. First, measuring cups and spoons are universal, but everyone's perception of a "large" tomato is different. What is large to one may seem medium to another. Second, many ingredients are now sold prepped to eliminate additional work, whether it be jarred minced garlic, packaged cut-up lettuce, or salad bar shredded vegetables. Although weighing ingredients is the most accurate method of measuring, most

homes are not equipped with the scales necessary to make this a practical means of calculation. But when an item is used whole or needs minimal prep, or if it is sold by weight, like cheese or meat, than a size or weight description is provided. An equivalency guide is included on page xvii to aid in shopping.

- Use these approximate guidelines for cutting descriptions:
  minced: $\frac{1}{16}$ inch or under
  chopped: $\frac{1}{8}$ inch to $\frac{1}{4}$ inch
  coarsely chopped: $\frac{1}{4}$ inch to $\frac{1}{2}$ inch
  thinly sliced: $\frac{1}{8}$ inch or under
  sliced: $\frac{1}{8}$ inch to $\frac{1}{4}$ inch
  thickly sliced: $\frac{1}{4}$ inch
  julienned : cut into 1- to 2-inch pieces and sliced thinly lengthwise
  cubed: cut into $\frac{1}{2} \times \frac{1}{2}$-inch or 1×1-inch squares

Planning Ahead:

- You can save valuable time by using a little foresight. Before shopping, look through your cupboards, refrigerator, and freezer, and plan your meals to use up what you have on hand.
- Keep your kitchen well stocked with staples for cooking in a pinch. Remember to replenish what you use by adding it to your shopping list immediately.
- Organize your kitchen to shorten your prep time. Divide your cupboard into sections and keep frequently used canned goods, condiments, cooking oils, and spices visible and arranged by categories. The easier it is to find things, the quicker it will be to make your meal.
- Prepare your vegetables at the beginning of the week. Chop several onions, slice carrots and celery, and mince a head of garlic. Then store each separately, in airtight containers,

until needed. Any leftover veggies are great in salads or simple stir-fries. If time is short, shop for pre-cut vegetables at your supermarket's salad bar.

- If you are preparing rice or pasta for a dinner, cook an extra batch to enhance a future one-pot meal. Save and freeze leftover rice from Chinese take-out meals. If you feel like adding rice to a dish, it's just a quick microwave away!

- If you find a recipe you enjoy, make a double batch and freeze half for a later date. Doubling a recipe does not double the work.

Keeping Clean:

- The more organized your kitchen is while you are preparing the recipe, the easier it will be to keep clean. After cooking, return things to their proper place so they will be accessible the next time you need them.

- Keep a trash receptacle close by and deposit all used wrappers and waste immediately. If a trash can isn't handy, place an empty box, grocery bag, or mixing bowl near your work space.

- Always use larger mixing bowls than you think will be necessary to eliminate messy spills and overflows. This also prevents the need to transfer ingredients to a larger bowl midway through the recipe, requiring additional cleanup.

Freezing:

- Most soups, stews, and casseroles freeze beautifully when wrapped airtight using foil, plastic wrap, zip-top bags, or plastic containers. Make sure the wrap and bags are intended for freezer use.

- Label and date everything before freezing so you can use it in a timely fashion. Keep a current list of freezer contents to refresh your memory.

Salads and Breads:

- A side salad and bread are the perfect complements to most one-pot dishes.
- Try making your own bread, or experiment with supermarket or bakery varieties until you find your favorites.
- Look for crusty French and Italian breads or a hearty multigrain loaf to round out your meal and help guests capture every last drop of your sensational soups, stews, and sauces.
- Serve breads from other countries—including pita, focaccia, garlic bread, bruschetta, and tortillas—to tie into international-theme dinners.
- For fun, serve a variety of different shaped breads, including rolls, fogossi (a shaped bread), and bread sticks.

2

POULTRY

30 Minutes or Less:

Mulligatawny Soup
Southwest Chicken
   Tortilla Soup
Moroccan Chicken with
   Couscous

Chicken Pesto Risotto
Chicken Caesar Salad
   Wrap
Thai Chicken Salad Wrap

60 Minutes or Less:

Chicken and Vegetables
Chicken Chili
Mediterranean Chicken
   and Rice
Brunswick Stew
Spicy Pepper Chicken
Curried Chicken and Rice

Chicken Cacciatore
Chicken and Barley Stew
Arroz con Pollo
Creamy Dijon Chicken
   Stew
Turkey, Potatoes,
   Tomatoes, and Cheese

oultry, long favored by cooks for its versatility, is also a nutritional winner. Low in fat and calories, as well as a good source of B_2, B_6, B_{12}, riboflavin, niacin, zinc, and magnesium, poultry is also widely available and relatively inexpensive. Whether you choose a whole chicken or Rock Cornish hens for roasting; a cut-up fryer for braising or stewing; or boneless breasts or thighs for easy sautés and soup-making, poultry is a great centerpiece for family one-pot dinners.

Poultry Tips:

- Always check the expiration date before buying packaged poultry. Look for plump, meaty pieces so you pay for bulk, not just bone or skin.
- Be aware of the possible bacterial contamination of poultry. Salmonella and campylobacter are the two pathogens most commonly associated with raw chicken. Before using chicken, carefully rinse it with cold water (making sure it doesn't spray all over the counters) and cut off any excess fat and skin. After cutting or handling raw chicken, always thoroughly wash your hands, counters, cutting boards, and knives with warm, soapy water. Store uncooked chicken separately from other ingredients to prevent cross-contamination. These bacteria are killed with proper cooking.
- Store poultry in your refrigerator. If you are unable to use poultry within three days or by its expiration date, it is best to freeze it. To prevent bacterial growth, always thaw chicken in your refrigerator or microwave, not at room temperature.
- If you find you have more chicken than you need for your meal, wrap, label, and store the extra in the freezer.
- For better browning, always pat the chicken dry with paper towels before searing. Sear chicken pieces a few at a

time—if you overcrowd the pan, the chicken will steam rather than brown.

- When cooking a cut-up fryer, remember that dark meat (the thighs and legs) generally takes about ten to fifteen minutes longer to cook than white meat. Check the pieces as they are cooking. If some are done before others, remove them and tent with aluminum foil to keep warm. Chicken is done when a meat thermometer inserted into the inner thigh registers 170 to 180 degrees and juices run clear, not pink.
- Even when cooking with all white meat or all dark meat, adjust the cooking time if you have pieces of greatly varying sizes. Larger pieces of meat will take longer to cook than smaller ones (sometimes an exceptionally big breast will take more time than a large piece of dark meat). Check pieces for doneness as they are cooking, or add smaller pieces ten minutes after larger pieces have been cooking. If you are using boneless and skinless chicken breasts of irregular thickness, either pound them for uniform density or alter their cooking times accordingly to prevent dried-out meat.
- Substitute individual chicken parts for a whole chicken if your family's preference is all white or all dark meat.
- To prevent tough and chewy chicken, cook at a simmer, not a boil.
- Before serving stews, use a soup spoon or paper towels to skim off any fat or froth that has risen to the surface, or run an ice cube over the surface to quickly solidify any liquid fat. If you are cooking and refrigerating the stew, the fat will harden when chilled and is easily removed.
- Add leftover chicken to vegetarian entreés for extra protein.

Mulligatawny Soup

2 tablespoons butter
1 cup chopped onions
1 cup chopped carrots
½ cup chopped celery
1 cup peeled, cored, and
    chopped Granny Smith
    apples
2 tablespoons all-purpose flour
1 tablespoon curry powder
⅛ teaspoon ground cloves
5 cups reduced-sodium
    chicken broth
1 cup peeled, seeded, and
    chopped ripe
    tomatoes, or 1 cup
    drained canned diced
    tomatoes
1 tablespoon freshly squeezed
    lemon juice
½ cup rice
1 pound boneless and skinless
    chicken breasts, cut
    into ½-inch pieces
1 teaspoon salt
½ teaspoon ground black
    pepper

This curried chicken soup, a classic eighteenth-century East Indian favorite, is flavored with apples, lemon, and cloves. Literally translated as "pepper water," Mulligatawny was originally made by Indian cooks for British colonialists, who later brought the recipe back to England and then to the United States. It is normally served with a side of rice, but this recipe cooks the rice right into the soup. Optional garnishes include a dollop of yogurt, grated apple, or a sprinkling of parsley.

Cooking Time: 30 minutes or less
Serves: 4

1. In a large stock pot over medium heat, add the butter. Add the onions, carrots, celery, and apples and cook until softened, 5 to 8 minutes, stirring occasionally.
2. Add the flour, curry, and cloves and cook for 1 to 2 minutes, stirring constantly.
3. Add the broth, tomatoes, and lemon juice and stir to combine. Bring to a boil.
4. Add the rice and stir to combine.

5. Reduce the heat, partially cover, and simmer for 10 minutes, stirring occasionally.

6. Add the chicken. Simmer for 5 to 10 minutes, or until the chicken and rice are cooked through. Season with salt and pepper.

Southwest Chicken Tortilla Soup

1 tablespoon vegetable oil
½ cup chopped onions
1 teaspoon minced garlic
½ teaspoon chili powder
⅛ teaspoon cayenne pepper
4 cups reduced-sodium
    chicken broth
1 cup canned Mexican-style
    stewed tomatoes
1 teaspoon salt
1 pound boneless and skinless
    chicken breasts, cut
    into ½-inch pieces
1 cup fresh or frozen corn
¼ cup thinly sliced scallions
2 tablespoons freshly
    squeezed lime juice
4 6-inch corn tortillas, lightly
    toasted and sliced into
    ½-inch strips, or 2
    cups crushed tortilla
    chips

This Mexican-inspired soup has found a loyal following north of the border. Full of tender chicken, corn, and tomatoes, it has a little spice and a lot of flavor. Garnish with sour cream or chopped cilantro, and serve with warm flour tortillas topped with melted Monterey Jack cheese and a tossed salad loaded with avocado.

Cooking Time: 30 minutes or less
Serves: 4

1. In a large stock pot over medium heat, add the oil. Add the onions and cook until softened, 3 to 5 minutes, stirring frequently.
2. Add the garlic, chili powder, and cayenne pepper and cook for 1 minute, stirring constantly.
3. Add the broth, tomatoes and their juice, and salt, and stir to combine and to break up the tomatoes. Bring to a boil.
4. Reduce the heat, cover, and simmer for 10 to 15 minutes, stirring occasionally.
5. Add the chicken and corn and simmer for 5 minutes.

6. Add the scallions and lime juice and cook for 1 minute, or until the chicken is cooked through.
7. Top each serving with the tortillas.

•••••••••••••••••

Variation:

Southwest Shrimp Tortilla Soup: *Substitute ¾ pound of peeled and deveined shrimp for the chicken. Add the shrimp in step 6 and cook for 1 to 2 minutes, or until just cooked through.*

•••••••••••••••••

Moroccan Chicken with Couscous

1 teaspoon salt
¼ teaspoon cayenne pepper
1 teaspoon ground ginger
1 teaspoon ground cumin
1 teaspoon ground cinnamon
½ teaspoon ground coriander
    (optional)
4 boneless and skinless
    chicken breasts (about
    1½ pounds)
2 tablespoons olive oil
1 cup finely chopped onions
½ cup finely chopped carrots
½ cup seeded and finely
    chopped red bell
    peppers
1 teaspoon minced garlic
2 cups reduced-sodium
    chicken broth
2 tablespoons freshly
    squeezed lemon juice
1½ cups couscous
½ cup rinsed and drained
    canned chickpeas
¼ cup pitted and halved green
    olives
½ cup pine nuts, lightly
    toasted (optional)

This fast and low-fat meal features chicken breasts coated with the spices of Morocco. At first glance these flavorings seem unusual partners: cinnamon and ginger, normally associated with baking; and cayenne, cumin, and coriander, normally found in savory Indian cooking. But when wed, they burst with exciting flavors. Couscous, this version jazzed up with onions, carrots, and red bell peppers, is a mainstay of this region.

Cooking Time: 30 minutes or less
Serves: 4

1. Combine the salt, cayenne pepper, ginger, cumin, cinnamon, and coriander. Coat the chicken with the spices.
2. In a large skillet over medium-high heat, add the oil. Add the chicken and brown, 4 to 5 minutes per side. Remove the chicken, cover with foil, and reserve.
3. Add the onions, carrots, red peppers, and garlic and cook until softened, 5 to 8 minutes, stirring frequently.
4. Add the broth and lemon juice and stir to combine. Bring to a boil.

5. Turn off the heat, add the couscous, chickpeas, and olives and stir to combine. Return the chicken to the skillet, cover, and let stand for 5 to 10 minutes.
6. Fluff the couscous and top with the pine nuts.

Chicken Pesto Risotto

4 to 5 cups reduced-sodium
    chicken broth
3 tablespoons butter
½ cup finely chopped onions
1 teaspoon minced garlic
½ pound boneless and skinless
    chicken breasts, cut
    into 1-inch pieces
1½ cups Arborio rice
½ cup dry white wine
½ cup pesto, ready-made or
    recipe, page 14
¼ cup shaved or grated
    Parmesan cheese

Risotto demands vigilance: The slow absorption of broth is integral to the creamy, yet firm, quality of the finished dish. But a beautiful restaurant-quality risotto, made with Italian Arborio rice, can be on your dinner table in half an hour or less, so it's definitely worth the effort. This Chicken Pesto Risotto is bursting with flavor. Make the pesto in the height of summer when basil is abundant, or use ready-made pesto in a pinch. One note: It is not essential to warm the broth first, but it does help maintain a constant cooking temperature.

Cooking Time: 30 minutes or less
Serves: 4

1. In a microwave, bring the broth to a simmer.
2. In a large saucepan or stock pot over medium heat, add the butter. Add the onions, garlic, and chicken and sauté for 3 to 5 minutes, or until the chicken begins to cook through, stirring frequently.
3. Add the rice. Stir constantly to coat with the butter, 1 minute.
4. Add the wine and stir until completely absorbed.
5. Begin slowly adding the broth, ½ cup at a time, stirring frequently. Wait until each addition is almost

completely absorbed before adding more, about 3 to 5 minutes for each addition. Continue to add broth, stirring frequently, for 20 to 25 minutes, or until the risotto has a creamy texture but is still al dente, slightly firm to the bite. You may not need to use all of the liquid.

6. Transfer the risotto to a serving dish. Stir in the pesto. Sprinkle with the Parmesan and serve immediately.

· · · · · · · · · · · · · · · ·

Variation:

Shrimp Pesto Risotto: *Substitute ¾ pound of peeled and deveined shrimp for the chicken. Proceed with the recipe through step 5. Add the shrimp after 15 minutes. Continue adding broth and stirring for another 5 to 8 minutes.*

· · · · · · · · · · · · · · · ·

Chicken Caesar Salad Wrap

Dressing:

1 clove garlic
½ cup olive oil
¼ cup mayonnaise
2 tablespoons freshly
    squeezed lemon juice
2 teaspoons Dijon mustard
1 teaspoon Worcestershire
    sauce
1 teaspoon anchovy paste,
    chopped anchovies,
    or salt
1 teaspoon ground black
    pepper

4 boneless and skinless
    chicken breasts (about
    1½ pounds)
1 tablespoon olive oil
4 10- to 12-inch flour tortillas

Salad:

5 cups packed chopped
    romaine lettuce
½ cup shaved or grated
    Parmesan cheese
1 cup croutons
1 cup chopped ripe tomatoes
    (optional)

Wraps, healthful and flavorful cross-cultural sandwiches, are currently the hottest category in casual dining. Tastes from all over the world mix and mingle in these trendy sandwiches. The Caesar wrap is a perfect example. The original Caesar salad was created by Italian chef Caesar Cardini in 1924 at his restaurant in Tijuana, Mexico. Many Americans frequented the border towns at this time because of Prohibition, and word of this tasty salad quickly traveled north with them. Its trademark dressing, loaded with garlic, lemon, and Parmesan cheese, is easy to make; but if time is short, substitute your favorite bottled dressing.

Cooking Time: 30 minutes or less
Serves: 4

1. Preheat the broiler or grill.
2. Prepare the dressing: In a food processor fitted with a metal chopping blade, with the motor running, add the garlic and purée. Add the oil, mayonnaise, lemon juice, mustard, Worcestershire sauce, anchovy paste, and pepper and process to combine. (You can also mix the dressing in a bowl using a wire whisk). Set aside.
3. Lightly brush the chicken with the oil. Broil or grill the chicken breasts, 4 to 5 minutes per side, or until cooked through. When cool, cut the chicken into thin strips and set aside.

4. If using a broiler, lower the heat to 350 degrees; if using a grill reduce heat to low. Wrap the tortillas in aluminum foil and place in the oven or on the grill to warm for 10 minutes. (Tortillas can also be wrapped in a damp towel and warmed in the microwave on high for 15 to 30 seconds).

5. Prepare the salad: In a large bowl, combine the lettuce and dressing. Add the cheese, croutons, tomatoes, and chicken and toss again.

6. Assemble the wraps: Place 1 to 1½ cups of salad in the center of each tortilla. Tuck the bottom of the tortilla up over the filling, fold both sides of the tortilla toward the center, and roll up. Be careful not to overstuff the wraps.

·················

Variation:

Shrimp Caesar Salad Wrap: *Substitute 1 pound of peeled and deveined shrimp for the chicken. Grill or broil the shrimp for 1 to 2 minutes per side, or until just cooked through.*

················

Thai Chicken Salad Wrap

Nowhere is the tortilla put to better use than in the making of giant wrapped sandwiches, known as "wraps." These flavorful sandwiches take the East-meets-West culinary concept to the next level: East not only meets West, but meets North and South as well. This Thai Chicken Salad Wrap, which teams crunchy greens and vegetables with grilled chicken and a sweet and spicy peanut sauce, is truly addictive. These flavors and textures will dance on your tongue, bring a big smile to your face, and leave you warm, happy, and well-fed. Save time by picking up some of these prepped veggies at your favorite salad bar.

Cooking Time: 30 minutes or less
Serves: 4

Dressing:

¼ cup peanut butter
2 tablespoons hoisin sauce
2 tablespoons reduced-sodium
    soy sauce
2 tablespoons reduced-sodium
    chicken broth
2 tablespoons honey
1 tablespoon dark sesame oil
1 tablespoon peeled and
    minced fresh ginger
1 teaspoon sugar
1 teaspoon Asian chili paste

4 boneless and skinless
    chicken breasts (about
    1½ pounds)
4 10- to 12-inch flour tortillas

Salad:

4 cups packed chopped
    lettuce
1 cup shredded carrots
1 cup chopped ripe tomatoes
    (optional)
½ cup shredded red cabbage
½ cup seeded and thinly
    sliced red bell peppers
½ cup coarsely chopped
    peanuts

1. Preheat the broiler or grill.
2. Prepare the dressing: In a microwave-safe bowl, combine the peanut butter, hoisin sauce, soy sauce, broth, honey, sesame oil, ginger, sugar, and chili paste. Microwave for 30 seconds to 1 minute, or until warm and easy to mix. (You can also mix dressing in a food processor). Set aside.
3. Lightly brush the chicken with ¼ cup of the dressing. Broil or grill the chicken breasts, 4 to 5 minutes per side, or until cooked through. When cool, cut the chicken into thin strips and set aside.

4. If using a broiler, lower the heat to 350 degrees; if using a grill, reduce heat to low. Wrap the tortillas in aluminum foil and place in the oven or on the grill to warm for 10 minutes. (Tortillas can also be wrapped in a damp towel and warmed in the microwave on high for 15 to 30 seconds.)

5. Prepare the salad: In a large bowl, combine the lettuce, carrots, tomato, red cabbage, red peppers, and remaining dressing. Add the chicken and peanuts and toss again.

6. Assemble the wraps: Place 1 to 1½ cups of salad in the center of each tortilla. Tuck the bottom of the tortilla up over the filling, fold both sides of the tortilla toward the center, and roll up. Be careful not to overstuff the wraps.

· · · · · · · · · · · · · · · ·

Variation:

Thai Shrimp Salad Wrap: *Substitute 1 pound of peeled and deveined shrimp for the chicken. Grill or broil the shrimp for 1 to 2 minutes per side, or until just cooked through.*

· · · · · · · · · · · · · · · ·

Chicken and Vegetables

4 boneless and skinless
    chicken breasts (about
    1½ pounds)
1 teaspoon salt
½ teaspoon ground black
    pepper
1 tablespoon olive oil
1 tablespoon butter
2 cups cleaned, julienned
    leeks (white part only)
2 cups small mushrooms,
    halved if large
2 cups quartered, sliced
    carrots (1-inch-thick
    pieces)
1 cup sliced celery (1-inch-
    thick pieces)
1 teaspoon minced garlic
1 teaspoon dried thyme
½ cup dry white wine or
    reduced-sodium
    chicken broth

This modern version of the classic French pot-au-feu, or "chicken-in-a-pot," includes the classic vegetables but makes use of boneless chicken breasts for an extra-short cooking time. With such easy preparation and execution, this healthful low-fat dinner is destined to become a tradition in your home.

Cooking Time: 60 minutes or less
Serves: 4

1. Sprinkle the chicken with salt and pepper.
2. In a large skillet over medium-high heat, add the oil and butter. Add the chicken and brown, 4 to 5 minutes per side. Remove the chicken and reserve.
3. Add the leeks, mushrooms, carrots, celery, and garlic and cook until softened, 5 to 8 minutes, stirring frequently.
4. Add the thyme and wine and stir to combine. Bring to a boil. Reduce the heat, cover, and simmer for 15 minutes.
5. Add the chicken, cover, and cook for 5 minutes, or until the chicken and vegetables are cooked through.

Chicken Chili

Chicken lovers rejoice! Here's a chili just for you. Using boneless chicken, this tasty treat cooks up quickly. Use different beans for variety—choose from white cannellini beans, black beans, or traditional pinto beans. Fresh jalapeños add some heat. Garnish with chopped cilantro, grated cheddar or Monterey Jack cheese, and avocado.

Cooking Time: 60 minutes or less
Serves: 4

1. In a large stock pot over medium heat, add the oil. Add the onions, red peppers, and jalapeños and sauté until softened, 5 to 8 minutes, stirring frequently.
2. Add the garlic and cook for 1 minute, stirring constantly.
3. Add the chicken and sauté until just cooked, 3 to 5 minutes.
4. Add the chili powder, cumin, oregano, salt, and cayenne pepper and stir to combine.
5. Add the broth and tomatoes and their juice. Bring to a boil.
6. Reduce the heat, cover, and simmer for 15 minutes, stirring occasionally.
7. Add the beans and simmer uncovered for 15 to 20 minutes, or until thickened and the flavors have melded, stirring occasionally.

2 tablespoons vegetable oil
1 cup coarsely chopped onions
½ cup seeded and coarsely chopped red bell peppers
2 tablespoons seeded and finely chopped fresh jalapeño peppers
2 teaspoons minced garlic
4 boneless and skinless chicken breasts or thighs, cut into 1-inch pieces (about 1½ pounds)
2 tablespoons chili powder
2 teaspoons ground cumin
1 teaspoon dried oregano
1 teaspoon salt
¼ teaspoon cayenne pepper (optional)
2 cups reduced-sodium chicken broth
1 14½-ounce can diced tomatoes
1 15¼-ounce can white beans, rinsed and drained
1 15¼-ounce can pinto beans, rinsed and drained

Mediterranean Chicken and Rice

1 teaspoon salt
½ teaspoon ground black
    pepper
4 boneless and skinless
    chicken breasts or
    thighs (about 1½
    pounds)
2 tablespoons olive oil
1 cup chopped onions
1 cup sliced mushrooms
1 tablespoon minced garlic
½ to 1 teaspoon red pepper
    flakes
1½ cups rice
½ cup dry white wine
2 cups reduced-sodium
    chicken broth
1 14½-ounce can diced
    tomatoes, drained, ½
    cup liquid reserved
2 tablespoons freshly
    squeezed lemon juice
2 tablespoons capers
¼ cup coarsely chopped green
    olives
½ cup coarsely chopped fresh
    basil (optional)

This delicious chicken and rice dish salutes the vibrant flavors of the Mediterranean. Typical of this region's style of cooking, the savory spices and vegetables—not a lot of fat or fillers—define and flavor the dish. Tangy lemon, capers, and olives mingle with a sublime mix of onions, mushrooms, garlic, and tomatoes for a harmonious mélange.

Cooking Time: 60 minutes or less
Serves: 4

1. Sprinkle the chicken with salt and pepper.
2. In a large skillet over medium-high heat, add the oil. Add the chicken and brown, 4 to 5 minutes per side. Remove the chicken and reserve.
3. Add the onions and mushrooms and sauté until softened, 5 to 8 minutes, stirring frequently.
4. Add the garlic and red pepper flakes and cook for 1 minute, stirring constantly.
5. Add the rice and stir to combine.
6. Add the wine, broth, and tomatoes and their reserved juice. Bring to a boil and stir to deglaze and dislodge any bits of food that have stuck to the bottom of the skillet.

7. Reduce the heat, cover, and simmer for 15 to 20 minutes, or until the rice is almost tender, stirring occasionally.

8. Add the lemon juice, capers, and olives and stir to combine. Add the reserved chicken, cover, and cook for 5 minutes, or until the chicken and rice are cooked through. Top with the basil.

· · · · · · · · · · · · · · · ·

Variation:

Mediterranean Shrimp and Rice: *Substitute 1 pound of peeled and deveined shrimp for the chicken. Cook the shrimp for 1 to 2 minutes per side, or until just cooked through.*

· · · · · · · · · · · · · · · ·

Brunswick Stew

¼ cup all-purpose flour
1 tablespoon salt
½ teaspoon ground black
    pepper
¼ teaspoon cayenne pepper
1 3- to 4-pound chicken, cut
    into 8 pieces
3 tablespoons olive oil
2 cups chopped onions
¼ pound ham, thickly sliced
    and cut into ½-inch
    pieces
1½ cups peeled potatoes cut
    into ½-inch cubes
2 cups reduced-sodium
    chicken broth
1 14½-ounce can diced
    tomatoes, drained
1 tablespoon Worcestershire
    sauce
4 dashes Tabasco or other hot
    red pepper sauce
1 cup fresh or frozen corn
1 cup fresh or frozen lima
    beans

Lima beans, once relegated to under-the-table pass-offs to the family dog, are now back in vogue, gracing entrées in the most trend-setting restaurants. Back in their disparaged days, the most common place you'd find them was in this tasty smoky-flavored Southern standard.

Cooking Time: 60 minutes or less
Serves: 4

1. Combine the flour, salt, black pepper, and cayenne pepper. Coat the chicken with the seasoned flour, reserving any excess.
2. In a large skillet, over medium-high heat, add the oil. Add the chicken and brown, 3 to 5 minutes per side. Remove the chicken and reserve. (You may need to do this in two or more batches).
3. Discard all but 1 tablespoon of fat from the skillet. Reduce the heat to medium and add the onions. Cook until softened, 3 to 5 minutes. Add the ham and potatoes and sauté for 3 minutes, stirring frequently.
4. Add any reserved flour and stir until it is absorbed into the onions, 1 to 2 minutes.
5. Add the broth, tomatoes, Worcestershire sauce, and Tabasco. Bring to a boil and stir to deglaze and dislodge any bits of food that have stuck to the bottom of the skillet. Keep stirring until slightly thickened.

6. Return the chicken to the skillet. Reduce the heat, cover, and simmer for 30 minutes, basting with the cooking liquid and turning the chicken occasionally.

7. Add the corn and lima beans and simmer uncovered for 5 to 10 minutes, or until the chicken and vegetables are cooked through.

Spicy Pepper Chicken

1 3- to 4-pound chicken, cut
    into 8 pieces
1 tablespoon salt
1 teaspoon ground black
    pepper
3 tablespoons olive oil
2 cups coarsely chopped
    onions
3 cups sliced bell peppers (a
    mix of red, yellow, and
    orange)
2 tablespoons seeded and
    finely chopped fresh
    jalapeño peppers
1 tablespoon minced garlic
½ pound prosciutto, thickly
    sliced and cut into
    thin, 1-inch-long strips
1 28-ounce can diced
    tomatoes, drained
2 tablespoons coarsely
    chopped fresh basil, or
    2 teaspoons dried
1 teaspoon orange zest
    (optional)

This French version of Chicken Cacciatore includes ingredients representative of the Basque region of Southwestern France—hot peppers, brightly colored bell peppers, garlic, and prosciutto. It's hearty enough to serve with a slab of crusty French bread, or you can try it over parsley rice or noodles coated with olive oil. Jalapeños vary in intensity, so use caution. When seeding or chopping hot chiles, wear rubber gloves to protect your hands from irritation. If you want more heat, add red pepper flakes before serving.

Cooking Time: 60 minutes or less
Serves: 4

1. Sprinkle the chicken with salt and pepper.
2. In a large skillet over medium-high heat, add the oil. Add the chicken and brown, 3 to 5 minutes per side. Remove the chicken and reserve. (You may need to do this in two or more batches).
3. Discard all but 1 tablespoon of fat from the skillet. Reduce the heat to medium and add the onions. Cook until softened, 3 to 5 minutes. Add the bell peppers, jalapeños, and garlic and cook for 5 minutes, stirring frequently.

4. Add the prosciutto, tomatoes, basil, and orange zest and stir to combine.

5. Return the chicken to the skillet. Reduce the heat, cover, and simmer for 30 to 40 minutes, or until the chicken and peppers are cooked through, basting with the cooking liquid and turning the chicken occasionally. If the sauce is too thin, remove the chicken and boil the sauce until it thickens.

Curried Chicken and Rice

1 3- to 4-pound chicken, cut
    into 8 pieces
1 tablespoon salt
½ teaspoon ground black
    pepper
3 tablespoons vegetable oil
2 cups chopped onions
2 teaspoons minced garlic
1 teaspoon peeled and minced
    fresh ginger
1½ cups basmati rice
3 tablespoons curry powder
1 teaspoon ground cumin
½ teaspoon red pepper flakes
3 cups reduced-sodium
    chicken broth
½ cup golden raisins
½ cup slivered almonds,
    lightly toasted

This fragrant and mild curry dish will please even the most timid eaters. Curry powder is actually a mixture of several spices, including cumin, coriander, fenugreek, red pepper, and turmeric. Its amalgamation was most likely a British invention, concocted by colonialists leaving the country who wanted to take a taste of India back home. In reality, curry powder is not representative of Indian cooking. There, different seasonings are combined for each dish and a standard curry blend is rarely, if ever, used. Because the spices in curry powder are ground, they tend to go stale; so for superior flavor, update your curry powder frequently. If basmati rice is unavailable, substitute your favorite variety.

Cooking Time: 60 minutes or less
Serves: 4

1. Preheat the oven to 375 degrees.
2. Sprinkle the chicken with salt and pepper.
3. In a large ovenproof skillet over medium-high heat, add the oil. Add the chicken and brown, 3 to 5 minutes per side. Remove the chicken and reserve. (You may need to do this in two or more batches).

4. Discard all but 1 tablespoon of fat from the skillet. Reduce the heat to medium and add the onions. Cook until softened, 3 to 5 minutes, stirring frequently.

5. Add the garlic and ginger and cook for 1 minute, stirring constantly.

6. Add the rice, curry powder, cumin, and red pepper flakes and stir to combine.

7. Add the broth. Bring to a boil, and stir to deglaze and dislodge any bits of food that have stuck to the bottom of the skillet.

8. Return the chicken to the skillet. Cover, place in the oven, and bake for 30 to 40 minutes, or until the rice is tender, the broth has been absorbed, and the chicken is cooked through.

9. Remove from the oven. Stir in the raisins and almonds.

Chicken Cacciatore

1 3- to 4-pound chicken, cut
    into 8 pieces
1 tablespoon salt
1 teaspoon ground black
    pepper
3 tablespoons olive oil
1 cup chopped onions
2 cups sliced bell peppers (a
    mix of red, yellow,
    orange, and/or green)
2 cups small mushrooms,
    quartered if large
2 teaspoons minced garlic
½ cup dry red wine
1 28-ounce can diced
    tomatoes, drained
1 teaspoon dried basil
½ teaspoon dried oregano
1 bay leaf

This robust Italian chicken braise is loaded with multicolored bell peppers, tomatoes, garlic, and mushrooms. While adding a salad and crusty bread makes this a complete meal, you could also serve it with pasta lightly tossed with capers in olive oil, or another Italian favorite, cornmeal polenta.

Cooking Time: 60 minutes or less
Serves: 4

1. Sprinkle the chicken with salt and pepper.
2. In a large skillet over medium-high heat, add the oil. Add the chicken and brown, 3 to 5 minutes per side. Remove the chicken and reserve. (You may need to do this in two or more batches).
3. Discard all but 1 tablespoon of fat from the skillet. Reduce the heat to medium and add the onions. Cook until softened, 3 to 5 minutes. Add the bell peppers, mushrooms, and garlic and cook for 5 minutes, stirring frequently.
4. Add the wine, tomatoes, basil, oregano, and bay leaf. Bring to a boil and stir to deglaze and dislodge any bits of food that have stuck to the bottom of the skillet.
5. Return the chicken to the skillet. Reduce the heat, cover, and simmer for 30 to 40 minutes, or until the chicken is cooked through, basting with the cooking liquid and turning the chicken occasionally. If the sauce is too thin, remove the chicken and boil the sauce until it thickens.

Chicken and Barley Stew

This healthful and flavorful stew combines an assortment of vegetables with barley, a nutritious grain that provides protein, niacin, thiamin, and potassium with very little sodium or fat. Studies have shown that this wonder grain also fights cholesterol production.

2 tablespoons vegetable oil
1 cup coarsely chopped
    onions
1 cup coarsely chopped
    carrots
1 cup coarsely chopped celery
1 cup sliced mushrooms
2 teaspoons minced garlic
5 cups reduced-sodium
    chicken broth
1 cup drained canned diced
    tomatoes
1 cup pearl barley
1 pound boneless and skinless
    chicken breasts, cut
    into ½-inch pieces
1 teaspoon salt
½ teaspoon ground black
    pepper

Cooking Time: 60 minutes or less
Serves: 4

1. In a large stock pot over medium-high heat, add the oil. Sauté the onions, carrots, celery, mushrooms, and garlic until softened, 5 to 8 minutes, stirring frequently.
2. Add the broth and tomatoes and stir to combine. Bring to a boil.
3. Add the barley and stir to combine.
4. Reduce the heat, cover, and simmer for 35 to 45 minutes, or until the barley is tender and the stew thickens, stirring occasionally.
5. Add the chicken and cook for 5 to 7 minutes, or until the chicken is cooked through. Season with salt and pepper.

Arroz con Pollo

1 3- to 4-pound chicken, cut
    into 8 pieces
1 tablespoon salt
½ teaspoon ground black
    pepper
3 tablespoons olive oil
1 cup chopped onions
1 cup seeded and chopped
    green bell peppers
1 cup seeded and chopped red
    bell peppers
1 teaspoon minced garlic
¼ pound ham, chopped
    (optional)
1½ cups rice
3 cups reduced-sodium
    chicken broth
1 teaspoon paprika
¼ teaspoon saffron (optional)
1 bay leaf
1 cup fresh or frozen peas
¼ cup pimentos (optional)

The ubiquitous arroz con pollo, Spanish for chicken and rice, is served all over the world, most notably in Spain, Cuba, and Latin America. This colorful dish's signature spice is saffron, which imparts its distinctive flavor and distinguishing yellow hue.

Cooking Time: 60 minutes or less
Serves: 4

1. Preheat the oven to 375 degrees.
2. Sprinkle the chicken with salt and pepper.
3. In a large ovenproof skillet over medium-high heat, add the oil. Add the chicken and brown, 3 to 5 minutes per side. Remove the chicken and reserve. (You may need to do this in two or more batches).
4. Discard all but 1 tablespoon of fat from the skillet. Reduce the heat to medium and add the onions, both bell peppers, garlic, and ham. Cook until softened, 5 to 8 minutes, stirring frequently.
5. Add the rice and stir to combine.
6. Add the broth. Bring to a boil and stir to deglaze and dislodge any bits of food that have stuck to the bottom of the skillet.

7. Add the paprika, saffron, and bay leaf and stir to combine.
8. Return the chicken to the skillet. Cover, place in the oven, and bake for 30 minutes.
9. Stir in the peas and pimentos, cover, and bake for 5 to 10 minutes, or until the rice is tender, the broth has been absorbed, and the chicken is cooked through.

Creamy Dijon Chicken Stew

1 3- to 4-pound chicken, cut into 8 pieces
1 tablespoon salt
1 teaspoon ground black pepper
3 tablespoons olive oil
2 cups cleaned and thinly sliced leeks (white part only)
2 cups sliced carrots (½-inch-thick pieces)
1½ cups sliced new potatoes
10 large cloves garlic, peeled
3 tablespoons all-purpose flour
1½ cups reduced-sodium chicken broth
1 cup dry white wine
½ cup Dijon mustard
2 teaspoons dried tarragon or herbs de Provençe (optional)
¼ cup whipping cream (optional)

In this flavorful medley, chicken is sautéed with garlic, leeks, and vegetables and then simmered in a Dijon mustard–white wine sauce. This tasty condiment, a mild mustard paste blended with wine, is named for the city of Dijon in central France.

Cooking Time: 60 minutes or less
Serves: 4

1. Sprinkle the chicken with salt and pepper.
2. In a large skillet, over medium-high heat, add the oil. Add the chicken and brown, 3 to 5 minutes per side. Remove the chicken and reserve. (You may need to do this in two or more batches).
3. Discard all but 1 tablespoon of fat from the skillet. Reduce the heat to medium and add the leeks, carrots, potatoes, and garlic. Cook until softened, 3 to 5 minutes, stirring frequently.
4. Add the flour and cook for 1 to 2 minutes, stirring constantly.
5. Add the broth, wine, mustard, and tarragon. Bring to a boil and stir to deglaze and dislodge any bits of food that have stuck to the bottom of the skillet. Keep stirring until slightly thickened.

6. Return the chicken to the skillet. Reduce the heat, cover, and simmer for 30 to 40 minutes, or until the chicken is cooked through, basting with the cooking liquid and turning the chicken occasionally.

7. Remove the chicken and vegetables to the serving bowl using a slotted spoon and cover with foil. Add the cream and simmer until the liquid thickens, 2 to 3 minutes, stirring constantly. Pour the sauce over the chicken.

• • • • • • • • • • • • • • •

Variation: *Although there is only a small amount of cream added, if you are watching your fat intake, or prefer a lighter dinner, omit the cream. If you omit the cream, boil the sauce until it thickens.*

• • • • • • • • • • • • • • •

Turkey, Potatoes, Tomatoes, and Cheese

1 tablespoon olive oil
3 cups peeled and thinly sliced
      potatoes
2 tablespoons freshly
      squeezed lemon juice
2 teaspoons minced garlic
1 teaspoon salt
½ teaspoon ground black
      pepper
1 cup reduced-sodium
      chicken broth
4 boneless and skinless turkey
      breast fillets (about 1
      pound)
1 egg, beaten
2 cups bread crumbs,
      homemade or
      packaged
½ cup dry white wine
1 large ripe tomato, sliced
      (about ½ pound)
1 teaspoon dried oregano
1 teaspoon dried basil
½ pound mozzarella cheese,
      grated or shredded

This layered casserole pairs tender turkey fillets with thinly sliced potatoes, tomatoes, herbs, and cheese. Turkey cutlets tend to be thinner than chicken, so be careful not to overcook them. If substituting chicken, pound the fillets between waxed paper for uniform thickness.

Cooking Time: 60 minutes or less
Serves: 4

1. Preheat the oven to 450 degrees.
2. Lightly coat a 13 × 9 × 2-inch baking pan with the oil. Arrange the potatoes in slightly overlapping rows. Top with the lemon juice and sprinkle with the garlic, salt, and pepper. Add the broth.
3. Cover with aluminum foil and bake for 10 minutes. Uncover and bake for 10 to 20 minutes, or until the potatoes have begun to brown and cook through.
4. Meanwhile, dip the turkey breasts in the egg and press into the bread crumbs to coat. Set aside.
5. Remove the pan from the oven and reduce the heat to 400 degrees.
6. Place the turkey breasts on top of the potatoes. Drizzle with the wine. Top each fillet with tomato slices. Sprinkle the oregano and basil on top of the tomatoes. Top with the mozzarella cheese.
7. Bake for 10 to 15 minutes, or until the turkey has cooked through and the cheese has melted. For added browning, place under the broiler for 1 to 2 minutes.

3
MEAT

30 Minutes or Less:

Pasta and Bean Soup
Steak Fajitas
Asian Steak and Noodles
Beef Burritos

Pasta with Prosciutto,
Vegetables, and Goat
Cheese
Ham and Vegetable
Frittata

60 Minutes or Less:

Chicken and Sausage
Jambalaya
Chili con Carne
Lamb, Leeks, Artichoke,
and Potato Casserole
Pork Chops with Potatoes
and Apples

Sausage, Peppers, and
Onions
Bacon and Barbecue Soup
Ham and Cheese Quiche
Ribollita

From quick stir-fries to slowly simmered stews, beef, pork, and lamb are an important and exciting part of our diet. Although red meat was shunned a few years ago for being unhealthful, as a result of new breeding and feeding practices, beef is now lower in fat, calories, and cholesterol than ever before and pork is now bred to be almost a third leaner than a decade ago. Protein-rich red meat provides important nutrients, including niacin, B vitamins, iron, and zinc.

The best method for cooking meat is based on the muscle density of the cut. Because tender prime cuts of meat toughen if overcooked, lean steaks are best when quickly grilled or combined with vegetables in simple sautés. The more muscled and fattier cuts are best adapted to long, slow cooking, which tenderizes and coaxes the flavor from every sinewy strand—and makes it impossible to prepare a meat stew in under an hour or two. While this is bad news for days when quick meals are needed, it is a wonderful and luxurious method of cooking for entertaining. Stews can be put up to simmer long before guests are due, allowing the time before company arrives to be stress-free.

Beef Tips:

- If you are unfamiliar with different cuts of meat, seek advice from a knowledgeable butcher. You can usually find meat-cutters in your local supermarket willing to share their wisdom.
- Check with your butcher before buying generically labeled "stew meat." It may actually be a leaner cut of meat packaged to look more appealing but will toughen with extended cooking. It is often more economical to cut your own stew meat from a larger piece of meat. If you do, be sure to account for added waste and bone weight when figuring out how much to buy.

- When buying beef, search for meat that is bright red. Look for marbling—flecks of fat within the meat. We are all "fat conscious" today, but we mustn't discount fat's benefits: added flavor, tenderness, and juiciness.
- Pork should be pink to pale red, not crimson. Avoid pork with blood or discoloration in the meat. When choosing prepared meats like ham or prosciutto, sample different quality brands to find the one you like best.
- We have become increasingly aware of bacterial contamination of meat. *E. coli* is the pathogen most commonly associated with raw beef. Before using meats, cut off excess fat and rinse with cold water (making sure it doesn't spray all over the counters). After cutting meat, always thoroughly wash your hands, counters, cutting boards, and knives with warm, soapy water. Store uncooked meat separately from other ingredients to prevent cross-contamination. These bacteria are killed with proper cooking. Never eat raw meat.
- Always check the expiration date before buying packaged meat, and store it in your refrigerator. If you are unable to use meat within three days or by its expiration date, it is best to freeze it. To prevent bacterial growth, always thaw meat in your refrigerator or microwave, not at room temperature.
- If you find you have more meat than you need for your meal, wrap, label, and store the extra in the freezer.
- For better browning, always pat the meat dry with paper towels before searing. Searing caramelizes the surface of the meat, adding flavor. When searing meat, don't overcrowd the pan or the meat will steam rather than brown, giving it an unappealing gray hue.
- When cutting meat for sautéing, slice against the grain for added tenderness.

- Use uniformly sized pieces of meat for more consistent cooking times.
- Meat stews should be cooked at a slow simmer, not a boil, to fully develop their character and flavor.
- Before serving stews, use a soup spoon or paper towels to skim off any fat or froth that has risen to the surface or run an ice cube over the surface to quickly solidify any liquid fat. If you are cooking and refrigerating the stew, the fat will harden when chilled and is easily removed.
- Most meat stews improve overnight and are even better reheated.
- Add leftover meat to vegetarian entrées for extra protein.

Pasta and Bean Soup

This classic Italian soup, known as pasta e fagioli *or* zuppa di fagioli, *came to worldwide attention with the song "That's Amore" in the movie* Moonstruck. *This tomato-based soup is studded with pasta, white beans, and pancetta—rolled Italian bacon. It's the perfect meal on a chilly night, served with toasted slices of Italian bread rubbed with garlic and drizzled with olive oil and a big green salad full of crunchy fennel.*

Cooking Time: 30 minutes or less
Serves: 4

1 tablespoon olive oil
¼ pound pancetta or prosciutto, chopped
1 cup finely chopped onions
¼ cup finely chopped celery
2 teaspoons minced garlic
1 teaspoon dried rosemary
6 cups reduced-sodium chicken broth
1 14½-ounce can diced tomatoes, drained
1½ cups small pasta shapes
1 15-ounce can cannellini or white beans, rinsed and drained
2 cups escarole, Swiss chard, or spinach leaves (optional)
⅓ cup grated Parmesan cheese (optional)

1. In a large stock pot over medium heat, add the oil. Sauté the pancetta for 8 to 10 minutes, or until lightly browned, stirring frequently.
2. Add the onions and celery and cook until softened, 3 to 5 minutes.
3. Add the garlic and rosemary and cook for 1 minute, stirring constantly.
4. Add the broth and tomatoes. Bring to a boil.
5. Add the pasta and cook for 5 to 8 minutes, or until almost tender, stirring occasionally.
6. Add the beans and escarole. Reduce the heat and simmer for 5 minutes. Season with salt and pepper to taste. Top each serving with the Parmesan cheese.

Steak Fajitas

¼ cup freshly squeezed lime
  juice
2 tablespoons olive oil
1 tablespoon minced garlic
1 teaspoon salt
1 teaspoon chili powder
1 pound top sirloin, thinly
  sliced
8 8- to 10-inch flour tortillas
2 tablespoons vegetable oil
1 large yellow onion, peeled
  and sliced (about ¾
  pound)
1 large red onion, peeled and
  sliced (about ¾ pound)
1 large red bell pepper, seeded
  and sliced (about ½
  pound)
1 large green bell pepper
  seeded and sliced
  (about ½ pound)
2 cups guacamole
¼ pound cheddar cheese,
  grated or shredded
1 cup tomato salsa
1 cup sour cream
1 cup rinsed and drained
  canned black beans

Fajitas are a fabulous party dish. They are simple to prepare and guests can roll up their sleeves and lend a helping hand. Marinated steak, bell peppers, and onions are wrapped in warmed tortillas and served with a variety of accompaniments— salsa, guacamole, black beans, sour cream, and grated cheddar cheese—so people can customize their fillings. The steak, onions, and peppers can also all be grilled on the barbecue for extra flavor.

Cooking Time: 30 minutes or less
Serves: 4

1. In a large baking pan or zip-top bag, combine the lime juice, olive oil, garlic, salt, chili powder, and steak. Marinate for at least 30 minutes, or up to 24 hours in the refrigerator.
2. Preheat the oven to 350 degrees.
3. Wrap the tortillas in aluminum foil and place in the oven to warm for 10 minutes. (Tortillas can also be wrapped in a damp towel and warmed in the microwave on high for 15 to 30 seconds).
4. In a large skillet over medium-high heat, add the vegetable oil. Sauté both onions for 3 to 5 minutes, stirring frequently. Add both bell peppers and cook for 5 to 8 minutes, until crisp-tender. Remove the vegetables and reserve.

5. Drain the marinade from the meat. Add the steak and sauté for 3 minutes. Return the vegetables to the skillet and stir to combine.
6. Serve the meat and vegetables with the tortillas, guacamole, cheese, salsa, sour cream, and black beans.

·················

Variations:

Shrimp Fajitas: *Substitute 1 pound of large peeled and deveined shrimp for the steak. Marinate the shrimp for 30 minutes. Cook for 1 to 2 minutes per side, or until just cooked through.*

Fish Fajitas: *Substitute 1 pound of thinly sliced mahi-mahi, swordfish, or wahoo for the steak. Marinate the fish for 30 minutes. Cook for 1 to 3 minutes per side, or until just cooked through.*

Chicken Fajitas: *Substitute 1 pound of thinly sliced boneless and skinless chicken breasts for the steak. Marinate the chicken for 30 minutes to 1 hour. Cook for 3 to 5 minutes per side, or until cooked through.*

·················

Asian Steak and Noodles

2 tablespoons vegetable oil
1 pound top sirloin, thinly
  sliced
2 3-ounce packages "Oriental"
  flavor instant ramen
  noodles, broken up
  into small pieces
2 cups broccoli florets, halved
  if large
1 cup thinly sliced carrots, cut
  diagonally
1 cup thinly sliced mushrooms
½ cup seeded and thinly
  sliced red bell peppers
2 cups water
½ teaspoon ground ginger
1 cup snow pea pods
½ cup sliced water chestnuts
½ cup fresh or frozen peas
2 tablespoons thinly sliced
  scallions

This Asian-flavored beef dish uses packaged instant ramen noodles. With the aid of this convenience, you can have a complete dinner on the table, packed with tender steak, vibrant veggies, and highly flavored noodles in under thirty minutes. This dish is also tasty with sliced boneless and skinless chicken breasts or large shrimp.

Cooking Time: 30 minutes or less
Serves: 4

1. In a large skillet over medium-high heat, add the oil. Cook the beef for 3 minutes. Remove the meat and toss with 1 seasoning packet from the noodles. Set aside.
2. Add the broccoli, carrots, mushrooms, and red peppers and sauté until almost cooked through, 8 to 10 minutes, stirring frequently.
3. Add the water, ginger, noodles, and remaining seasoning packet and stir to combine. Bring to a boil.
4. Add the snow pea pods, water chestnuts, and peas. Reduce the heat and simmer for 5 to 8 minutes, or until the noodles are tender, stirring occasionally.
5. Add the beef and scallions and stir to combine. Cook for 1 minute.

Variations:

Asian Chicken and Noodles: *Substitute 1 pound of thinly sliced boneless and skinless chicken breasts for the steak. Cook the chicken for 3 to 5 minutes, or until cooked through.*

Asian Shrimp and Noodles: *Substitute 1 pound of large peeled and deveined shrimp for the steak. Cook the shrimp for 1 to 2 minutes per side, or until just cooked through.*

Beef Burritos

4 10- to 12-inch flour tortillas
1 tablespoon vegetable oil
1 cup finely chopped onions
1¼ pounds lean ground beef
1 tablespoon chili powder
1 teaspoon ground cumin
1 teaspoon salt
3 cups coarsely chopped
      spinach leaves
      (optional)
1¼ cups chunky tomato salsa
1 cup fresh or frozen corn
¼ pound cheddar cheese,
      grated or shredded

In this south-of-the-border treat, lean ground beef, vegetables, and tasty seasonings are tossed in a skillet and then wrapped in warm tortillas. It's a fast, easy, and inexpensive family meal that will be on your table in less than thirty minutes. More important, it helps disguise vegetables from children who fear anything healthful! Have lots of toppings handy. Extra salsa, sour cream, shredded lettuce, chopped tomatoes, and guacamole all make great add-ons.

Cooking Time: 30 minutes or less
Serves: 4

1. Preheat the oven to 350 degrees.
2. Wrap the tortillas in aluminum foil and place in the oven to warm for 10 minutes. (Tortillas can also be wrapped in a damp towel and warmed in the microwave on high for 15 to 30 seconds).
3. In a large skillet over medium-high heat, add the oil. Add the onions and cook until softened, 3 to 5 minutes, stirring frequently.
4. Add the beef, chili powder, cumin, and salt. Cook, breaking up the meat, until the beef is no longer pink, 8 to 10 minutes, stirring frequently. Drain any excess fat from the skillet.

5. Add the spinach, salsa, and corn and cook until heated through, 3 to 5 minutes. Remove from the heat and stir in the cheese.

6. Spoon one-quarter of the beef into the center of each tortilla and add any toppings. Tuck the bottom of the tortilla up over the filling, fold both sides of the tortilla toward the center, and roll up. Be careful not to over-stuff the burrito.

· · · · · · · · · · · · · · · ·

Variation:

Turkey Burritos: *Substitute 1¼ pounds of ground turkey for the beef.*

· · · · · · · · · · · · · · · ·

Pasta with Prosciutto, Vegetables, and Goat Cheese

½ cup drained and coarsely chopped oil-packed sun-dried tomatoes

¼ cup olive oil

¼ pound prosciutto, ham, or salami, thinly sliced

¼ teaspoon red pepper flakes

2 cloves garlic, peeled

2 cups broccoli florets, halved if large

¾ pound spaghetti or other pasta

1 cup fresh or frozen peas

½ cup thinly sliced fresh basil

¼ pound goat cheese, crumbled

1 teaspoon salt

½ teaspoon ground black pepper

¼ cup grated Parmesan cheese

This colorful dish teams emerald broccoli, peas, and basil with crimson sun-dried tomatoes, strips of rosy prosciutto, steaming pasta, and creamy goat cheese. Delicious, healthful, and filling, it's a winning trifecta for cooks in a hurry. When cooking both the vegetables and the pasta in the same pot, it is helpful to have a pasta set with a removable insert. Otherwise, a strainer with a long handle will do.

Cooking Time: 30 minutes or less
Serves: 4

1. In the serving bowl, combine the sun-dried tomatoes, oil, prosciutto, and red pepper flakes. Set aside.
2. In a large pot over high heat, put the water up to boil for the pasta.
3. When the water is boiling, blanch the garlic for 30 to 45 seconds. (For easy blanching, skewer the garlic or use a mesh spoon to scoop it out). Rinse the garlic under cold water, pat dry, mince, and add to the serving bowl.
4. Add the broccoli and cook for 3 to 4 minutes, or until crisp-tender. Remove to the serving bowl.
5. Add the pasta and cook for 7 minutes. Add the peas and cook for 1 to 2 minutes, or until the pasta is al dente. Drain, reserving 2 to 3 tablespoons of pasta water.

6. Combine the pasta, reserved pasta water, basil, goat cheese, salt, and pepper with the sun-dried tomato mixture and stir to combine. Top with the Parmesan cheese.

· · · · · · · · · · · · · · · · ·

Variation:

Pasta with Shrimp, Prosciutto, Vegetables, and Goat Cheese: *Add ¾ pound of peeled and deveined shrimp in step 5 before adding the pasta. Cook the shrimp for 1 to 2 minutes, or until just cooked through. Remove to the serving bowl.*

Pasta with Vegetables and Goat Cheese: *For a vegetarian dish, omit the prosciutto.*

· · · · · · · · · · · · · · · · ·

Ham and Vegetable Frittata

1 tablespoon butter
½ cup coarsely chopped
    mushrooms
¼ cup finely chopped red
    onions
¼ cup seeded and finely
    chopped green or red
    bell peppers
8 eggs
¼ pound ham, chopped
2 ounces Swiss cheese, grated,
    or 2 ounces brie, sliced
    into 1-inch pieces
½ teaspoon salt
¼ teaspoon ground black
    pepper

After years of hard knocks, eggs are finally receiving the nutritional recognition they deserve. In addition to being an inexpensive source of protein, eggs are especially attractive for hurried cooks because they are quickly prepared. This light dinner, reminiscent of the classic American "Western omelet," adapts perfectly to the ease of frittata cooking. Substitute any vegetables or seasonings to make it your own creation. I highly recommend using a nonstick pan, which allows you to move the frittata easily during cooking.

Cooking Time: 30 minutes or less
Serves: 4

1. Preheat the oven to 350 degrees.
2. In a 10- or 11-inch nonstick, ovenproof skillet over medium-high heat, add the butter. Sauté the mushrooms, onions, and bell peppers until softened, 3 to 5 minutes, stirring frequently.
3. Meanwhile, in a medium bowl, beat the eggs. Add the ham, cheese, salt, and pepper.
4. Reduce the heat to medium. Pour the eggs on top of the vegetables. Cook without stirring for 1 minute, or until the eggs are almost set on the bottom. Continue cooking, using a spatula to lift the edges of the frittata toward the center of the skillet, while gently tilting the pan so the uncooked eggs run underneath the bot-

tom of the frittata. Cook for 30 to 40 seconds and repeat the process several times until the egg on top is
still wet, but not runny.

5. Place in the oven. Bake for 3 to 7 minutes, or until
the top is just set. Do not overcook.
6. Remove from the oven, run a spatula around the skillet edge to loosen the frittata, and slide or invert it
onto a serving plate.

Chicken and Sausage Jambalaya

1 2- to 2½-pound chicken, cut
    into 8 pieces
1 tablespoon salt
1 teaspoon ground black
    pepper
3 tablespoons vegetable oil
1 cup chopped onions
1 cup seeded and chopped
    green bell peppers
2 teaspoons minced garlic
1 14½-ounce can diced
    tomatoes, drained
½ pound smoked andouille
    sausage, or Louisiana
    smoked sausage, or
    kielbasa, halved
    lengthwise and sliced
    ½-inch thick
1 teaspoon dried thyme
¼ teaspoon cayenne pepper
1 bay leaf
3 cups reduced-sodium
    chicken broth
1½ cups rice

> *Jambalaya is as much a part of New Orleans as Mardi Gras and Zydeco music. The name for this spicy Cajun–Creole dish is derived from two French words—jambon for ham and a là for on top of—and the African word for rice, ya. Like much of Cajun cooking, it makes the most of ingredients found on hand—and there are as many variations of jambalaya as there are bars on Bourbon Street. This version features chicken and sausage, but ham and shrimp are two other popular additions.*

Cooking Time: 60 minutes or less
Serves: 4

1. Sprinkle the chicken with salt and pepper.
2. In a large skillet over medium-high heat, add the oil. Add the chicken and brown, 3 to 5 minutes per side. Remove the chicken and reserve. (You may need to do this in two or more batches).
3. Discard all but 1 tablespoon of the fat from the skillet. Reduce the heat to medium and add the onions, green peppers, and garlic. Cook until softened, 5 to 8 minutes, stirring frequently.

Meat

4. Add the tomatoes, sausage, thyme, cayenne pepper, and bay leaf and stir to combine.
5. Add the broth. Bring to a boil and stir to deglaze and dislodge any bits of food that have stuck to the bottom of the skillet.
6. Add the rice and stir to combine.
7. Return the chicken to the skillet. Reduce the heat, cover, and simmer for 30 to 40 minutes, or until the rice is tender, the broth has been absorbed, and the chicken is cooked through, stirring occasionally.

Chili con Carne

2 tablespoons vegetable oil
1 cup coarsely chopped
    onions
1 cup seeded and coarsely
    chopped green bell
    peppers
2 teaspoons minced garlic
1½ pounds lean ground beef
2 cups canned crushed
    tomatoes
2 cups reduced-sodium beef
    broth
3 tablespoons chili powder
1 teaspoon ground cumin
1 teaspoon salt
½ teaspoon cayenne pepper
½ teaspoon dried oregano
1 15¼-ounce can kidney
    beans, rinsed and
    drained

Contrary to popular belief, Chili con Carne is an American invention, not an import from south of the border. Texans lay claim to its origin, but its true beginnings are undocumented. What is well known is its overwhelming popularity, as evidenced by the number of festivals held in its honor, the monumental number of recipe variations, and the worshipping of its heat and spice by "chiliheads" all over the world. This classic meat and bean chili is the quintessential party fare. It's a snap to prepare, and the recipe can easily be doubled or tripled to accommodate a crowd of hungry eaters. You can vary the seasonings to make it as potent as you want. If you like your chili super hot, add some extra cayenne pepper, jalapeño peppers, or Tabasco. Make sure you have lots of toppings on hand: sour cream, grated cheddar cheese, chopped red onions, cilantro, ripe tomatoes, and lime are all naturals. Serve with a big salad and cornbread or tortilla chips, and it's a party.

Cooking Time: 60 minutes or less
Serves: 4

1. In a large stock pot over medium heat, add the oil. Add the onions and green peppers and sauté until softened, 3 to 5 minutes, stirring frequently.

Meat

2. Add the garlic and cook for 1 minute, stirring constantly.
3. Add the ground beef and cook for 5 to 8 minutes, or until just cooked through, using a fork or spatula to break up the meat into small pieces.
4. Add the tomatoes, broth, chili powder, cumin, salt, cayenne pepper, and oregano and stir to combine. Bring to a boil.
5. Add the kidney beans. Reduce the heat and simmer for 45 minutes, or until thickened and the flavors have melded, stirring occasionally.

•••••••••••••••••

Variation:

Turkey Chili: *Substitute ground turkey for the beef.*

•••••••••••••••••

Lamb, Leek, Artichoke, and Potato Casserole

8 1-inch-thick lamb chops, trimmed of excess fat (about 2½ pounds)
1 tablespoon minced garlic
2 tablespoons olive oil
3 cups cleaned, julienned leeks (white part only)
6 cups peeled and thinly sliced potatoes
1 teaspoon dried thyme
1 teaspoon salt
½ teaspoon ground black pepper
1 cup reduced-sodium chicken broth
2 cups frozen or canned artichoke hearts, halved

Tender lamb chops are paired with flavorful leeks and smothered with potatoes and artichoke hearts in this easy stove-to-oven casserole. Leeks, a milder member of the onion family, resemble giant scallions. When sautéed, they impart a delicate and sweet flavor that enhances whatever they are cooked with.

Cooking Time: 60 minutes or less
Serves: 4

1. Preheat the oven to 425 degrees.
2. Rub the lamb chops with the garlic.
3. In a large ovenproof skillet over medium-high heat, add the oil. Add the lamb chops and brown, 2 minutes per side. (You may need to do this in two or more batches). Remove the lamb and reserve.
4. Add the leeks and sauté until softened, 3 to 5 minutes, stirring frequently.
5. Add the potatoes, thyme, salt, and pepper and stir to combine.
6. Add the broth. Bring to a boil.
7. Add the lamb and artichokes to the skillet, cover, and place in the oven. Bake for 10 to 15 minutes. Uncover, baste with the cooking liquid, and bake for 10 to 15 minutes, or until the lamb and potatoes are cooked through.

Pork Chops with Potatoes and Apples

In this autumnal dish, delicately seasoned pork is a natural match for apples and potatoes. Pork, once maligned as high in fat, is now bred to be much leaner. In fact, it now has 50 percent less fat than it did twenty years ago. So enjoy "the other white meat" in this delicious stove-to-oven meal.

Cooking Time: 60 minutes or less
Serves: 4

1. Preheat the oven to 425 degrees.
2. Sprinkle the pork chops with the salt, thyme, sage, and pepper.
3. In a large ovenproof skillet over medium-high heat, add the butter. Add the pork chops and brown, 2 minutes per side. Remove the pork and reserve.
4. Add the onions and sauté until softened, 3 to 5 minutes, stirring frequently.
5. Stir in the mustard. Top with the potatoes, apples, broth, and apple juice and stir to combine. Bring to a boil.
6. Cover, place in the oven, and bake for 10 minutes. Uncover, stir, and bake for 10 to 15 minutes, or until the potatoes are tender.
7. Return the pork to the skillet, cover, and bake for 7 to 12 minutes, or until the pork is cooked through.

4 1-inch-thick boneless pork chops, trimmed of excess fat (about 1½ to 2 pounds)
1 teaspoon salt
1 teaspoon dried thyme
1 teaspoon dried sage
½ teaspoon ground black pepper
2 tablespoons butter
1 cup chopped onions
2 teaspoons Dijon mustard
4 cups peeled and thinly sliced potatoes
4 cups peeled, cored, and thinly sliced Granny Smith apples
½ cup reduced-sodium chicken broth
½ cup apple juice or cider

Sausage, Peppers, and Onions

2 tablespoons olive oil
1½ pounds hot or sweet
　　Italian sausage, sliced
　　1½ inches thick
1 large yellow onion, peeled
　　and sliced ½ inch thick
　　(about ¾ pound)
2 large bell peppers (red,
　　yellow, orange, and/or
　　green), sliced ½ inch
　　thick (about 1 pound)
1 tablespoon minced garlic
1 28-ounce can Italian plum
　　tomatoes
½ cup dry red wine
2 teaspoons dried oregano
1 teaspoon dried basil
1 teaspoon fennel seeds
　　(optional)
¼ teaspoon red pepper flakes
1 teaspoon salt
½ teaspoon ground black
　　pepper

For me, the aromatic and tasty combination of sausage, peppers, and onions always stirs memories of strolling by Fenway Park, the great Boston baseball field. There, food vendors lined the streets leading up to the stadium, filling historic Kenmore Square with tempting aromas, none more intoxicating than this winning combination. Whether the Red Sox won or lost, if a sausage sandwich was enjoyed, the evening was not a total disappointment. Make sure to serve crusty rolls on the side.

Cooking Time: 60 minutes or less
Serves: 4

1. In a large skillet over medium-high heat, add the oil. Add the sausage and brown on all sides, 8 to 10 minutes. (You may need to do this in two or more batches). Remove the sausage and reserve.
2. Discard all but 1 tablespoon of fat from the skillet. Reduce the heat to medium and add the onions. Cook until softened, 3 to 5 minutes. Add the bell peppers and garlic and cook for 5 minutes, stirring frequently.
3. Add the tomatoes and their juice, wine, oregano, basil, fennel seeds, and red pepper flakes and stir to combine and to break up any large pieces of tomato.

Bring to a boil and stir to deglaze and dislodge any bits of food that have stuck to the bottom of the skillet.

4. Return the sausage to the skillet. Reduce the heat, cover, and simmer for 30 minutes, stirring occasionally. Season with salt and pepper.

· · · · · · · · · · · · · · · ·

Variation:

Turkey Sausage, Onions, and Peppers: *Substitute turkey or chicken sausage for the Italian sausage.*

· · · · · · · · · · · · · · · ·

Bacon and Barbecue Soup

½ pound bacon, cut into 2-
    inch pieces
2 cups sliced mushrooms
1 cup coarsely chopped
    onions
3½ cups reduced-sodium
    chicken broth
1 28-ounce can diced
    tomatoes
1 15-ounce can tomato sauce
¼ cup barbecue sauce
2 tablespoons red wine
    vinegar
1 tablespoon coarsely chopped
    fresh Italian parsley
    (optional)
1 teaspoon chili powder
1 teaspoon salt
½ teaspoon ground black
    pepper
2 cups medium-sized shell
    noodles or other pasta
    shape

This soup was created by George V. Jackson at the age of eight. Jackson, as he is known to friends and family, learned to fend for himself in the kitchen at an early age. Now fifty years have passed and time hasn't altered his recipe. Although Jackson calls his creation "vinegar soup," his grandsons, for whom he now cooks, refer to it as "Grandpa's Bacon Soup" when asking for seconds. Because the barbecue sauce adds such a distinctive flavor, I call it Bacon and Barbecue Soup.

Cooking Time: 60 minutes or less
Serves: 4

1. In a large stock pot over medium heat, sauté the bacon until cooked but not crisp, 6 to 8 minutes, stirring frequently.
2. Discard all but 1 tablespoon of fat from the skillet. Add the mushrooms and onions and cook until softened, 5 to 8 minutes, stirring frequently.
3. Add the broth, tomatoes and their juice, tomato sauce, barbecue sauce, vinegar, parsley, chili powder, salt, and pepper and stir to combine. Bring to a boil.

4. Reduce the heat, partially cover, and simmer for 30 minutes, stirring occasionally.

5. Bring to a boil and add the noodles. Stir to combine. Cook for 7 to 11 minutes, or until the noodles are cooked through, stirring occasionally. This soup will thicken as it stands. If necessary, add extra broth or water to achieve the desired consistency.

Ham and Cheese Quiche

Crust:

1 ¼ cups all-purpose flour
¼ teaspoon salt
½ cup (1 stick) unsalted
        butter, chilled and cut
        into ½-inch pieces
2 to 4 tablespoons ice water

Filling:

4 eggs
1 cup cream or milk
1 cup milk
½ teaspoon salt
¼ teaspoon ground black
        pepper
½ pound ham, chopped
¼ cup finely chopped red
        onions
5 ounces Swiss cheese, grated
        or shredded

Contrary to popular belief, real men do eat quiche . . . and what's more, they usually ask for seconds. Quiche has a real place in a busy household. It can be prepared in minutes and be on the table within the hour. Served with a salad loaded with crispy vegetables, this classic meal will never go out of style. Make your own crust or buy a pre-made crust and fit it into a 9-inch pie plate.

Cooking Time: 60 minutes or less
Serves: 4

1. Prepare the crust: In a food processor fitted with a metal chopping blade, mix the flour and salt (5 seconds). Add the butter and pulse until the mixture resembles coarse meal (10 short pulses). Sprinkle the minimum amount of water over the mixture and pulse until distributed throughout the dough and the crumbs start sticking together (5 to 10 pulses). Process just until the dough holds together, adding the remaining water if necessary. Do not allow the dough to form a ball.
2. Scrape the dough onto the work surface. Shape the dough into a 1-inch-thick disc. Wrap the dough tightly with plastic wrap and refrigerate for 30 minutes, or until it is firm enough to roll out.
3. Preheat the oven to 450 degrees.

4. Roll out the dough and fit into a 9-inch pie pan. Prick the dough with a fork and bake for 5 to 10 minutes, or until lightly browned. Remove from the oven and reduce the temperature to 350 degrees.

5. Prepare the filling: Meanwhile, in a medium bowl, beat the eggs, cream, milk, salt, and pepper. Add the ham and onions and stir to combine. Set aside.

6. Line the partially baked pie crust with the cheese. Add the egg mixture.

7. Bake for 40 to 50 minutes, or until the eggs are set and the center doesn't jiggle. If the crust begins to brown before the quiche is ready, cover it with aluminum foil to prevent burning. Let stand 5 to 10 minutes before serving.

Ribollita

2 tablespoons olive oil
¼ pound pancetta or
    prosciutto, chopped
1 cup chopped onions
1 cup thinly sliced leeks
    (white part only)
½ cup coarsely chopped
    carrots
½ cup coarsely chopped celery
2 teaspoons minced garlic
½ head Savoy cabbage, thinly
    sliced
6 cups reduced-sodium
    chicken broth
1 14½-ounce can diced
    tomatoes
1 cup rinsed and drained
    canned cannellini or
    small white beans
¼ cup coarsely chopped fresh
    basil
1 teaspoon salt
½ teaspoon ground black
    pepper
2 cups 1-inch cubed stale
    crusty sourdough,
    French, or Italian
    bread
½ cup grated Parmesan
    cheese

This peasant-style bread and vegetable soup is a mainstay of Tuscan dining. Ribollita, which means "reboiled," originated in the days when cooks traditionally stretched out their minestrone soup for a second serving by adding leftover bread. It is much debated whether Ribollita is best enjoyed right after cooking in its more liquid state, or if it is even better after standing or reheating, when the bread expands and the soup takes on a thick porridge-like consistency.

Cooking Time: 60 minutes or less
Serves: 4

1. Heat the oil in a large stock pot. Sauté the pancetta over medium heat for 8 to 10 minutes, or until lightly browned, stirring frequently.
2. Add the onions, leeks, carrots, celery, and garlic and cook until softened, 5 to 8 minutes, stirring occasionally.
3. Add the cabbage and cook for 2 to 3 minutes, stirring constantly.
4. Add the broth and tomatoes and their juice. Bring to a boil.
5. Add the beans, basil, salt, and pepper. Reduce the heat and simmer for 20 minutes, stirring occasionally.
6. Add the bread and cook for 5 minutes. Top each serving with the Parmesan cheese.

Meat

4

SEAFOOD

30 Minutes or Less:

Oriental Shrimp and
Vegetable Pasta
Shrimp and Asparagus
Risotto
Beer-Battered Fish Tacos
Seafood Stew
Coconut Fish and Shrimp
Stew

Spicy Shrimp with Dried-
Fruit Pilaf
Shrimp and Feta Cheese
Thai Shrimp and Jasmine
Rice
Shrimp and White Bean
Stew
Thai Shrimp and Cello-
phane Noodles

60 Minutes or Less:

Oven-Baked Fish with
Roasted Vegetables
Bouillabaisse
Shrimp and Sausage
Gumbo
Paella

Manhattan Clam
Chowder
New England Clam and
Fish Chowder
Smoked Salmon and Goat
Cheese Quiche
Cioppino

We have not always been a piscivorous nation. But as we become more health conscious, seafood is playing a bigger role in our diet. While many of us grew up associating seafood with soggy fish sticks and smelly kitchens, we now have to revise our perceptions. With so many varieties of seafood widely available, and newly perfected "quick" cooking techniques like grilling and stir-frying, fried and breaded is no longer the only option. Now fish is no longer cooked to a rubbery death, and we can celebrate its moist, firm texture and superior flavor.

Seafood is gracing our dinner tables with greater regularity—and for good reason. Seafood is high in protein and low in calories and saturated fats. It provides B vitamins, phosphorus, potassium, iron, zinc, calcium, iodine, and omega-3 fatty acids. These acids reduce blood clots, prevent heart disease, and lower cholesterol. In addition to its great nutritional value, seafood is quick cooking and requires very little added fat for its preparation.

In this chapter, you'll find fast and temptingly easy shrimp recipes and a variety of full-flavored seafood stews, stirfries, and soups.

A word of warning: Seafood, especially shellfish, can be quite pricey, but there are many ways around this. Most recipes allow a lot of flexibility when selecting fish. Inexpensive mussels are easily substituted when clams are costly, and several options are given for fish fillets so you can take advantage of whichever one is on sale. Splurge for special occasions and conserve on others.

Seafood Tips:

- Unfortunately, specialty fish markets are becoming a thing of the past. To offset this, supermarket fish departments are offering greater variety and are becoming more knowledgeable about different types of fish. Check out different markets to see which has the best quality, variety, and price.

- Buy fresh fish rather than frozen or previously frozen whenever possible. The exception is shrimp, which has almost always been previously frozen.
- Seafood should smell clean and sweet. It should never smell "fishy" or have an unpleasant or ammonia-like odor. Fish should look firm, moist, and translucent. Avoid slimy, dried-out, or discolored fish. Mussels, clams, and oysters should be alive, clean, free of debris, and have tightly closed, intact shells.
- Store seafood in your refrigerator. It is best to consume fish within twenty-four to thirty-six hours of its purchase. Always thaw and marinate seafood in the refrigerator, not at room temperature, to prevent bacterial growth.
- Before using seafood, rinse it with cold water (making sure it doesn't spray all over the counters) to remove surface bacteria. After cutting seafood, always thoroughly wash your hands, counters, cutting boards, and knives with warm, soapy water. Store uncooked seafood separately from other ingredients to prevent cross-contamination.
- When cooking clams, oysters, or mussels in their shells, always discard any that do not open. Unopened shells most likely mean that they were dead before cooking and they could harbor bacteria.
- Do not overcook seafood—it will become hard, rubbery, and lose much of its flavor. Remember that fish will continue to cook after it is removed from the heat, especially when surrounded by hot broth in a soup or stew. Food safety specialists recommend that fish be cooked until the flesh is opaque and flakes easily. It should have an internal temperature of 145 degrees.
- When a recipe calls for a firm white fish, choose from cod, scrod, monkfish, sea bass, halibut, orange roughy, haddock, or snapper.

Oriental Shrimp and Vegetable Pasta

⅓ cup peanut oil
¼ cup reduced-sodium soy
 sauce
¼ cup rice vinegar
2 tablespoons dark sesame oil
1 tablespoon sugar
1 tablespoon peeled and
 minced fresh ginger
½ to 1 teaspoon hot chili oil
 or red pepper flakes
2 cloves garlic, peeled
2½ cups sliced asparagus (1-
 inch-long pieces)
¾ pound medium shrimp,
 peeled and deveined
¾ pound angel hair pasta
½ cup fresh or frozen peas
½ cup seeded and thinly
 sliced red bell peppers
 (1-inch pieces)
½ cup coarsely chopped
 roasted salted peanuts
 or cashews
2 tablespoons thinly sliced
 scallions

This easy-to-put-together dinner features quickly blanched vegetables, shrimp, and angel hair pasta tossed in a light Asian dressing and topped with chopped peanuts. Most grocery stores now carry a wide variety of Asian spices and condiments, so cooking restaurant favorites at home has never been easier. Look for thin asparagus for extra-quick cooking. When cooking both vegetables and pasta in the same pot, it is helpful to have a pasta set with a removable insert. Otherwise, a strainer with a long handle will do.

Cooking Time: 30 minutes or less
Serves: 4

1. In the serving bowl, combine the peanut oil, soy sauce, rice vinegar, sesame oil, sugar, ginger, and chili oil. Set aside.
2. In a large pot over high heat, put the water up to boil for the pasta.
3. When the water is boiling, blanch the garlic for 30 to 45 seconds. (For easy blanching, skewer the garlic or use a mesh spoon to scoop it out). Rinse the garlic under cold water, pat dry, mince, and add to the serving bowl.
4. Add the asparagus and cook for 3 to 5 minutes, or until crisp-tender. Remove to the serving bowl.

5. Add the shrimp and cook for 1 to 2 minutes, or until just cooked through. Remove to the serving bowl. Stir to coat the shrimp and asparagus with the dressing.

6. Add the pasta and cook for 4 minutes. Add the peas and cook for 1 to 2 minutes, or until the pasta is al dente. Drain and add the pasta and peas to the serving bowl. Stir well to combine. Top with the red peppers, peanuts, and scallions.

....

Variations:

Oriental Vegetarian Pasta: *Substitute 4 cups of broccoli florets for the shrimp. In step 4, add the broccoli and cook for 2 minutes before adding the asparagus.*

Oriental Pasta with Tofu: *For added protein, add a 6-ounce package of tofu, drained and cut into cubes, to the dressing.*

....

Shrimp and Asparagus Risotto

4 cups clam juice mixed with 1 cup of water, or 4 to 5 cups reduced-sodium chicken broth
2 tablespoons butter
½ cup finely chopped onions
1½ cups Arborio rice
½ cup dry white wine
2 cups sliced asparagus (1-inch-long pieces)
¾ pound shrimp, peeled and deveined
¼ pound prosciutto, finely chopped
1 cup grated Parmesan cheese
½ teaspoon ground black pepper

Risotto, a slow-cooking creamy rice dish, is a mainstay of Northern Italian cooking. Its essence is Arborio rice, a short-grain, highly glutinous rice grown in the Po Valley of Northern Italy. What makes Arborio rice exceptional is its ability to absorb liquid while retaining its firmness. The secret to perfect risotto is the slow and steady sequential additions of broth. One note: It is not essential to warm the broth first, but it does help maintain a constant cooking temperature. Look for thin asparagus spears for more even cooking.

Cooking Time: 30 minutes or less
Serves: 4

1. In a microwave, bring the broth to a simmer.
2. In a large saucepan or stock pot over medium heat, add the butter. Add the onions and sauté until softened, 2 to 3 minutes, stirring frequently.
3. Add the rice. Stir constantly to coat with the butter, 1 minute.
4. Add the wine and stir until completely absorbed.
5. Add the asparagus, reserving the tips. Stir to combine.
6. Begin slowly adding the broth, ½ cup at a time, stirring frequently. Wait until each addition is almost completely absorbed before adding more, about 3 to 5 minutes for each addition.

Seafood

7. After 15 minutes, add the reserved asparagus tips, shrimp, and prosciutto. Stir to combine and to prevent sticking. Continue to add broth, stirring frequently, for 5 to 8 minutes, or until the risotto has a creamy texture but is still al dente, slightly firm to the bite. You may not need to use all of the liquid.
8. Add the Parmesan cheese and pepper and stir vigorously to combine. Serve immediately.

·················

Variation:

Chicken and Asparagus Risotto: *Substitute ½ pound of boneless and skinless chicken breasts, cut into 1-inch pieces, for the shrimp. In step 2, add the onions and chicken and sauté for 3 to 5 minutes, or until the chicken begins to cook through.*

·················

Beer-Battered Fish Tacos

8 6-inch corn tortillas
1½ cups all-purpose flour
½ teaspoon salt
¼ teaspoon ground black
    pepper
1 to 1¼ cups beer
3 cups vegetable oil
1½ pounds cod, flounder, or
    other white fish fillets,
    cut crosswise into 1-
    inch-wide strips
¼ cup sour cream
¼ cup mayonnaise
1 cup fresh tomato salsa,
    ready-made or recipe,
    page 175
2 cups cabbage, shredded
1 cup guacamole (optional)
¼ pound cheddar cheese,
    grated or shredded
    (optional)
1 lime, cut into eighths

One of the best culinary rewards for moving to Southern California was the discovery of Mexico's Baja cuisine, especially fish tacos. Irresistible fried fish fillets, surrounded by crunchy shredded cabbage and drizzled with creamy white sauce and salsa, are enclosed in warm corn tortillas. The flavors and textures are in perfect symmetry. Once you try them, you'll be singing "California, here I come!"

Cooking Time: 30 minutes or less
Serves: 4

1. Preheat the oven to 350 degrees.
2. Wrap the tortillas in aluminum foil and place in the oven to warm for 10 minutes. (Tortillas can also be wrapped in a damp towel and warmed in the microwave on high for 15 to 30 seconds).
3. In a medium bowl, combine 1 cup of the flour, salt, and pepper. Gradually whisk in the beer to form a medium-thick, smooth batter. (Batter can also be mixed in a food processor or blender).
4. In a medium saucepan or skillet, heat the oil to 375 degrees. The oil should be at least 1 inch deep.
5. Dust the fish with the remaining ½ cup flour. Working in batches, dip the fish into the batter, coating each piece completely and allowing any excess batter to drip off.

6. Fry the fish, 2 to 3 pieces at a time, for 3 to 5 minutes, or until golden and crispy. Using tongs, turn the fish twice to ensure even cooking. Transfer the fish to paper towels and repeat with remaining pieces.

7. Meanwhile, combine the sour cream and mayonnaise. Spread 1 tablespoon of sour cream sauce on each tortilla. Top with 1 to 2 tablespoons of salsa, ¼ cup of cabbage, fish, 2 tablespoons of guacamole, 2 tablespoons of cheddar cheese, and a squeeze of lime; or to taste.

·················

Variation:

Shrimp Tacos: *Substitute 1 pound of large shrimp, peeled and deveined, for the fish. Fry the shrimp for 2 to 4 minutes, or until golden and crispy.*

·················

Seafood Stew

2 tablespoons olive oil
1 cup finely chopped onions
½ cup finely chopped carrots
½ cup finely chopped celery
1 tablespoon minced garlic
1 cup dry white wine
1 cup clam juice
1 28-ounce can diced
    tomatoes, drained
1 pound firm white fish, cut
    into 1-inch pieces
12 mussels, scrubbed and
    debearded
12 littleneck or small clams,
    scrubbed
12 shrimp, peeled and
    deveined
1 teaspoon salt
½ teaspoon ground black
    pepper
2 tablespoons chopped fresh
    Italian parsley
    (optional)

This fast and easy seafood stew features a variety of fish and shellfish served in a garlic–tomato broth. It is simple enough for a family dinner and elegant enough for guests. Choose whichever firm white fish looks good at the market: cod, sea bass, halibut, or orange roughy are all delicious. The secret to the success of all seafood stews is not to overcook the seafood, so use care when cooking.

Cooking Time: 30 minutes or less
Serves: 4

1. In a large stock pot over medium heat, add the oil. Sauté the onions, carrots, celery, and garlic until softened, 5 to 8 minutes, stirring frequently.
2. Add the wine, clam juice, and tomatoes and stir to combine. Bring to a boil.
3. Reduce the heat, cover, and simmer for 15 minutes, stirring occasionally.
4. Add the fish, mussels, and clams and cook for 3 to 5 minutes, or until the mussel and clam shells begin to open. Add the shrimp and cook for 1 to 2 minutes, or until the seafood is just cooked through.
5. Season with salt and pepper. Sprinkle with the parsley.

Coconut Fish and Shrimp Stew

This savory fish stew is a Brazilian specialty. White fish fillets are marinated in lime juice and hot peppers and simmered with vibrant vegetables in creamy coconut milk. This mild stew is traditionally made with cod, although haddock, orange roughy, or scrod are all pleasing.

Cooking Time: 30 minutes or less
Serves: 4

1. In a medium bowl, add the fish, lime juice, and jalapeños and stir to combine. Set aside.
2. In a large stock pot or large skillet over medium heat, add the oil. Sauté the onions, both bell peppers, and garlic until softened, 5 to 8 minutes, stirring frequently.
3. Add the clam juice, coconut milk, and rice. Cover and simmer for 10 minutes, stirring occasionally.
4. Add the fish and its marinade, tomatoes, and green beans. Cook uncovered for 5 minutes, stirring occasionally.
5. Add the shrimp and cook for 1 to 2 minutes, or until the seafood is just cooked through.
6. Season with salt and pepper. Sprinkle with cilantro.

1 pound cod, or other white fish, cut into 1-inch pieces
3 tablespoons freshly squeezed lime juice
1 tablespoon seeded and minced fresh jalapeño peppers
2 tablespoons olive oil
1 cup chopped onions
½ cup seeded and chopped green bell peppers
½ cup seeded and chopped red bell peppers
1 tablespoon minced garlic
2 cups clam juice
1 cup canned unsweetened coconut milk, stirred vigorously to blend
½ cup rice (preferably jasmine or basmati)
2 cups seeded and chopped ripe plum tomatoes
1 cup trimmed and sliced green beans (1-inch pieces)
1 pound shrimp, peeled and deveined
1 teaspoon salt
½ teaspoon ground black pepper
¼ cup chopped fresh cilantro (optional)

Spicy Shrimp with Dried-Fruit Pilaf

1 pound large shrimp, peeled
    and deveined
1 teaspoon paprika
1 teaspoon ground ginger
½ teaspoon ground cinnamon
¼ teaspoon cayenne pepper
2 tablespoons olive oil
1 tablespoon butter
1 cup finely chopped onions
1½ cups rice
3 cups reduced-sodium
    chicken broth
½ cup chopped dried apricots
½ cup currants or golden
    raisins
¼ cup dried cranberries
    (optional)
1 tablespoon orange zest
1 teaspoon salt
½ cup slivered almonds,
    lightly toasted

This Mediterranean entrée combines fragrantly seasoned shrimp with a fruity rice pilaf. A pilaf refers to rice that has been cooked in oil or butter, usually with seasonings or onions, before being simmered in liquid. The name originally came from the Persian pilau.

Cooking Time: 30 minutes or less
Serves: 4

1. In a medium bowl, combine the shrimp, paprika, ginger, cinnamon, and cayenne pepper.
2. In a large skillet over medium-high heat, add the oil. Add the shrimp and cook for 1 minute per side. Remove the shrimp and reserve.
3. Melt the butter in the skillet. Add the onions and sauté until softened, 3 to 5 minutes, stirring frequently.
4. Add the rice and stir to combine. Cook for 1 minute, stirring frequently.
5. Add the broth. Bring to a boil and stir to deglaze and dislodge any bits of food or seasonings that have stuck to the bottom of the skillet.
6. Add the apricots, currants, cranberries, orange zest, and salt and stir to combine.

7. Reduce the heat, cover, and simmer for 15 to 20 minutes, or until the rice is almost tender, stirring occasionally.
8. Add the shrimp and stir to combine. Cover and cook for 2 minutes. Top with the almonds.

· · · · · · · · · · · · · · · · ·

Variation:

Chicken with Dried-Fruit Pilaf: *Substitute 1 to 1½ pounds of skinless and boneless chicken breasts for the shrimp and brown for 4 to 5 minutes per side. Remove the chicken, cover with foil, and reserve until step 8.*

· · · · · · · · · · · · · · · ·

Shrimp and Feta Cheese

3 tablespoons olive oil
1½ pounds large shrimp,
    peeled and deveined
1 cup finely chopped onions
2 teaspoons minced garlic
1 28-ounce can diced
    tomatoes, drained
½ cup dry white wine
1 tablespoon freshly squeezed
    lemon juice
1 teaspoon salt
½ teaspoon ground black
    pepper
⅛ teaspoon cayenne pepper
½ pound feta cheese,
    crumbled

Big tasty shrimp find their match in this Greek in-spired union of feta cheese, garlic, and tomatoes cooked to bubbly perfection. Serve with warm pita bread and a cucumber, red onion, and kalamata olive salad tossed with red wine vinaigrette. It also is great with buttered rice.

Cooking Time: 30 minutes or less
Serves: 4

1. Preheat the oven to 400 degrees.
2. In a large ovenproof skillet over medium heat, add the oil. Sauté the shrimp for 15 to 30 seconds per side, or until they just turn pink. Remove the shrimp and reserve.
3. Add the onions and cook until softened, 3 to 5 minutes.
4. Add the garlic and cook for 1 minute, stirring constantly.
5. Add the tomatoes, wine, lemon juice, salt, black pepper, and cayenne pepper and stir to combine. Bring to a boil.
6. Cook for 5 to 8 minutes, or until thickened, stirring frequently.

7. Arrange the shrimp on top of the tomato sauce. Cover with the feta cheese.
8. Bake for 10 to 15 minutes, or until the tomatoes are bubbly, the shrimp is cooked through, and the feta has melted. For added browning, place under the broiler for 1 to 2 minutes.

Thai Shrimp and Jasmine Rice

2 tablespoons vegetable oil
1 pound large shrimp, peeled and deveined
2 tablespoons seeded and finely chopped fresh jalapeño peppers
1 tablespoon minced garlic
1 tablespoon peeled and minced fresh ginger
1½ cups jasmine or basmati rice, rinsed and drained
1½ cups clam juice
1 cup unsweetened coconut milk, stirred vigorously to combine
2 tablespoons freshly squeezed lemon juice
1 teaspoon lemon zest
1 cup seeded and chopped ripe plum tomatoes
½ cup thinly sliced scallions
½ cup chopped roasted salted peanuts
2 tablespoons freshly squeezed lime juice
1 teaspoon salt
¼ cup coarsely chopped fresh basil (optional)

This Far East risotto-like dish combines the aromatic and evocative flavorings of Thai cooking in the spirit of sanuk, *a joyous sense of well-being. Fusing the best from many Asian cultures, Thai cuisine finds harmony between delicate and assertive flavors. Jasmine rice, a fragrant long-grain white rice indigenous to Thailand, cooks quickly and requires less liquid than its fluffier and better-known American cousin, converted rice.*

Cooking Time: 30 minutes or less
Serves: 4

1. In a large skillet over medium-high heat, add the oil. Sauté the shrimp, jalapeños, garlic, and ginger for 2 minutes, stirring frequently. Remove the shrimp and reserve.
2. Add the rice and cook for 1 minute, stirring constantly. Add the clam juice, coconut milk, and lemon juice and stir to combine. Bring to a boil.
3. Reduce the heat, cover, and simmer for 12 to 15 minutes, stirring occasionally.
4. Add the shrimp, lemon zest, and tomatoes and stir to combine. Cook for 5 minutes, or until the rice is tender, the broth has been absorbed, and the shrimp is cooked through.
5. Remove from the heat. Add the scallions, peanuts, lime juice, and salt and stir to combine. Sprinkle with the basil.

Shrimp and White Bean Stew

This quick-cooking Tuscan-style stew is an extraordinary medley of tastes, textures, and colors. Succulent sautéed shrimp are married with salty and mellow pancetta, tomatoes, beans, and basil. While the flavors fuse, each ingredient maintains its own identity.

Cooking Time: 30 minutes or less
Serves: 4

3 tablespoons olive oil
¼ pound pancetta, chopped (optional)
1½ pounds shrimp, peeled and deveined
3 cups rinsed and drained canned cannellini beans
1 cup seeded and chopped ripe plum tomatoes, or 1 cup drained canned diced tomatoes
½ cup clam juice
2 tablespoons coarsely chopped fresh basil
2 teaspoons minced garlic
1 teaspoon salt
½ teaspoon ground black pepper

1. In a large skillet over medium heat, add the oil. Sauté the pancetta for 8 to 10 minutes, or until lightly browned, stirring frequently.
2. Add the shrimp and cook for 30 seconds per side.
3. Add the beans, tomatoes, clam juice, basil, garlic, salt, and pepper. Cook until heated through, 5 to 8 minutes.

• • • • • • • • • • • • • • •

Variation:

Meatless Shrimp and White Bean Stew: *For non-meat eaters, omit the pancetta.*

• • • • • • • • • • • • • • •

Thai Shrimp and Cellophane Noodles

¼ pound dried cellophane
  noodles
3 tablespoons vegetable oil
1 pound large shrimp, peeled
  and deveined
3 cups cubed Japanese
  eggplant
2 cups trimmed and sliced
  green beans (1-inch-
  long pieces)
1 tablespoon seeded and finely
  chopped fresh jalapeño
  peppers (optional)
1 14½-ounce can plus 1 cup
  unsweetened coconut
  milk, stirred vigorously
  to blend
1 to 2 tablespoons Thai red
  curry paste
1 teaspoon salt
1 cup fresh or frozen peas
2 tablespoons thinly sliced
  scallions
2 tablespoons coarsely
  chopped fresh basil
  (optional)

In this creamy dish, juicy shrimp, cellophane noodles, and vegetables are simmered in a spicy curry–coconut sauce. Cellophane noodles—also known as mung bean noodles, bean threads, saifun, or glass noodles—are sold dried in tightly looped skeins and then soaked in hot water to soften. These versatile noodles are only one of the many varieties used in Thai cooking. Luckily, with supermarkets offering a wide range of international foods, these clear thin noodles, curry paste, and coconut milk are easier to find than ever before.

Cooking Time: 30 minutes or less
Serves: 4

1. In a medium bowl, place the noodles and add enough hot water to cover. Let stand until the noodles are pliable, 10 to 15 minutes. Drain, rinse with cold water, and drain again. Set aside.

2. Meanwhile, in a large skillet over medium-high heat, add the oil. Add the shrimp and cook for 1 minute per side. Remove the shrimp and reserve.

3. Add the eggplant, green beans, and jalapeños and cook until softened, 5 to 8 minutes, stirring frequently.

4. Add the coconut milk, curry paste to taste (2 table-spoons is *hot!*), and salt and stir to combine. Reduce the heat and simmer for 15 minutes, or until the vegetables are tender and the sauce thickens slightly, stirring occasionally.
5. Add the reserved shrimp, noodles, and peas. Cook for 2 to 5 minutes, or until the shrimp and vegetables are cooked through, stirring frequently.
6. Sprinkle with the scallions and basil.

Oven-Baked Fish
with Roasted Vegetables

6 ripe plum tomatoes, sliced
¼-inch thick (about
1 pound)
2 cups cleaned and thinly
sliced leeks (white part
only)
2 cups thickly sliced zucchini
2 cups thinly sliced new
potatoes
1 cup seeded and thinly sliced
bell peppers (red,
orange, or yellow)
2 cups thinly sliced shiitake or
other mushrooms
2 teaspoons minced garlic
3 tablespoons olive oil
1 teaspoon dried thyme
2 tablespoons freshly
squeezed lemon juice
2 tablespoons coarsely
chopped fresh basil
(optional)
1 teaspoon lemon zest
1 teaspoon balsamic vinegar
(optional)
1 tablespoon salt
4 6-ounce skinless fish fillets
(salmon, sea bass, cod,
or flounder)
½ teaspoon ground black
pepper
½ cup toasted bread crumbs,
homemade or
packaged

Roasting vegetables at high temperatures cara-melizes their natural sugars and brings out their in-herent sweetness. This dish highlights its flavorful vegetables and is balanced by the addition of sim-ply seasoned fish fillets. Look for fillets of uniform thickness to ensure even cooking, or bake fish for varying lengths of time to prevent overcooking thinner fillets.

Cooking Time: 60 minutes or less
Serves: 4

1. Preheat the oven to 450 degrees.
2. In a 13 × 9 × 2-inch baking pan, combine the toma-toes, leeks, zucchini, potatoes, bell peppers, mush-rooms, and garlic. Drizzle with 2 tablespoons of the oil and toss to combine. Sprinkle with the thyme.
3. Roast the vegetables for 25 to 30 minutes, or until they begin to soften and brown. Add the lemon juice, basil, lemon zest, vinegar, and 1 teaspoon of the salt and toss to combine.
4. Lightly coat the fish with the remaining 1 tablespoon oil and sprinkle with the remaining 2 teaspoons salt, pepper, and bread crumbs.
5. Arrange the fish over the vegetables and roast for 10 to 15 minutes, or until the fish is cooked through.

Bouillabaisse

The signature ingredients of this famous Provençal fish stew are monkfish, a firm white fish; fennel, a licorice-flavored bulb; and saffron, a distinctive spice from Spain. Harvesting saffron's delicate threads is so labor intensive it is regarded as the world's most expensive seasoning. Luckily, this fabulous stew only requires a small amount. Serve this with bruschetta rubbed with garlic and drizzled with olive oil.

Cooking Time: 60 minutes or less
Serves: 4

1. In a large stock pot over medium heat, add the oil. Sauté the leeks, fennel, onions, and garlic until softened, 7 to 10 minutes, stirring frequently.
2. Add the tomatoes and their juice, thyme, fennel seeds, bay leaf, and orange peel and stir to combine. Simmer for 5 minutes.
3. Add the clam juice and saffron and stir to combine. Bring to a boil.
4. Reduce the heat, cover, and simmer for 20 minutes, stirring occasionally.
5. Add the monkfish and clams and cook for 3 to 5 minutes, or until the clam shells begin to open. Add the shrimp and cook for 1 to 2 minutes, or until the seafood is just cooked through.
6. Sprinkle with the parsley.

¼ cup olive oil
2 cups cleaned and thinly sliced leeks (white part only)
2 cups coarsely chopped fresh fennel
1 cup finely chopped onions
1 tablespoon minced garlic
1 28-ounce can diced tomatoes
1 teaspoon dried thyme
½ teaspoon dried fennel seeds
1 bay leaf
1 3-inch strip orange peel (optional)
3 cups clam juice
¼ teaspoon saffron
1 pound monkfish, or other firm white fish, cut into 1-inch pieces
2 pounds littleneck or small clams, scrubbed
1 pound shrimp, peeled and deveined
2 tablespoons finely chopped fresh Italian parsley (optional)

Shrimp and Sausage Gumbo

3 tablespoons vegetable oil
3 tablespoons all-purpose flour
2 cups finely chopped onions
1 cup seeded and finely
    chopped green bell
    peppers
½ cup finely chopped celery
1 teaspoon minced garlic
2 cups clam juice
1 14½-ounce can diced
    tomatoes, drained
½ pound smoked andouille
    sausage, smoked
    Louisiana sausage, or
    kielbasa, halved
    lengthwise and sliced
    ¼-inch thick
½ teaspoon cayenne pepper
1 bay leaf
1 cup thickly sliced okra
1 pound shrimp, peeled and
    deveined

Few things mean New Orleans like beignets, po' boys, and Louisiana's trademark gumbo. The secret to gumbo's distinctive flavor is the roux, a mahogany-colored, slow-cooked mixture of flour and oil that is found in many Cajun dishes. Cajuns, descendants of French Acadians who settled in central Louisiana's bayou country after being forced out of Nova Scotia in 1785, became major influences in the area's cooking style. This gumbo, loaded with shrimp, andouille sausage, and okra, is a hearty soup on its own or more of a stew if rice is added. Make sure to have all your vegetables prepped and ready to go. Serve Tabasco on the side for those who like it hot!

Cooking Time: 60 minutes or less
Serves: 4

1. In a large soup pot, over high heat, add the oil. When the oil is very hot, almost smoking, add the flour and stir constantly until the mixture turns a deep reddish-brown, 2 to 5 minutes. You will smell the flour cooking, and it may smell as if something is almost burning, but don't be alarmed.

2. Reduce the heat to medium-high and immediately add the onions, green peppers, celery, and garlic. Cook until softened, 5 to 8 minutes, stirring constantly.

3. Add the clam juice, tomatoes, sausage, cayenne pepper, and bay leaf and stir to combine. Bring to a boil.
4. Reduce the heat, cover, and simmer for 10 minutes, stirring occasionally.
5. Add the okra and simmer uncovered for 10 minutes, stirring occasionally.
6. Add the shrimp and simmer for 1 to 2 minutes, or until just cooked through.

• • • • • • • • • • • • • • • •

Variation:

Shrimp, Sausage, and Rice Gumbo: *Add ½ cup of rice in step 4.*

• • • • • • • • • • • • • • • •

Paella

1 tablespoon olive oil
½ pound hot or sweet Italian
    sausage, sliced ½ inch
    thick
4 chicken legs or thighs
1 cup chopped onions
1 cup seeded and chopped
    green bell peppers
2 teaspoons minced garlic
⅛ teaspoon red pepper flakes
1½ cups rice
2½ cups reduced-sodium
    chicken broth
1 cup canned diced tomatoes
½ teaspoon saffron (optional)
1 bay leaf
12 littleneck or small clams,
    scrubbed
12 mussels, scrubbed and
    debearded
12 shrimp, peeled and
    deveined
1 teaspoon salt
½ teaspoon ground black
    pepper

Paella, the signature dish of the Valencia region of Spain, is named for the broad, shallow pan in which it is traditionally cooked. It began as a peasant dish, made primarily of rice, vegetables, and with luck, a few scraps of fish. Now paella is made with a wide variety of seafood, in addition to chicken, sausage, and pork. This version uses clams, mussels, and shrimp, but you can choose your favorite seafood to complete this dish—or if you'd rather, you can leave the seafood out entirely.

Cooking Time: 60 minutes or less
Serves: 4

1. In a large skillet over medium-high heat, add the oil. Add the sausage and cook, 5 to 8 minutes, turning often.
2. Add the chicken and brown, 3 to 5 minutes per side. Continue cooking for 5 minutes, turning the chicken and sausage frequently. Push the meat to the side.
3. Reduce the heat to medium and add the onions, green peppers, garlic, and red pepper flakes. Cook until softened, 5 to 8 minutes, stirring frequently.

4. Add the rice and stir to combine.
5. Add the broth, tomatoes and their juice, saffron, and bay leaf and stir to combine.
6. Cover and simmer for 20 minutes.
7. Add the clams and mussels, stir to combine, cover, and cook for 3 to 5 minutes, or until the clam and mussel shells begin to open. Add the shrimp and cook for 1 to 2 minutes, or until the shellfish is just cooked through.
8. Season with salt and pepper.

Manhattan Clam Chowder

¼ pound bacon or salt pork,
    chopped
2 cups peeled, cubed potatoes
1 cup finely chopped onions
1 cup finely chopped celery
1 teaspoon dried basil
½ teaspoon dried thyme
2 cups clam juice
1 28-ounce can diced
    tomatoes
2 6¼-ounce cans minced
    clams
1 teaspoon salt
½ teaspoon ground black
    pepper

The battle of chowders between New England's creamy white and the Big Apple's red is ongoing. Manhattan's version is less sinful, substituting tomatoes for heavy cream, but is equally delicious. Like its nemesis, it is even better if you use fresh clams.

Cooking Time: 60 minutes or less
Serves: 4

1. In a large stock pot over medium-low heat, sauté the bacon until brown and crisp, 8 to 10 minutes, stirring frequently. Try not to scorch the bottom of the pot.
2. Discard all but 1 tablespoon of fat. Add the potatoes, onions, celery, basil, and thyme and sauté until softened, 5 to 8 minutes, stirring frequently.
3. Add the clam juice, tomatoes and their juice, and juice from the clams (reserving the clams), and stir to combine. Bring to a boil.
4. Reduce the heat, partially cover, and simmer for 15 to 20 minutes, or until the potatoes are tender, stirring occasionally.
5. Add the reserved clams. Cook over very low heat until heated through, 1 to 2 minutes. Do not boil. Season with salt and pepper.

••••••••••••••••

Variation:

Manhattan Clam Chowder with Fresh Clams: *Substitute 24 fresh clams for the canned clams. Just steam them in 1 cup of water until they open, reserve the broth, and chop the clams. Proceed with the directions, substituting the broth for clam juice, and adding the cooked clams just before serving. For a more rustic presentation, leave some or all of the clams in their shells for guests to remove.*

••••••••••••••••

New England Clam and Fish Chowder

¼ pound bacon or salt pork, chopped
2 cups peeled, cubed potatoes
½ cup finely chopped onions
¼ cup finely chopped celery
½ teaspoon dried thyme
1 tablespoon all-purpose flour
1 cup clam juice
2 6¼-ounce cans minced clams
1 pound cod, or other firm white fish, cut into 1-inch pieces
1 cup heavy cream
1 cup milk, or half and half, or heavy cream
1 teaspoon salt
½ teaspoon white or black pepper

Creamy and rich, studded with clams, fish, and potato chunks, New England clam chowder is as integral a part of the Northeast as Boston accents, the Celtics, and summertime clambakes on the beach. It's even better if you use fresh clams or quahogs.

Cooking Time: 60 minutes or less
Serves: 4

1. In a large stock pot over medium-low heat, sauté the bacon until brown and crisp, 8 to 10 minutes, stirring frequently. Try not to scorch the bottom of the pot.
2. Discard all but 1 tablespoon of fat. Add the potatoes, onions, celery, and thyme and sauté until softened, 5 to 8 minutes, stirring frequently.
3. Sprinkle with the flour and stir to combine.
4. Add the clam juice and juice from the clams (reserving the clams) and stir to combine. Bring to a boil.
5. Reduce the heat, partially cover, and simmer for 10 to 15 minutes, or until the potatoes are just tender, stirring occasionally.
6. Add the cod and simmer for 5 to 8 minutes, or until the fish and potatoes are cooked through.
7. Add the cream, milk, and reserved clams. Cook over very low heat until heated through, 1 to 2 minutes. Do not boil. Season with salt and pepper.

· · · · · · · · · · · · · · · ·

Variation:

New England Clam Chowder with Fresh Clams: *Substitute 24 fresh clams for the canned clams. Steam the clams in 1 cup of water or wine until they open, reserve the broth, and chop the clams. Proceed with the directions, substituting the broth for clam juice, and adding the cooked clams just before serving. For a more rustic presentation, leave some or all of the clams in their shells for guests to remove.*

· · · · · · · · · · · · · · · ·

Smoked Salmon and Goat Cheese Quiche

Crust:

1¼ cups all-purpose flour
¼ teaspoon salt
½ cup (1 stick) unsalted
    butter, chilled and cut
    into ½-inch pieces
2 to 4 tablespoons ice water

Filling:

4 eggs
1 cup cream or milk
1 cup milk
½ teaspoon salt
¼ teaspoon ground black
    pepper
1 tablespoon finely chopped
    fresh dill
3 tablespoons finely chopped
    fresh chives
¼ pound goat cheese,
    crumbled
¼ pound smoked salmon,
    coarsely chopped

Quiche, a custard filling nestled in a pastry crust, hails from the Alsace and Lorraine regions of France. This elegant quiche updates the classic French rendering with today's most popular ingredients. In this version, lightly salted smoked salmon is the perfect foil for creamy goat cheese and piquant dill and chives. Make your own crust or buy a ready-made crust and fit it into a 9-inch pie plate.

Cooking Time: 60 minutes or less
Serves: 4

1. Prepare the crust: In a food processor fitted with a metal chopping blade, mix the flour and salt (5 seconds). Add the butter and pulse until the mixture resembles coarse meal (10 short pulses). Sprinkle the minimum amount of water over the mixture and pulse until distributed throughout the dough and the crumbs start sticking together (5 to 10 pulses). Process just until the dough holds together, adding the remaining water if necessary. Do not allow the dough to form a ball.

2. Scrape the dough onto the work surface. Shape the dough into a 1-inch-thick disc. Wrap the dough tightly with plastic wrap and refrigerate for 30 minutes, or until it is firm enough to roll out.

3. Preheat the oven to 450 degrees.
4. Roll out the dough and fit into a 9-inch pie pan. Prick the dough with a fork and bake for 5 to 10 minutes, or until lightly browned. Remove from the oven and reduce the temperature to 350 degrees.
5. Prepare the filling: Meanwhile, in a medium bowl, beat the eggs, cream, milk, salt, and pepper. Add the dill and chives and stir to combine. Set aside.
6. Line the partially baked pie crust with the cheese. Top with the smoked salmon. Add the eggs.
7. Bake for 40 to 50 minutes, or until the eggs are set and the center doesn't jiggle. If the crust begins to brown before the quiche is ready, cover it with aluminum foil to prevent burning. Let stand 5 to 10 minutes before serving.

Cioppino

3 tablespoons olive oil
2 cups finely chopped onions
1 cup seeded and finely
    chopped green bell
    peppers
1 cup seeded and finely
    chopped red bell
    peppers
1 tablespoon minced garlic
1 cup dry red wine
1 cup clam juice
1 28-ounce can diced
    tomatoes
3 tablespoons tomato paste
1 teaspoon dried oregano
1 teaspoon dried basil
1 pound firm white fish, cut
    into 1-inch pieces
3 pounds cleaned mixed
    shellfish (mussels,
    shrimp, clams, crab
    claws, scallops, cut-up
    lobster)
1 teaspoon salt
½ teaspoon ground black
    pepper
¼ cup chopped fresh Italian
    parsley or fresh basil

Cioppino, a fisherman's stew that hails from San Francisco, is our nation's version of France's classic bouillabaisse. Plan to get your fingers messy—this richly flavored stew is loaded with shellfish. Choose from crab legs, scallops, clams, mussels, shrimp, or lobster, and whichever white fish is your favorite. If you like a little spice, add a few shakes of cayenne pepper.

Cooking Time: 60 minutes or less
Serves: 4

1. In a large stock pot over medium heat, add the oil. Sauté the onions, both bell peppers, and garlic until softened, 7 to 10 minutes, stirring frequently.
2. Add the wine, clam juice, tomatoes and their juice, tomato paste, oregano, and basil and stir to combine. Bring to a boil.
3. Reduce the heat, cover, and simmer for 30 minutes, stirring occasionally.
4. Add the fish and shellfish and cook for 5 to 7 minutes, or until the fish is cooked through and clam and/or mussel shells have opened. (If using shrimp or scallops, add during the last 1 to 2 minutes of cooking).
5. Season with the salt and pepper. Sprinkle with the parsley or basil.

5

VEGETARIAN

30 Minutes or Less:

Gazpacho
Cucumber and Yogurt
    Soup
Minestrone Soup
Mexican Tortilla Lasagna
Vegetarian Couscous
Vegetable Frittata
Pasta with Pesto
Pasta with Tomatoes,
    Basil, and Garlic
Pasta with Broccoli, Garlic,
    and Toasted Walnuts
Cheese Pizza
Bean and Cheese Enchi-
    ladas in Green Sauce
Tomato and Basil Frittata

60 Minutes or Less:

Lentil-Vegetable Soup
Butternut Squash and
    Apple Soup
Ratatouille
Black Bean and Butternut
    Squash Chili
Eggplant and Vegetable
    Tian
Chile Relleno Phyllo Bake
Spinach and Ricotta
    Lasagna
Tomato, Goat Cheese, and
    Pesto Tart

The bounty of the garden has never been so grand. Not only is there increased variety, but there is greater recognition and appreciation of flavor. Vine-ripened tomatoes fill our supermarket bins, nudging out the plastic hothouse variety from years past. Where bland iceberg used to rule the lettuce roost, now dozens of tasty greens compete for shelf space. The white button mushroom need no longer feel lonely—his companions, the shiitake, portobello, oyster, and porcini are all tucked in nearby. This remarkable transformation was brought about by professional chefs (most notably Alice Waters of Chez Panisse in Berkeley, California) who designed their meals by what was fresh at the market that day and encouraged local farmers to grow organic vegetables with improved taste. With the advent of "designer" and organic produce and a new focus on cooking with vegetables, we are actually tasting vegetables as they were meant to be prepared: fresh and robust instead of overcooked and lifeless.

Vegetarian Tips:

- The United States government has revised the Food Guide Pyramid based on the latest nutritional research. This pyramid, which displays the relative importance of various food groups to the overall diet, deems the most significant component of a healthful diet to be grain products—bread, cereal, rice, and pasta—followed by vegetables and fruit. This shows the value of vegetarian entrées as part of a sensible overall eating pattern. Strict vegetarian diets can be healthy for adults and children if the proper balance of protein, calories, fat, and essential nutrients, especially B_{12}, are met.
- Beans and grains are an inexpensive and filling source of cholesterol-free protein. Low in fat, calories, and sodium, yet high in soluble and insoluble fiber, beans and grains are

great sources of complex carbohydrates and provide many valuable nutrients to vegetarian entrées.

- Eggs are a good source of protein, iron, zinc, and vitamins A, B, and D and have only 75 calories. Egg consumption dropped dramatically in response to the American Heart Association's concern that dietary cholesterol affects total cholesterol. But recent scientific research rebuts that premise and indicates that the consumption of saturated fat, not dietary cholesterol, influences the level of cholesterol in the blood. One large egg contains only 5 grams of total fat, of which only 1.5 grams are saturated.

- Support your local growers. Search out farmers' markets in your area and use ingredients in the heart of their growing season. In the spring and summer, find recipes that make use of the plethora of fresh tomatoes, basil, and summer squashes. In the fall and winter, look for dishes that use hearty eggplants, potatoes, broccoli, and winter squashes.

- Try organic vegetables for freshness and flavor, unless their cost is prohibitive.

- Choose crisp, unblemished vegetables that feel heavy, a sign that they are succulent and in their prime.

- Store most fresh vegetables in a cold, moist environment, either in their plastic bags or in a refrigerator crisper, and use them as soon as possible. Store onions, garlic, and potatoes in a cool cupboard. Once they are cut, place in the refrigerator. Do not refrigerate tomatoes, or their taste and texture will diminish.

- Always rinse vegetables thoroughly before using. Many vegetables are sprayed with pesticides and are picked under unsanitary conditions. If vegetables have been waxed, wash them with a mild detergent and rinse thoroughly before using. It is not necessary to peel carrots or potatoes after washing. Their skins contain important nutrients that are lost when pared. Use your own preference and time constraints when preparing these vegetables. Mushrooms, which tend to absorb a lot of water, should be quickly rinsed and dried or wiped with a damp cloth.

- If you use a food processor to chop vegetables with a high water content, like onions or bell peppers, pulse a small portion at a time to avoid turning them to pulp. Use the slicing blades to quickly cut carrots and mushrooms.

Gazpacho

Served cold, this Spanish soup, loaded with chunky fresh vegetables, is just the thing for hot summer evenings. Be sure to allow at least two hours for the soup to chill and for the flavors to come together. For an impressive presentation, garnish the soup with seasoned croutons; chopped yellow tomatoes, yellow peppers, or cucumbers; thinly sliced scallions; or poached shrimp.

Cooking Time: None
Serves: 4

1 large clove garlic
1 small red onion, peeled and quartered (about ¼ pound)
1 large green bell pepper, seeded and quartered (about ½ pound)
1 large red bell pepper, seeded and quartered (about ½ pound)
1 large cucumber, peeled, seeded, and quartered (about 1 pound)
1 28-ounce can Italian plum tomatoes
2 tablespoons olive oil
2 tablespoons red wine vinegar
2 teaspoons salt
½ teaspoon ground black pepper
½ teaspoon sugar
¼ teaspoon Tabasco or other hot red pepper sauce
2 cups tomato juice

1. In a food processor fitted with a metal chopping blade, with the motor running, purée the garlic. Add the onion and pulse until coarsely chopped. Add both bell peppers and cucumber and pulse until coarsely chopped.
2. Add the tomatoes and their juice, oil, vinegar, salt, pepper, sugar, and Tabasco. Pulse for 30 seconds, or until all of the vegetables are chopped but still chunky. Do not overprocess. (If this is too much bulk for your food processor, you may need to do this in two or more batches).
3. Transfer the soup to a large bowl. Add the tomato juice and stir to combine.
4. Cover and refrigerate for at least 2 hours.

Cucumber and Yogurt Soup

1 large clove garlic
⅛ cup chopped fresh dill
4 cups peeled, seeded, and
    coarsely chopped
    cucumbers
2 cups unflavored yogurt
2 cups water
1 tablespoon olive oil
1 tablespoon honey
2 teaspoons salt
1 teaspoon ground black
    pepper

This cold soup is perfect on a sweltering summer's day, when the mere thought of heating up your kitchen makes you sweat. It is quickly prepared in a food processor, so you can make it in the morning before heading out, stick it in the refrigerator, and have it ready on your return. Served with crusty French bread and a big crunchy salad topped with goat cheese, it's the perfect way to chill out after a long steamy day. Try topping it with chopped walnuts, chives, mint, or added dill.

Cooking Time: None
Serves: 4

1. In a food processor fitted with a metal blade, with the motor running, purée the garlic and dill.
2. Add the cucumbers and pulse until finely chopped.
3. Add the yogurt, water, oil, honey, salt, and pepper. Pulse until combined. Transfer to a large bowl, cover, and refrigerate for at least 2 hours. If the soup thickens too much, dilute with ice cubes.

Minestrone Soup

Make minestrone soup a staple in summer when gardens are overflowing with zucchini, spinach, and beans. You can let your imagination run wild when preparing the soup—add whatever is plentiful to make it your own!

Cooking Time: 30 minutes or less
Serves: 4

1. In a large stock pot over medium heat, add the oil. Sauté the leeks until softened, 3 to 5 minutes, stirring frequently.
2. Add the carrots, celery, and zucchini and cook until softened, 5 to 8 minutes, stirring occasionally.
3. Add the broth, tomatoes and their juice, oregano, basil, salt, and pepper and stir to combine.
4. Bring to a boil and cook for 5 minutes.
5. Add the pasta and green beans and cook for 5 minutes, stirring occasionally.
6. Reduce the heat, add the spinach, peas, and chickpeas and simmer for 5 minutes, stirring occasionally.
7. Top each serving with some of the Parmesan cheese.

2 tablespoons olive oil
4 cups cleaned and thinly sliced leeks (white part only)
1 cup thickly sliced carrots
1 cup thickly sliced celery
1 cup thickly sliced zucchini
6 cups vegetable broth or reduced-sodium chicken broth
1 28-ounce can diced tomatoes
1 tablespoon dried oregano
1 tablespoon dried basil
1 teaspoon salt
½ teaspoon ground black pepper
½ cup small pasta shapes or orzo
1 cup trimmed and sliced green beans (1-inch pieces)
1 cup spinach leaves
½ cup fresh or frozen peas
½ cup rinsed and drained canned chickpeas
⅓ cup grated Parmesan cheese

Mexican Tortilla Lasagna

2 14½-ounce cans Mexican-style stewed tomatoes
1⅓ cups chopped fresh cilantro (optional)
1 4-ounce can diced green chiles, drained
15 6-inch corn tortillas
1 15¼-ounce can black beans, rinsed and drained, or refried pinto beans
1½ pounds Monterey Jack or cheddar cheese, grated or shredded
1½ cups sour cream
1 3¾-ounce can sliced and pitted black olives, drained

Like its Italian counterpart, this Mexican-inspired casserole layers tomato sauce and cheese. But instead of noodles, it uses corn tortillas as its base. This casserole is a bit spicy, so cut back on the chiles if you're cooking for sensitive palates. A bit of history: The recommended cheese, Monterey Jack, was developed in 1882 by David Jacks, a dairy farmer in Monterey, California, using an old recipe from the early mission days of the late 1700s.

Cooking Time: 30 minutes or less
Serves: 4 to 6

1. Preheat the oven to 375 degrees.
2. In a food processor fitted with a metal chopping blade, pulse the tomatoes, cilantro, and chiles to combine.
3. In a 13 × 9 × 2-inch baking pan, spread ½ cup of the tomato sauce over the bottom of the dish. Cover with 5 tortillas. You will need to cut 1 tortilla in half to cover the bottom completely.
4. Top with half of the beans, 2 cups of cheese, and 1½ cups of tomato sauce.
5. Cover the sauce with 5 tortillas. Top with the remaining beans, 2 cups of cheese, and 1½ cups of tomato sauce.
6. Cover the sauce with the remaining tortillas. Top with the remaining sauce and cheese.

Vegetarian

7. Cover with aluminum foil and bake for 15 minutes. Uncover and bake for 10 to 15 minutes, or until the cheese has melted and the casserole has heated through.
8. Remove from the oven. Cover with the sour cream and sprinkle with the olives. Let stand for 2 minutes before serving.

Vegetarian Couscous

Vegetables:

2 tablespoons olive oil
1 cup coarsely chopped red
    onions
1 teaspoon minced garlic
1 cup chopped turnips
    (optional)
1 cup thinly sliced carrots
1 cup seeded and coarsely
    chopped red bell
    peppers
1 cup drained canned diced
    tomatoes
1 teaspoon salt
½ teaspoon ground cumin
½ teaspoon curry powder
¼ teaspoon red pepper flakes
¼ teaspoon ground allspice
    (optional)
¼ teaspoon ground cinnamon
1½ cups vegetable broth or
    reduced-sodium
    chicken broth
2 cups thinly sliced zucchini
1 cup trimmed and sliced
    green beans (1-inch
    pieces)
4 cups spinach leaves
    (optional)
½ cup rinsed and drained
    canned chickpeas

(ingredients continue)

Couscous, long associated with Moroccan and Middle-Eastern dining, is believed by many to be a rice-like grain. This misconception is due primarily to its preparation and appearance—like rice, once it is combined with a liquid, it becomes a filling and fluffy side dish. But couscous is actually a form of pasta, made with semolina flour and water.

Cooking Time: 30 minutes or less
Serves: 4

1. Prepare the vegetables: In a large skillet over medium heat, add the oil. Add the onions and garlic and cook until softened, 3 to 5 minutes, stirring frequently.
2. Add the turnips, carrots, red peppers, tomatoes, salt, cumin, curry powder, red pepper flakes, allspice, cinnamon, and broth and stir to combine. Bring to a boil.
3. Reduce the heat, cover, and simmer for 10 minutes, stirring occasionally.
4. Add the zucchini, green beans, spinach, and chickpeas and cook for 5 to 10 minutes, or until the vegetables are crisp-tender, stirring occasionally.

5. Meanwhile, prepare the couscous: In a microwave, bring the broth to a boil. Add the butter and stir to combine. Combine the couscous, salt, and pepper in the serving bowl, pour the broth on top, and cover with aluminum foil for 5 to 10 minutes.
6. Fluff the couscous, top with the vegetables and their juice, and sprinkle with the almonds.

Couscous:

1½ cups vegetable broth or reduced-sodium chicken broth
2 tablespoons butter
1½ cups couscous
1 teaspoon salt
½ teaspoon ground black pepper
¼ cup almond slivers, lightly toasted

Vegetable Frittata

1 tablespoon olive oil
1 cup grated, shredded, or finely chopped new potatoes
½ cup thinly sliced mushrooms
½ cup coarsely chopped zucchini
¼ cup finely chopped red onions
¼ cup seeded and finely chopped red bell peppers
1 cup coarsely chopped spinach leaves
8 eggs
2 ounces Asiago, Fontina, or other hard cheese, grated or shredded
1 teaspoon salt
½ teaspoon dried thyme
¼ teaspoon ground black pepper

Frittatas are the Italian equivalent of France's ethereal omelets. But some major differences make frittatas a lot more attractive for cooks. A frittata is cooked first on the stove and then finished in the oven, eliminating any flipping gymnastics. This process results in an egg delight that is just firm and set, unlike an omelet, which is slightly moist and runny. I highly recommend using a nonstick pan, which allows you to move the frittata easily during cooking.

Cooking Time: 30 minutes or less
Serves: 4

1. Preheat the oven to 350 degrees.
2. In a 10- or 11-inch nonstick, ovenproof skillet over high heat, add the oil. Sauté the potatoes for 5 minutes, stirring frequently.
3. Reduce the heat to medium-high and add the mushrooms, zucchini, onions, and red peppers. Cook until softened, 5 to 8 minutes, stirring occasionally.
4. Add the spinach and cook for 2 minutes, or until wilted.

5. Meanwhile, in a medium bowl, beat the eggs. Add the cheese, salt, thyme, and pepper.

6. Reduce the heat to medium. Pour the eggs on top of the vegetables. Cook without stirring for 1 minute, or until the eggs are almost set on the bottom. Continue cooking, using a spatula to lift the edges of the frittata toward the center of the skillet, while gently tilting the pan so the uncooked eggs run underneath the bottom of the frittata. Cook for 30 to 40 seconds and repeat the process several times until the egg on top is still wet, but not runny.

7. Place in the oven. Bake for 3 to 7 minutes, or until the top is just set. Do not overcook.

8. Remove from the oven, run a spatula around the skillet edge to loosen the frittata, and slide or invert it onto a serving plate.

Pasta with Pesto

3 cloves garlic, peeled
¾ pound linguine or other
    pasta
2 cups packed fresh basil
¼ cup pine nuts or walnuts,
    lightly toasted
½ cup extra-virgin olive oil
½ cup grated Parmesan
    cheese
1 teaspoon salt
½ teaspoon ground black
    pepper

Garnish:

1 cup Parmesan cheese,
    grated (optional)
¼ cup pine nuts, lightly
    toasted (optional)

Homemade pesto sings of summer. This simple blend of fresh basil, garlic, rich and fruity extra-virgin olive oil, cheese, and nuts blossoms into a full-flavored coating that turns pasta from simple to spectacular. Make a more distinctive pesto by quickly blanching the garlic to cut its bitterness and by toasting the nuts to add depth to their flavor. For stronger flavor, use basil-infused oil. Make extra pesto in season to store in your freezer and you can enjoy this favorite all year.

Cooking Time: 30 minutes or less
Serves: 4

1. In a large pot over high heat, put the water up to boil for the pasta.
2. When the water is boiling, blanch the garlic for 30 to 45 seconds. (For easy blanching, skewer the garlic or use a mesh spoon to scoop it out). Rinse the garlic under cold water and pat dry. Set aside.
3. Add the pasta and cook for 7 to 11 minutes, or until al dente. Drain, reserving 2 to 3 tablespoons of pasta water.
4. Meanwhile, in a food processor fitted with a metal chopping blade, with the motor running, add the reserved garlic and purée. Add the basil and nuts and process to combine. With the motor running, slowly

pour the oil down the feed tube. Scrape down the sides of the bowl. Add the cheese, salt, and pepper and process to combine.

5. In the serving bowl, combine the pasta, reserved pasta water, and pesto. Top with the cheese and nuts.

••••••••••••••••

Variation:

Pasta with Shrimp and Pesto: *Add ½ pound of peeled and deveined shrimp in step 3 before adding the pasta. Cook the shrimp for 1 to 2 minutes, or until just cooked through. Remove to the serving bowl.*

••••••••••••••••

Pasta with Tomatoes, Basil, and Garlic

5 cups coarsely chopped ripe
   tomatoes, juice
   reserved
⅓ cup extra-virgin olive oil
1 teaspoon balsamic vinegar
   (optional)
1 tablespoon salt
1 teaspoon ground black
   pepper
2 cloves garlic, peeled
¾ pound spaghetti, linguine,
   or other pasta
1 cup packed coarsely
   chopped fresh basil
½ cup grated Parmesan
   cheese

This pasta pays homage to summer's most winning combination—ripe and luscious fresh tomatoes and fragrant basil. This combination, so good in so many dishes, is simply outstanding when combined with pasta, extra-virgin olive oil, and garlic. Do not attempt this out of season. Hothouse tomatoes are simply no match for the juicy boys of summer.

Cooking Time: 30 minutes or less
Serves: 4

1. In a large pot over high heat, put the water up to boil for the pasta.
2. In the serving bowl, combine the tomatoes and their juice, oil, vinegar, salt, and pepper. Set aside.
3. When the water is boiling, blanch the garlic for 30 to 45 seconds. (For easy blanching, skewer the garlic or use a mesh spoon to scoop it out). Rinse the garlic under cold water, pat dry, mince, and add to the serving bowl.
4. Add the pasta to the pot and cook for 7 to 11 minutes, or until al dente.
5. Drain the pasta, add to the serving bowl, and stir to combine. Add the basil and stir again. Top with the Parmesan cheese.

Vegetarian

....

Variation:

Pasta with Shrimp, Tomatoes, and Basil: *Add ½ pound of peeled and deveined shrimp in step 4 before adding the pasta. Cook the shrimp for 1 to 2 minutes, or until just cooked through. Remove to the serving bowl.*

....

Pasta with Broccoli, Garlic, and Toasted Walnuts

⅓ cup extra-virgin olive oil
10 large cloves garlic, peeled and smashed
½ teaspoon red pepper flakes (optional)
6 cups broccoli florets
¾ pound ziti or other pasta
1 tablespoon butter
2 teaspoons salt
½ teaspoon ground black pepper
½ cup grated Parmesan cheese
1 cup coarsely chopped walnuts, lightly toasted

After its humiliation during the Bush administration, broccoli has come back with a vengeance. There are few vegetables as healthful and as tasty as this versatile cruciferous plant, especially when it's flavored with garlic, extra-virgin olive oil, and Parmesan cheese. While many pasta dishes utilize the summer's harvest, broccoli is a wonderful winter alternative. The longer the garlic and oil can stand, the stronger the taste will be. If you have bottled garlic-flavored oil, use that instead of making your own. When cooking both vegetables and pasta in the same pot, it is helpful to have a pasta set with a removable insert. Otherwise, a strainer with a long handle will do.

Cooking Time: 30 minutes or less
Serves: 4

1. In the serving bowl, combine the oil, garlic, and red pepper flakes. Set aside.
2. In a large pot over high heat, put the water up to boil for the pasta.
3. When the water is boiling, add the broccoli and cook for 4 to 6 minutes, or until crisp-tender. Remove to the serving bowl.

4. Add the pasta and cook for 9 to 11 minutes, or until al dente. Drain, reserving 2 to 3 tablespoons of pasta water.

5. Remove the garlic from the oil and discard garlic. Add the pasta, reserved pasta water, butter, salt, and pepper to the serving bowl and stir to combine. Top with the Parmesan cheese and walnuts.

· · · · · · · · · · · · · · · · ·

Variation:

Pasta with Shrimp and Broccoli: *Add ½ pound of peeled and deveined shrimp in step 4 before adding the pasta. Cook the shrimp for 1 to 2 minutes, or until just cooked through. Remove to the serving bowl.*

· · · · · · · · · · · · · · · ·

Cheese Pizza

Pizza Dough:

1 cup very warm water (about 110 degrees)

1 package (2½ teaspoons) active dry yeast

3 cups flour (all-purpose, bread, or a combination)

1 teaspoon salt

2 tablespoons olive oil, plus extra for greasing the bowl

1 to 2 tablespoons cornmeal (optional for sprinkling)

Toppings:

⅔ cup pizza, pasta, or other sauce

½ pound mozzarella cheese, grated or shredded

½ cup grated Parmesan cheese

It would be unconscionable to exclude America's greatest fast food in a book about quick and easy family dinners that require only one pot or pan. Pizza is the quintessential family meal. This dough takes less than five minutes to make in a food processor and can be left to rise in the refrigerator while you are at work; but if time is short, use store-bought dough or a 12-inch Boboli. Be adventurous with toppings. Here are some suggestions: Substitute tomato sauce with ripe tomatoes, roasted garlic paste, pesto, or tapenade; replace some or all of the mozzarella cheese with goat, Fontina, or Gorgonzola cheese; experiment adding different vegetables and herbs, including mushrooms, red onions, artichoke hearts, slivered garlic, bell peppers, olives, spinach, red pepper flakes, and fresh basil. Meat lovers should add deli salami, prosciutto, or ham or recycle leftover sausage, hamburger, or chicken.

Cooking Time: 30 minutes or less
Serves: 4

1. Prepare the dough: In a food processor fitted with a metal chopping blade, sprinkle the yeast over warm water and let it stand for 5 minutes to dissolve. Add the flour, salt, and oil and process until the dough

Vegetarian

forms a ball and cleans the sides of the bowl, 20 to 30 seconds. The dough will be slightly sticky.

2. Transfer the dough to a lightly oiled large bowl and rotate to coat all sides. Cover the bowl with plastic wrap or a clean cloth and leave it to double in size, 45 minutes to 1 hour, or place it in the refrigerator for 4 or more hours.

3. When the dough has risen, preheat the oven to 450 degrees. If you have a pizza stone, top it with the cornmeal and put it in the oven for preheating; if not, lightly coat a baking sheet or pizza pan with the cornmeal and set aside.

4. Turn the dough out onto a lightly floured surface. Punch down and knead briefly to deflate the air bubbles. Let the dough rest for 15 minutes.

5. Roll or stretch the dough on a lightly floured surface until it measures 12 inches in diameter. Transfer the dough to the pizza stone, baking sheet, or pizza pan.

6. Top with the sauce, cheeses, and any additional toppings.

7. Bake for 15 to 20 minutes, or until the edges and bottom are browned and the cheese has melted.

Bean and Cheese Enchiladas in Green Sauce

12 6-inch corn tortillas

1 15-ounce container ricotta cheese

1½ pounds Monterey Jack, or cheddar cheese, grated or shredded

4 cups tomatillo (green) salsa, or taco sauce

1 4-ounce can diced green chiles, drained

2 15¼-ounce cans black beans, rinsed and drained

¼ cup chopped scallions

¼ cup chopped fresh cilantro (optional)

Mexican-style food lends itself to one-pot dishes because it efficiently and deliciously combines proteins, carbohydrates, and fiber. This simple casserole combines two cheeses, black beans, and tomatillo salsa. Tomatillos are a green, firm tomato-like fruit grown mostly in Mexico and Southern California. Covered by a thin, papery husk, they are sometimes called Chinese lantern plants. Tomatillos are tart when eaten raw, but have a fresh, lemony flavor when cooked. As with other Mexican entrées, have extra salsa, sour cream, and guacamole on hand for toppings. If tomatillo salsa is unavailable, tomato salsa can be substituted.

Cooking Time: 30 minutes or less
Serves: 4 to 6

1. Preheat the oven to 350 degrees.
2. Wrap the tortillas in aluminum foil and place in the oven to warm for 10 minutes. (Tortillas can also be wrapped in a damp towel and warmed in the microwave on high for 15 to 30 seconds).
3. In a large bowl, combine the ricotta, 4 cups of the Monterey Jack cheese, 1 cup of tomatillo sauce, chiles, black beans, scallions, and cilantro. Set aside.

4. In a 13 × 9 × 2-inch baking pan, spread 1 cup of tomatillo salsa over the bottom of the dish.

5. Spoon ½ cup of filling into the center of a warmed tortilla. Roll up the tortilla to enclose the filling. Place the filled tortillas, seam side down, into the baking dish. Repeat with the remaining tortillas and filling, placing the tortillas close together and along the side of the pan to fit them all. Top with the remaining sauce and cheese.

6. Bake uncovered for 25 to 30 minutes, or until the enchiladas are heated through.

Tomato and Basil Frittata

1 tablespoon butter
¼ cup minced shallots
8 eggs
1 cup seeded and chopped
    ripe tomatoes
¼ cup coarsely chopped fresh
    basil
1 teaspoon salt
¼ teaspoon ground black
    pepper
¼ pound goat cheese,
    crumbled
2 tablespoons grated
    Parmesan cheese

Come August, if your garden is like mine, basil grows wild with aromatic wonder and ruby red tomatoes weigh down vines climbing toward the heavens. This open-faced omelet celebrates the abundance of summertime garden treasures. Frittatas are perfect for a simple dinner, savored on a blistering evening, or as a light meal after a heavy lunch. Be sure to use the ripest, most flavorful tomatoes you can find. I recommend using a nonstick pan, which allows the frittata to be easily moved during cooking.

Cooking Time: 30 minutes or less
Serves: 4

1. Preheat the oven to 350 degrees.
2. In a 10- or 11-inch nonstick, ovenproof skillet over medium-high heat, add the butter. Sauté the shallots until softened, 3 to 5 minutes, stirring frequently.
3. Meanwhile, in a medium bowl, beat the eggs. Add the tomatoes, basil, salt, and pepper. Gently add the goat cheese.

4. Reduce the heat to medium. Pour the egg mixture on top of the shallots. Cook without stirring for 1 minute, or until the eggs are almost set on the bottom. Continue cooking, using a spatula to lift the edges of the frittata toward the center of the skillet, while gently tilting the pan so the uncooked eggs run underneath the bottom of the frittata. Cook for 30 to 40 seconds and repeat the process several times until the egg on top is still wet, but not runny.
5. Sprinkle the Parmesan cheese on top of the frittata.
6. Place in the oven. Bake for 3 to 7 minutes, or until the top is just set. Do not overcook.
7. Remove from the oven, run a spatula around the skillet edge to loosen the frittata, and slide or invert it onto a serving plate.

Lentil-Vegetable Soup

2 tablespoons olive oil or
　　vegetable oil
2 cups coarsely chopped
　　onions
1 cup coarsely chopped
　　carrots
½ cup coarsely chopped celery
1½ cups dried lentils
8 cups vegetable broth or
　　reduced-sodium
　　chicken broth
1 28-ounce can diced
　　tomatoes
1 teaspoon dried thyme
1 cup dry white wine
1 teaspoon salt
½ teaspoon ground black
　　pepper

Lentils, one of the quickest-cooking dried legumes, date back to the ancient Greeks and Romans. Because lentils don't need to be presoaked, this soup can be prepared with little notice. I like to top the soup with a sprinkling of Parmesan or cheddar cheese.

Cooking Time: 60 minutes or less
Serves: 4

1. In a large stock pot over medium heat, add the oil. Sauté the onions, carrots, and celery until softened, 5 to 8 minutes, stirring frequently.
2. Add the lentils, broth, tomatoes and their juice, and thyme and stir to combine. Bring to a boil.
3. Reduce the heat, cover, and simmer for 40 to 45 minutes, or until the lentils are tender, stirring occasionally.
4. Add the wine, salt, and pepper, stir to combine, and cook for 5 minutes.

Butternut Squash and Apple Soup

This soup reminds me of the best of autumn: the plentiful squash that line the vines around Halloween and the trees weighed down with apples waiting to be picked and transformed into pies, crisps, and this wonderful soup.

2 tablespoons butter
1 cup finely chopped onions
1 teaspoon ground ginger
½ teaspoon ground cinnamon
½ teaspoon ground nutmeg
7 cups peeled, seeded, and coarsely chopped butternut squash
2 cups peeled, cored, and coarsely chopped Granny Smith apples
3 cups vegetable broth, or reduced-sodium chicken broth
½ to 1 cup apple juice
1 teaspoon salt
½ teaspoon ground black pepper

Cooking Time: 60 minutes or less
Serves: 4

1. In a large stock pot over medium heat, add the butter. Add the onions and cook until softened, 3 to 5 minutes, stirring frequently. Add the ginger, cinnamon, and nutmeg and stir to combine.
2. Add the squash, apples, and broth and stir to combine. Bring to a boil.
3. Reduce the heat, cover, and simmer for 20 to 30 minutes, or until the squash is very tender, stirring occasionally.
4. In a food processor fitted with a metal chopping blade, purée the soup. (You may need to do this in two or more batches).
5. Return the soup to the pot and add ½ cup of the apple juice. Stir to combine and heat through. Season with salt and pepper. If the soup is too thick, add the remaining apple juice to achieve the desired consistency.

Ratatouille

¼ cup olive oil
2 cups cleaned and thinly sliced leeks (white part only)
1 cup seeded and coarsely chopped green bell peppers
1 cup seeded and coarsely chopped red bell peppers
1 tablespoon minced garlic
4 cups 1-inch-cubed eggplant
1½ cups sliced zucchini
1 28-ounce can diced tomatoes
1 teaspoon salt
1 bay leaf
½ cup rinsed and drained canned chickpeas
2 tablespoons thinly sliced fresh basil (optional)
¼ pound cheddar cheese, grated or shredded

This hearty vegetable stew originated in the Provençe region of France. It's loaded with the bounty of the summer harvest: zucchini, eggplant, bell peppers, and fresh basil. To provide a little extra protein, I add some chickpeas and cheddar cheese. Many cooks top the stew with eggs and briefly bake it.

Cooking Time: 60 minutes or less
Serves: 4

1. In a large stock pot over medium heat, add the oil. Sauté the leeks, both bell peppers, and garlic until softened, 5 to 8 minutes, stirring frequently.
2. Add the eggplant and cook for 10 minutes, stirring frequently. Add the zucchini and cook for 5 minutes, stirring frequently.
3. Add the tomatoes and their juice, salt, bay leaf, and chickpeas and stir to combine.
4. Reduce the heat, cover, and simmer for 30 minutes, or until the vegetables are tender, stirring occasionally.
5. Sprinkle with the basil and cheddar cheese.

Black Bean and Butternut Squash Chili

Here's a chili, loaded with spices, beans, and veggies. It's a welcome treat on a chilly evening, and it's also great reheated the next day. Feel free to adjust the spices to get the proper amount of fire. Don't forget the toppings and chips, warm tortillas, or cornbread to complete the meal.

2 tablespoons vegetable oil
2 cups coarsely chopped
    onions
1 cup seeded and coarsely
    chopped red bell
    peppers
1 tablespoon seeded and finely
    chopped fresh jalapeño
    peppers
2 teaspoons minced garlic
5 cups peeled, seeded, and
    cubed butternut
    squash
1 cup vegetable broth or
    reduced-sodium
    chicken broth
1 14½-ounce can diced
    tomatoes
1 15¼-ounce can black beans,
    rinsed and drained
2 tablespoons chili powder
2 teaspoons ground cumin
1 teaspoon dried oregano
1 teaspoon salt
1 cup fresh or frozen corn
¼ pound cheddar or
    Monterey Jack cheese,
    grated or shredded
    (optional)
4 tablespoons sour cream
    (optional)

Cooking Time: 60 minutes or less
Serves: 4

1. In a large stock pot over medium heat, add the oil. Add the onions, red peppers, and jalapeños and sauté until softened, 5 to 8 minutes, stirring frequently.
2. Add the garlic and cook for 1 minute, stirring constantly.
3. Add the squash, broth, tomatoes and their juice, black beans, chili powder, cumin, oregano, and salt and stir to combine. Bring to a boil.
4. Reduce the heat, cover, and simmer for 30 minutes, stirring occasionally.
5. Add the corn and cook for 5 to 10 minutes, or until the vegetables are tender, stirring occasionally.
6. Top each serving with cheese and sour cream.

Eggplant and Vegetable Tian

1 large red onion, thinly sliced
    (about 10 ounces)
5 tablespoons olive oil
2 teaspoons salt
1 teaspoon dried thyme
1 medium eggplant, thinly
    sliced (about ¾ pound)
1 medium yellow squash or
    zucchini, thinly sliced
    (about ⅓ pound)
2 large ripe tomatoes, thinly
    sliced (about 1 pound)
¼ cup chopped fresh basil
½ pound goat cheese,
    crumbled
¼ cup bread crumbs,
    homemade or
    packaged
2 tablespoons grated
    Parmesan cheese

A tian is both the name of a casserole cooked in a shallow clay pot as well as the name of the pot itself. This vegetarian specialty is found primarily in the Provençe region of France. This tian features hearty eggplant, summer squash, red onions, tomatoes, and goat cheese, but you can adapt it to show off whatever is plentiful in your garden or at the farmers' market.

Cooking Time: 60 minutes or less
Serves: 4 to 6

1. Preheat the oven to 350 degrees.
2. In a large shallow decorative ovenproof dish, or a 13 × 9 × 2-inch baking pan, arrange the onions in a single layer. Drizzle with 1 tablespoon of the oil, ½ teaspoon salt, and ¼ teaspoon thyme. Top with a layer of the eggplant slices. Drizzle with 1 tablespoon of oil, ½ teaspoon salt, and ¼ teaspoon thyme. Top with a layer of the squash slices. Drizzle with 1 tablespoon of oil, ½ teaspoon salt, and ¼ teaspoon thyme. Top with the tomato slices. Drizzle with 1 tablespoon of oil, ½ teaspoon salt, and ¼ teaspoon thyme.

3. Cover with aluminum foil and bake for 45 minutes. Remove the foil, sprinkle with the basil and goat cheese, and drizzle with the remaining tablespoon of oil. Top with the bread crumbs and Parmesan cheese. Bake uncovered for 10 to 15 minutes, or until the cheese has melted. For added browning, place under the broiler for 1 to 2 minutes.

4. Remove from the oven. Cover with aluminum foil and let stand for 10 minutes before serving.

Chile Relleno Phyllo Bake

3 eggs
½ pound cream cheese, room
    temperature
1 cup ricotta cheese
2 7-ounce cans whole green
    chiles, drained
¼ cup coarsely chopped fresh
    cilantro (optional)
¼ cup thinly sliced scallions
½ pound cheddar cheese,
    grated or shredded
½ cup (1 stick) butter, melted
    or very soft
12 sheets phyllo dough,
    defrosted and cut in
    half widthwise
2 cups fresh tomato salsa,
    ready-made or recipe,
    page 175 (optional)

Creamy chile-studded custard is spread between layers of buttery phyllo dough in this dressed-up version of the classic Mexican dish. Ready-made phyllo dough (also known as filo or fillo), tissue-paper thin sheets of pastry, makes a distinctively crispy and light crust. It does take patience to work with phyllo, as it is fragile and crumbles easily; but because multiple layers are used, mistakes are invisible to the eye and palate. A salad of shredded lettuce, chopped tomatoes, jicama, grapefruit slices, and avocado in a creamy citrus vinaigrette is a nice accompaniment.

Cooking Time: 60 minutes or less
Serves: 4

1. Preheat the oven to 350 degrees.
2. In a food processor fitted with a metal chopping blade, combine the eggs, cream cheese, and ricotta. Add the chiles, cilantro, scallions, and cheddar cheese and pulse to combine. (This can also be mixed in a large bowl).

Vegetarian

3. Lightly butter the bottom and sides of a $13 \times 9 \times 2$-inch baking pan. Cover with 7 sheets of the phyllo, brushing each sheet with butter before adding the next.

4. Spread half of the cheese mixture on top of the phyllo. Top with 7 sheets of phyllo, brushing each sheet with butter before adding the next. Top with the remaining cheese mixture. Top with 10 layers of phyllo, brushing each sheet with butter before adding the next. Lightly brush the top sheet with butter.

5. Bake for 45 minutes, or until lightly browned and cooked through. Let stand for 5 minutes before serving.

Spinach and Ricotta Lasagna

1 15-ounce container ricotta
cheese
3 cups coarsely chopped
spinach leaves
1 cup finely chopped fresh
basil
½ to 1 teaspoon red pepper
flakes (optional)
4 cups prepared pasta sauce
1 cup water
½ pound lasagna noodles
1 pound mozzarella cheese,
grated or shredded
1½ cups grated Parmesan
cheese

Now that most lasagna noodles do not need to be precooked, making this hearty pasta dish is easier than ever. To keep the noodles from drying out, add a little water to the tomato sauce before baking. Be as creative as you want, adding more vegetables or precooked meat to the ricotta cheese filling and spicing up your pasta sauce to make this dish your own. For a fresh taste, instead of using jarred sauce, ask your favorite Italian restaurant if they sell their homemade tomato sauce.

Cooking Time: 60 minutes or less
Serves: 4 to 6

1. Preheat the oven to 350 degrees.
2. In a medium bowl, combine the ricotta, spinach, basil, and red pepper flakes.
3. In a $13 \times 9 \times 2$-inch baking pan, mix 1 cup of the pasta sauce and ½ cup of the water and spread over the bottom of the pan.
4. Cover the bottom of the pan with some of lasagna noodles. You will need to overlap or break some noodles to cover the bottom completely.

5. Top with half of the ricotta mixture, 1 cup of the pasta sauce, and half of the mozzarella cheese. Sprinkle with ½ cup of the Parmesan cheese.
6. Cover the cheese with another layer of noodles. Top with the remaining ricotta mixture, 2 cups of pasta sauce, and ½ cup of water.
7. Top with the remaining mozzarella and Parmesan cheeses.
8. Cover with aluminum foil and bake for 30 minutes. Check to make sure the sides are not drying out. If necessary, pour a few tablespoons of water or sauce into the corners.
9. Uncover and bake for 15 to 25 minutes, or until the lasagna is heated through and the cheese is bubbly. Let stand for 5 to 10 minutes before serving.

Tomato, Goat Cheese, and Pesto Tart

Crust:

1¼ cups all-purpose flour
¼ teaspoon salt
½ cup (1 stick) unsalted but-
    ter, chilled and cut into
    ½-inch pieces
2 to 4 tablespoons ice water

Filling:

4 eggs
1 cup cream or milk
1 cup milk
½ cup pesto, ready-made or
    recipe, page 114
½ teaspoon salt
½ teaspoon ground black
    pepper
¼ pound goat cheese,
    crumbled
2 medium red, orange, and/or
    yellow ripe tomatoes,
    thinly sliced (about ½
    pound)

Creamy goat cheese mingles with basil pesto and fresh tomatoes in this delightful tart. It tastes and looks like summertime, with vibrant colors and vivid flavors. Search your farmers' market to find yellow or orange tomatoes to add to its colorful presentation. Make your own crust or buy a ready-made crust and fit it into a 9-inch pie plate.

Cooking Time: 60 minutes or less
Serves: 4

1. Prepare the crust: In a food processor fitted with a metal chopping blade, mix the flour and salt (5 seconds). Add the butter and pulse until the mixture resembles coarse meal (10 short pulses). Sprinkle the minimum amount of water over the mixture and pulse until distributed throughout the dough and the crumbs start sticking together (5 to 10 pulses). Process just until the dough holds together, adding the remaining water if necessary. Do not allow the dough to form a ball.

2. Scrape the dough onto the work surface. Shape the dough into a 1-inch-thick disc. Wrap the dough tightly with plastic wrap and refrigerate for 30 minutes, or until it is firm enough to roll out.

3. Preheat the oven to 450 degrees.

4. Roll out the dough and fit into a 9-inch pie pan. Prick the dough with a fork and bake for 5 to 10 minutes, or until lightly browned. Remove from the oven and reduce the temperature to 350 degrees.

5. Prepare the filling: Meanwhile, in a medium bowl, beat the eggs, cream, milk, pesto, salt, and pepper. Set aside.

6. Line the partially baked pie crust with the goat cheese. Add the egg mixture.

7. Bake for 30 minutes, or until just set. Top with the tomatoes, placed in slightly overlapping concentric circles. Bake for 10 to 20 minutes, or until the eggs are set and the center doesn't jiggle. If the crust begins to brown before the tart is ready, cover it with aluminum foil to prevent burning. Let stand 5 to 10 minutes before serving.

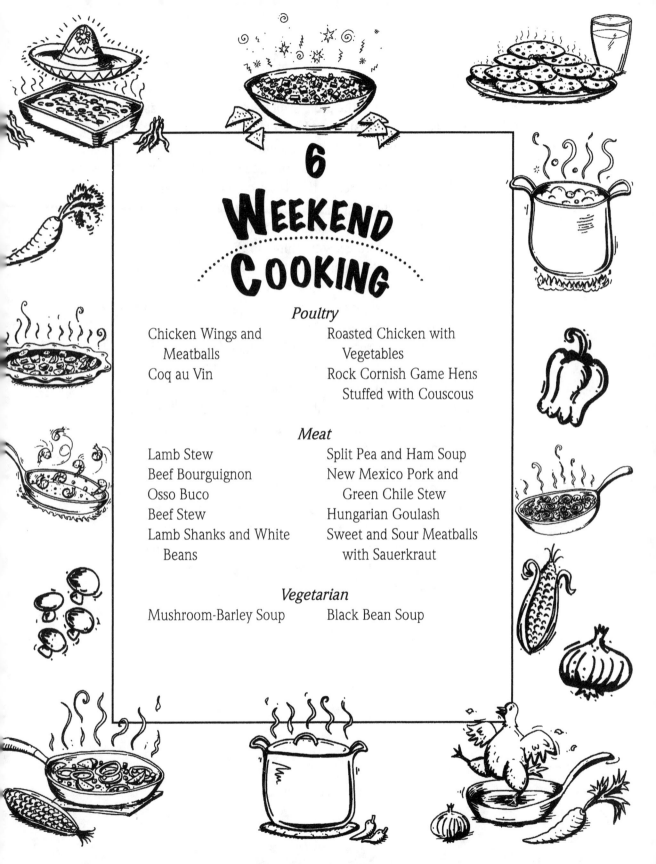

6
WEEKEND COOKING

Poultry

Chicken Wings and
  Meatballs
Coq au Vin

Roasted Chicken with
  Vegetables
Rock Cornish Game Hens
  Stuffed with Couscous

Meat

Lamb Stew
Beef Bourguignon
Osso Buco
Beef Stew
Lamb Shanks and White
  Beans

Split Pea and Ham Soup
New Mexico Pork and
  Green Chile Stew
Hungarian Goulash
Sweet and Sour Meatballs
  with Sauerkraut

Vegetarian

Mushroom-Barley Soup

Black Bean Soup

As working moms, weekends are our time to kick back, relax, and enjoy our children. With the week behind us, and two days full of the promise of freedom (and errands, and errands, and errands), Saturday and Sunday let us reclaim our lives, set our own schedules, and move at our own pace.

During this brief reprieve from being perpetually hurried and harried, meal preparation takes on a more leisurely nature. We can enjoy recipes that require longer cooking times, thus liberating ourselves from last minute scurrying. Instead of the usual rush to get something on the table, these meals permit us to start dinner in advance. We can put our feet up and enjoy a stress-free period before eating, while savoring the tantalizing aromas that presage the promise of something wonderful to come.

These meals, reminiscent of childhood Sunday dinners, allow time for hearty stews to gently bubble away on the stove, infusing gravy and vegetables with gusto while slowly tenderizing morsels of meat. Roasted chicken becomes crackley crisp, golden, and juicy. Healthful bean and vegetable soups blossom as flavors bloom and the legumes ready their nutritious goodness.

Weekends are also the perfect time to anticipate our needs for the coming week and lay the groundwork for weekday dinners. Whether we prepare an extra meal to serve later, double a recipe to store in the freezer, or simply chop extra vegetables to use later, we'll find a little planning goes a long way towards future peace of mind!

Chicken Wings and Meatballs

This dish was a childhood standard in my house. It's fun for kids with tiny fingers to pick up the chicken wings and tiny meatballs and get down and dirty enjoying this dish.

Cooking Time: Over 60 minutes
Serves: 4

1 slice white bread, crust
    removed
¼ cup milk
1 pound lean ground beef or
    ground turkey
2 tablespoons vegetable oil
2 pounds chicken wings or
    wing drumettes,
    trimmed of excess skin
1 8-ounce can tomato soup
1 cup water
2 teaspoons Italian seasoning
1 teaspoon salt
½ teaspoon ground black
    pepper
8 small new potatoes,
    quartered if large
    (about 1 pound)
8 pearl or boiling onions,
    peeled
1 cup fresh or frozen peas

1. In a medium bowl, soak the bread in milk until saturated. Squeeze the milk from the bread and discard the excess liquid. Mash the bread with the beef. Form small meatballs, 1 to 1½ inches in diameter. Set aside.

2. In a large skillet over medium-high heat, add the oil. Brown the chicken on all sides, 3 to 5 minutes. (You may need to do this in two or more batches). Remove the chicken and reserve.

3. Discard any fat from the skillet. Add the soup, water, Italian seasoning, salt, and pepper and stir to combine. Bring to a boil.

4. Return the chicken to the pot. Top with the meatballs. Reduce the heat, cover, and simmer for 1 hour, stirring occasionally.

5. Add the potatoes and onions and cook for 20 to 25 minutes. Add the peas and cook for 1 to 2 minutes.

Coq au Vin

¼ pound bacon, coarsely
    chopped
1 3- to 4-pound chicken, cut
    into 8 pieces
8 pearl or boiling onions,
    peeled
2 cups small mushrooms,
    halved if large
3 tablespoons all-purpose flour
2 teaspoons minced garlic
1 teaspoon dried thyme
2 cups Burgundy or dry red
    wine
1 cup reduced-sodium
    chicken broth
12 baby carrots, or 2 cups
    sliced carrots (1-inch-
    thick pieces)
12 small new potatoes,
    quartered if large
    (about 1½ pounds)

This aromatic chicken stew celebrates the cuisine of the Burgundy region of France and its coveted export, the dry full-bodied wines of the region. This one-pot meal can be prepared the night before, refrigerated, and then placed in the oven the next day for its final cooking. For a modern twist on this classic dish, experiment by using exotic mushrooms like shiitakes or portobellos instead of domestic button mushrooms. Make sure to serve lots of crusty bread so you don't miss a single drop.

Cooking Time: Over 60 minutes
Serves: 4

1. In a large stock pot or skillet over medium-high heat, sauté the bacon until brown and crisp, 8 to 10 minutes, stirring frequently. Transfer the bacon to paper towels, using a slotted spoon.
2. Add the chicken and brown, 3 to 5 minutes per side. Remove the chicken and reserve. (You may need to do this in two or more batches).
3. Discard all but 2 tablespoons of fat from the pot. Add the onions and mushrooms. Cook until browned, 8 to 10 minutes, stirring occasionally. Do not overcrowd the pot.

4. Add the flour, garlic, and thyme and cook for 1 to 2 minutes, stirring constantly.
5. Add the wine and broth. Bring to a boil and stir to deglaze and dislodge any bits of food that have stuck to the bottom of the pot.
6. Return the bacon and chicken to the pot. (If desired, refrigerate overnight at this point). Add the carrots and potatoes.
7. Reduce the heat, cover, and simmer for 1 hour, or until the chicken is cooked through and the vegetables are tender, basting with the cooking liquid and turning the chicken occasionally.

Roasted Chicken with Vegetables

1 3- to 4-pound chicken,
    giblets, excess fat, and
    excess skin removed
1 lemon, halved
2 tablespoons butter, melted
    or very soft
1 tablespoon dried rosemary
1 tablespoon salt
½ teaspoon ground black
    pepper
10 cloves garlic, peeled
4 large carrots, halved
    lengthwise and cut
    into 2-inch pieces
    (about 1 pound)
3 large onions, peeled and
    quartered (about 2¼
    pounds)
3 large celery stalks, trimmed
    and cut into 2-inch
    pieces (about ½
    pound)
8 small new potatoes,
    quartered if large
    (about 1 pound)
2 sweet potatoes, halved
    lengthwise and cut
    into 2-inch pieces
    (about 1 pound)
2 tablespoons olive oil
1 cup reduced-sodium
    chicken broth

This time-honored dinner will warm hearts, appetites, and kitchens on a cold winter's night. After a short prep, all you have to do is wait for its intoxicating aroma to overtake your home. For added browning, flip the chicken midway through cooking. Whether it's a family meal or a guests-only dinner party, no one ever outgrows this favorite.

Cooking Time: Over 60 minutes
Serves: 4

1. Preheat the oven to 450 degrees.
2. Let the chicken stand at room temperature for 30 minutes before cooking.
3. Rub the chicken with one lemon half and then lightly coat with the butter. Sprinkle with the rosemary, salt, and pepper.
4. Place the chicken in a large roasting pan on a vertical roaster or a V-shaped rack. Surround the chicken with the garlic, carrots, onions, celery, potatoes, and sweet potatoes. Drizzle the oil, juice from the remaining lemon half, and broth over the vegetables and toss to combine.
5. Roast the chicken for 20 minutes.
6. Reduce the heat to 350 degrees and stir the vegetables. Bake for 1¼ to 1½ hours, until the chicken is cooked through, stirring the vegetables every 30 minutes. The chicken is ready when a meat thermometer

inserted into the inner thigh registers between 170 and 180 degrees and juices run clear, not pink.

7. Remove the pan from the oven and let the chicken rest for 10 to 15 minutes.

8. Carve or cut the chicken into pieces and serve with the vegetables.

·················

Variation:

Herbed Roast Chicken: *For added flavor and a dramatic presentation, loosen the skin around the breast and insert fresh herbs (rosemary, thyme, and sage are all nice additions) or slivers of garlic.*

·················

Rock Cornish Game Hens Stuffed with Couscous

Stuffing:

1 cup reduced-sodium chicken broth

1 cup peeled, cored, and finely chopped apples

⅔ cup couscous

3 tablespoons currants, or raisins

1 teaspoon lemon zest

1 teaspoon salt

¼ cup pine nuts, lightly toasted

Hens:

4 1-pound Cornish game hens, or 2 larger hens, giblets, excess fat, and excess skin removed

1 tablespoon butter, melted or very soft

1 tablespoon dried thyme

1 teaspoon salt

½ teaspoon ground black pepper

2 large onions, peeled and quartered (about 1½ pounds)

2 large carrots, halved lengthwise and cut into 2-inch pieces (about ½ pound)

2 cups Brussels sprouts, trimmed and halved (optional)

2 tablespoons olive oil

¼ to ½ cup reduced-sodium chicken broth

2 cups trimmed green beans

Rock Cornish game hens, an American crossbreed between white Plymouth Rock hens and Cornish gamecocks, are a nice departure from traditional chicken dinners. They are elegant when presented, yet their preparation is not demanding. Most Cornish hens are between five and six weeks old, weigh around one to two pounds, and have less fat and calories than older chickens. These are stuffed with fruity couscous and then roasted alongside vegetables. When cooking a stuffed bird, add 15 minutes to the cooking time.

Cooking Time: Over 60 minutes
Serves: 4

1. Preheat the oven to 450 degrees.
2. Prepare the stuffing: In a microwave, bring the broth to a boil.
3. In a medium bowl, combine the apples, couscous, currants, lemon zest, and salt. Pour in the broth. Cover with aluminum foil and let stand for 5 to 10 minutes, or until the broth is absorbed. Add the pine nuts and toss to combine. Set aside.
4. Prepare the hens: Rub the hens with the butter and sprinkle with the thyme, salt, and pepper.
5. Loosely stuff each hen with between ⅓ and ½ cup of the couscous mixture. Tie the legs together at the ankles with kitchen string to secure.

6. In a large roasting pan or on a rack in a large roasting pan, place the hens. Surround the hens with the onions, carrots, and Brussels sprouts. Drizzle the oil and ¼ cup broth over the vegetables and toss to combine.

7. Roast the hens for 20 minutes.

8. Reduce the heat to 350 degrees. Add the green beans and stir the vegetables to combine. If the vegetables begin to dry out, add another ¼ cup broth.

9. Bake for 30 to 40 minutes for 1-pound birds, or 55 to 65 minutes for larger birds, or until the hens are cooked through, stirring the vegetables every 30 minutes. The hens are ready when a meat thermometer inserted into the thigh registers between 170 and 180 degrees and juices run clear, not pink.

10. Remove the pan from the oven and let the hens rest for 5 to 10 minutes. If serving larger birds, cut them in half. Serve with the stuffing and vegetables.

Lamb Stew

2 tablespoons butter
1½ pounds boneless lamb
shoulder or stew meat,
cut into 1½-inch
pieces
2 tablespoons all-purpose flour
2 cups reduced-sodium beef
broth
12 pearl or boiling onions,
peeled
12 small new potatoes,
quartered if large
(about 1½ pounds)
12 baby carrots, or 2 cups
sliced carrots (1-inch
pieces)
1 cup turnips, peeled and cut
into 1-inch pieces
(optional)
1 teaspoon dried thyme
½ teaspoon dried rosemary
½ teaspoon dried sage
(optional)
1 bay leaf
2 cups trimmed and cut green
beans
1 teaspoon salt
½ teaspoon ground black
pepper

Lamb stew is actually a classic French dish named navarin printanier, *or "spring lamb," because it is most frequently made in the spring when lambs are young, tender, and flavorful. Lamb is braised and then baked with baby vegetables until the stew's flavor becomes something greater than its individual ingredients. This recipe was given to me my mother, Bert Hoberman.*

Cooking Time: Over 60 minutes
Serves: 4

1. Preheat the oven to 350 degrees.
2. In a large ovenproof stock pot over medium-high heat, add the butter. Brown the lamb on all sides, 3 to 5 minutes. Do not overcrowd the meat. (You may need to do this in two or more batches).
3. Add the flour and stir until it is absorbed into the meat, 1 to 2 minutes.
4. Add the broth. Bring to a boil and stir to deglaze and dislodge any bits of lamb that have stuck to the bottom of the pot and to incorporate the flour. Scrape your stirring spoon to free any flour that has adhered to it.

5. Add the onions, potatoes, carrots, turnips, thyme, rose-mary, sage, and bay leaf. The liquid will just barely cover the stew. Cover and place in the oven. After 10 to 15 minutes, check to make sure the stew is gently simmering. If necessary, adjust the oven temperature to correct.

6. Bake for 1¼ hours. Add the green beans and bake for 15 minutes, or until the meat and vegetables are tender.

7. Remove from the oven and skim off any fat. Season with salt and pepper.

Beef Bourguignon

¼ pound bacon, coarsely
    chopped
1½ pounds boneless beef
    chuck, cut into 1½-
    inch pieces
2 teaspoons salt
½ teaspoon ground black
    pepper
1 tablespoon all-purpose flour
16 pearl or boiling onions,
    peeled
2 cups sliced carrots (1-inch
    thick)
1 tablespoon minced garlic
1½ cups reduced-sodium beef
    broth
¼ cup Cognac (optional)
2 cups Burgundy or dry red
    wine
2 cups small mushrooms,
    halved if large
1 teaspoon dried thyme

This enticing classic hails from the Burgundy region of France. Hearty beef, onions, carrots, and mushrooms are slowly simmered in a luscious red wine sauce for a truly succulent stew. Don't scrimp on the wine. For optimum flavor, use a drinkable dry red that you would enjoy on its own. Make sure there's lots of crusty French bread so you won't miss a single drop of this rich, robust gravy.

Cooking Time: Over 60 minutes
Serves: 4

1. Preheat the oven to 325 degrees.
2. In a large ovenproof stock pot over medium heat, sauté the bacon until brown and crisp, 8 to 10 minutes, stirring frequently. Transfer the bacon to paper towels, using a slotted spoon. Set aside.
3. Sprinkle the beef with the salt and pepper and coat with the flour. Brown the beef on all sides, 3 to 5 minutes. Do not overcrowd the meat. Remove the meat and reserve in a large bowl. (You may need to do this in two or more batches).
4. Add the onions and carrots and cook until lightly browned, 5 to 8 minutes, stirring frequently.
5. Add the garlic and cook for 1 minute, stirring constantly. Transfer the vegetables to the bowl with the beef. Set aside.

6. Add the broth and Cognac to the pot. Bring to a boil and stir to deglaze and dislodge any bits of food that have stuck to the bottom of the pot. Boil for 5 minutes, or until the broth begins to reduce.

7. Return the bacon, beef, and vegetables with their juices to the pot. Add the wine, mushrooms, and thyme. The liquid will just barely cover the stew. Cover and place in the oven. After 10 to 15 minutes, check to make sure the stew is gently simmering. If necessary, adjust the oven temperature to correct.

8. Bake for 1¼ to 1½ hours, or until the meat and vegetables are tender.

9. Remove from the oven and skim off any fat.

Osso Buco

4 meaty veal or lamb shanks
(about 3 pounds)
2 teaspoons salt
1 teaspoon ground black
pepper
2 tablespoons olive oil
1 cup coarsely chopped
onions
1 cup coarsely chopped
carrots
¼ cup coarsely chopped celery
2 teaspoons minced garlic
1 cup reduced-sodium
chicken broth
½ cup dry white wine
1 14½-ounce can diced
tomatoes
2 tablespoons chopped fresh
Italian parsley
2 teaspoons lemon zest
1 teaspoon minced garlic

Translated, the name of this northern Italian dish means "bone with a hole filled with marrow," which is a slightly crude but apt description of what makes this delicacy so popular: the flavorful bone marrow. The traditional garnish for osso buco is gremolata, a mixture of lemon zest, parsley, and garlic. While this braise is definitely a meal in itself, risotto Milanese (saffron risotto) is a traditional accompaniment. If you don't enjoy veal, you can make osso buco with lamb shanks.

Cooking Time: Over 60 minutes
Serves: 4

1. Preheat the oven to 325 degrees.
2. Sprinkle the meat with the salt and pepper.
3. In a large ovenproof skillet over medium-high heat, add the oil. Brown the shanks on all sides, 8 to 10 minutes. Do not overcrowd the meat. Remove the meat and reserve.
4. Add the onions, carrots, celery, and garlic and sauté until softened, 5 to 8 minutes, stirring frequently.
5. Add the broth, wine, and tomatoes and their juice and stir to combine. Bring to a boil and stir to deglaze and dislodge any bits of food that have stuck to the bottom of the skillet.

6. Return the shanks to the skillet and distribute them between the vegetables. Cover and place in the oven. After 10 to 15 minutes, check to make sure the stew is gently simmering. If necessary, adjust the oven temperature to correct.
7. Bake for 1¼ to 1½ hours, or until the meat and vegetables are tender, turning the shanks after 45 minutes. Remove from the oven, turn the shanks, and let stand for 5 to 10 minutes.
8. Meanwhile, prepare the gremolata. Combine the parsley, lemon zest, and garlic until blended. Sprinkle on top of the Osso Buco.

Beef Stew

2 pounds beef chuck, cut into
   1½-inch pieces
1 teaspoon salt
½ teaspoon ground black
   pepper
2 tablespoons vegetable oil
2 cups coarsely chopped
   onions
2 teaspoons minced garlic
2 tablespoons all-purpose flour
1 cup dry red wine
1 cup reduced-sodium beef
   broth
1 teaspoon dried thyme
1 bay leaf
3 cups peeled and halved new
   potatoes
3 cups sliced carrots (½-inch-
   thick pieces)
1 cup fresh or frozen peas
   (optional)

Hearty chunks of beef are seared to caramelize and seal in flavorful juices, mixed with an aromatic assortment of vegetables, and then placed in the oven to maintain a gentle simmer. As the stew slowly cooks, the connective tissue in the beef breaks down, making the meat so tender you can cut it with a spoon. The addition of the wine, broth, and vegetables adds sublime flavor. Who says beef stew is boring?

Cooking Time: Over 60 minutes
Serves: 4

1. Preheat the oven to 275 degrees.
2. Sprinkle the beef with salt and pepper.
3. In a large ovenproof stock pot over medium-high heat, add the oil. Brown the beef on all sides, 3 to 5 minutes. Do not overcrowd the meat. Remove the meat and reserve. (You may need to do this in two or more batches).
4. Add the onions and sauté until softened, 3 to 5 minutes, stirring frequently. Reduce the heat to medium and add the garlic. Cook for 1 minute, stirring constantly.
5. Add the flour and stir until it is absorbed into the onions, 1 to 2 minutes.

6. Add the wine, broth, thyme, and bay leaf. Bring to a boil and stir to deglaze and dislodge any bits of food that have stuck to the bottom of the pot and to incorporate the flour. Scrape your stirring spoon to free any flour that has adhered to it.
7. Return the beef and its juice to the pot. The liquid will just barely cover the stew. Cover and place in the oven. After 10 to 15 minutes, check to make sure the stew is gently simmering. If necessary, adjust the oven temperature to correct.
8. Bake for 1 hour. Remove the pot from the oven. Check to make sure the broth has not evaporated. If necessary, add a little hot water. Add the potatoes and carrots, cover, and return to the oven.
9. Bake for 1 to 1½ hours, or until the meat is tender. Add the peas and bake for 1 to 2 minutes.
10. Remove from the oven and skim off any fat.

Lamb Shanks and White Beans

4 meaty lamb shanks (about 3
  pounds)
2 teaspoons salt
1 teaspoon ground black
  pepper
2 tablespoons olive oil
1 cup coarsely chopped
  onions
1 cup coarsely chopped
  carrots
1 tablespoon minced garlic
2 teaspoons dried rosemary
1 teaspoon dried thyme
1 cup dry red wine or white
  wine
1 cup reduced-sodium
  chicken broth
1 28-ounce can diced
  tomatoes
2 15-ounce cans cannellini or
  small white beans,
  rinsed and drained

Tender braised lamb is slow-cooked with creamy white beans and seasoned with rosemary and thyme for a taste sensation. This is a wonderful dish for entertaining because it can be prepared ahead of time and left on the stove while you enjoy your guests.

Cooking Time: Over 60 minutes
Serves: 4

1. Sprinkle the lamb with salt and pepper.
2. In a large skillet over medium-high heat, add the oil. Brown the lamb on all sides, 8 to 10 minutes. Do not overcrowd the meat. Remove the lamb and reserve.
3. Add the onions, carrots, garlic, rosemary, and thyme and sauté until softened, 5 to 8 minutes, stirring frequently.
4. Add the wine, broth, and tomatoes and their juice. Bring to a boil and stir to deglaze and dislodge any bits of food that have stuck to the bottom of the skillet.
5. Return the shanks to the skillet and spoon the tomatoes and liquids over the lamb.
6. Reduce the heat, cover, and simmer for 1 hour, turning the lamb shanks after 30 minutes.
7. Add the beans and cook uncovered for 45 minutes to 1 hour, or until the meat is tender and the cooking liquid thickens, stirring and turning the lamb occasionally.

Split Pea and Ham Soup

This thick and creamy soup has "comfort" written all over it. So hearty and rich with peas, veggies, and ham it is almost like a stew. For a vegetarian soup, leave out the ham and substitute vegetable broth for the chicken broth.

9 cups reduced-sodium chicken broth
2 cups dried split peas
1 large meaty ham bone, or ½ pound thickly cut country ham, chopped
1 cup coarsely chopped onions
1 cup coarsely chopped carrots
1 cup coarsely chopped celery
½ teaspoon dried thyme
1 teaspoon salt
½ teaspoon ground black pepper

Cooking Time: Over 60 minutes
Serves: 4 to 6

1. In a large stock pot over high heat, combine the broth and split peas. Bring to a boil for 2 minutes. Remove from the heat, cover, and let stand for 1 hour.
2. Add the ham bone or ham, onions, carrots, celery, and thyme. Bring to a boil.
3. Reduce the heat, cover, and simmer for 1½ to 2 hours, or until the peas are tender, stirring occasionally.
4. If using a ham bone, remove it and cut the meat into bite-size pieces. Return the ham to the pot.
5. Add the salt and pepper. This soup will thicken as it stands. If necessary, add extra broth or water to achieve the desired consistency.

New Mexico Pork and Green Chile Stew

2 tablespoons vegetable oil
1½ pounds boneless pork shoulder, loin end, or butt, cut into 1-inch pieces
1½ cups chopped onions
1 tablespoon minced garlic
2 tablespoons all-purpose flour
3 cups reduced-sodium chicken broth
1 cup Mexican-style canned diced tomatoes, drained (optional)
2 teaspoons dried oregano
½ teaspoon ground cumin
2 cups thickly sliced carrots
2 cups peeled, ¾-inch-cubed potatoes
⅓ cup seeded and coarsely chopped fresh jalapeño peppers, or 1 4-ounce can green chiles, drained and chopped
1 teaspoon salt
½ teaspoon ground black pepper

From the heart of the Southwest comes this rich and fragrant stew, seasoned with green chiles, onions, and garlic. Serve it with warm tortillas or corn bread, fresh from the oven, and a salad brimming with chunks of avocado and tomato. A note of caution: When seeding and chopping fresh chiles, wear rubber gloves and keep your hands away from your eyes.

Cooking Time: Over 60 minutes
Serves: 4

1. In a large stock pot over medium-high heat, add the oil. Brown the pork on all sides, 3 to 5 minutes. Do not overcrowd the meat. Remove the meat and reserve. (You may need to do this in two or more batches).
2. Add the onions and sauté until softened, 3 to 5 minutes, stirring frequently. Reduce the heat to medium and add the garlic. Cook for 1 minute, stirring constantly.
3. Add the flour and stir until it is absorbed into the onions, 1 to 2 minutes.
4. Add the broth, tomatoes, oregano, and cumin. Bring to a boil and stir to deglaze and dislodge any bits of food that have stuck to the bottom of the pot and to incorporate the flour. Scrape your stirring spoon to free any flour that has adhered to it.

5. Return the pork and its juice to the pot, reduce the heat, cover, and simmer for 1 hour, stirring occasionally.
6. Add the carrots, potatoes, and jalapeños and cook for 20 to 30 minutes, or until the vegetables and pork are tender.
7. Remove from the oven and skim off any fat. Season with salt and pepper.

Hungarian Goulash

1 tablespoon butter
1 cup chopped onions
1 tablespoon sweet paprika
1 teaspoon minced garlic
1 teaspoon caraway seeds
1 teaspoon dill seed (optional)
¼ teaspoon marjoram
    (optional)
1½ pounds boneless beef
    chuck, cut into 1½-
    inch pieces
2 tablespoons all-purpose flour
2 cups reduced-sodium beef
    broth
2 tablespoons tomato paste
1 tablespoon Worcestershire
    sauce (optional)
2 cups peeled, 1-inch-cubed
    potatoes
1 teaspoon salt
½ teaspoon ground black
    pepper
4 tablespoons sour cream

The defining ingredient for this European stew is sweet paprika. It's worth searching out Hungarian paprika for a more authentic taste. Although the ingredient list may appear a little long, this robust favorite is easy to put together. While goulash can be served over buttered egg noodles, here it is cooked with potatoes and simply garnished with a dollop of sour cream.

Cooking Time: Over 60 minutes
Serves: 4

1. In a large stock pot over medium-high heat, add the butter. Add the onions and sauté until softened, 3 to 5 minutes, stirring frequently. Reduce the heat to medium and add the paprika, garlic, caraway seeds, dill seed, and marjoram. Cook for 1 minute, stirring constantly.

2. Add the beef and stir to combine. Cook for 2 minutes, stirring frequently.

3. Add the flour and stir until it is absorbed into the onions and beef, 1 to 2 minutes.

4. Add the broth, tomato paste, and Worcestershire sauce. Bring to a boil and stir to deglaze and dislodge any bits of food that have stuck to the bottom of the pot and to incorporate the flour. Scrape your stirring spoon to free any flour that has adhered to it.

5. Reduce the heat, cover, and simmer for 1 hour, stirring occasionally.
6. Add the potatoes, cover, and simmer for 30 to 45 minutes, or until the meat is tender, stirring occasionally. Season with salt and pepper.
7. Top each serving with 1 tablespoon of the sour cream.

Sweet and Sour Meatballs with Sauerkraut

Sauce:

1 cup chopped onions
½ cup packed brown sugar
½ cup raisins
1 15-ounce can tomato sauce
1 pound sauerkraut

Meatballs:

2 slices white bread, crusts
    removed
½ cup milk
2 pounds lean ground beef or
    ground turkey
1 cup finely chopped onions
2 tablespoons brown sugar
1 teaspoon salt
½ teaspoon ground black
    pepper
2 tablespoons vegetable oil

My husband insisted I include this favorite from his childhood. His mom had this recipe in her family for generations. With four kids to feed, one-pot meals were a standard in this busy family. Ruth sometimes served this with mashed potatoes, but it is filling on its own.

Cooking Time: Over 60 minutes
Serves: 4

1. Prepare the sauce: In a medium bowl, mix the onions, brown sugar, raisins, tomato sauce, and sauerkraut. Set aside.
2. Prepare the meatballs: In a large bowl, soak the bread in the milk until saturated. Squeeze the milk from the bread and discard the excess liquid. Mash the bread with the beef. Add the onions, brown sugar, salt, and pepper and stir to combine. Form meatballs 1½ to 2 inches in diameter.
3. In a stock pot over medium heat, add the oil. Lightly brown the meatballs on all sides, 5 to 8 minutes. (You may need to do this in two or more batches). Remove the meatballs and reserve.
4. Discard any fat from the pot. Spoon half of the sauce into the pot. Top with half of the meatballs. Repeat with the remaining sauce and meatballs.
5. Cover and simmer, stirring occasionally, for 1½ hours, or until the meat is cooked through.

Mushroom-Barley Soup

First cultivated in ancient Egypt, barley dates back to between 6000 B.C. and 5000 B.C. A popular offering to the gods, barley was found alongside other "treasures" in the tomb of King Tut. For a richer mushroom flavor, add ¼ to ½ ounce of dried porcini mushrooms that have been soaked for 30 minutes in 1 cup of the broth.

2 tablespoons vegetable oil
1 cup finely chopped onions
1 cup finely chopped carrots
½ cup finely chopped celery
1 teaspoon garlic, minced
5½ cups coarsely chopped
    mushrooms
8 cups vegetable broth or
    reduced-sodium
    chicken broth
½ cup pearl barley
1 tablespoon finely chopped
    fresh dill (optional)
1 teaspoon salt
½ teaspoon ground black
    pepper

Cooking Time: Over 60 minutes
Serves: 4

1. In a large stock pot over medium heat, add the oil. Sauté the onions, carrots, celery, and garlic until softened, 5 to 8 minutes, stirring frequently.
2. Increase the heat. Add the mushrooms and cook for 5 to 8 minutes, or until the mushrooms give off most of their liquid, stirring frequently.
3. Add the broth. Bring to a boil for 5 minutes.
4. Add the barley and stir to combine. Reduce the heat, cover, and simmer for 40 to 50 minutes, or until the barley is tender and the soup thickens, stirring occasionally.
5. Season with the dill, salt, and pepper.

Black Bean Soup

2 tablespoons olive oil or
    vegetable oil
2 cups finely chopped onions
1 cup finely chopped carrots
½ cup finely chopped celery
2 teaspoons minced garlic
2 cups dried black beans,
    soaked overnight and
    drained
8 cups vegetable broth or
    reduced-sodium
    chicken broth
2 teaspoons ground cumin

This hearty soup is a popular Cuban specialty. For a show-stopping presentation, top with a dollop of sour cream or crème fraîche, chopped red onions, cilantro, or hard-boiled egg, grated cheddar cheese, or thinly sliced lemons. For more heat, add some chopped jalapeños. For a meaty soup, cook a ham hock with the beans and shred the meat into the soup right before serving.

Cooking Time: Over 60 minutes
Serves: 4

1. In a large stock pot over medium heat, add the oil. Sauté the onions, carrots, celery, and garlic until softened, 5 to 8 minutes, stirring frequently.
2. Add the black beans, broth, and cumin and stir to combine. Bring to a boil.
3. Reduce the heat, cover, and simmer for 1½ to 2 hours, or until the beans are tender, stirring occasionally.
4. For a thicker soup, purée 3 cups of soup in a food processor and add back into the pot, or use an immersion blender to purée the beans directly in the pot.

7
SALADS

Chunky Salad

Antipasto

Fresh Tomato, Basil, and Mozzarella Salad

Spinach, Bacon, and Mushroom Salad

Coleslaw

Tomato Salsa

Caesar Salad

Greek Salad

Mediterranean Salad

Pear, Walnut, Blue Cheese, and Arugula Salad

Just as vegetarian dishes have profited by the demand for more flavorful and nutritious produce, salads have reaped similar benefits. No longer simply a side dish, salads have become as inventive as the main course—in many instances, they have replaced the main course!

Be creative when making your salad. Go for flavor, color, and texture. Look beyond the standard iceberg-and-tomato combination. With so many lettuces providing superior and distinctive flavors and offering different degrees of crunch, it is easy to build a salad that has great balance and interest. Use a variety of greens and combine them with a huge spectrum of accompaniments, including vegetables in season, fresh or dried fruits, creamy or sharp cheeses, and crunchy nuts, seeds, or croutons.

With more flavorful ingredients starring in the salad bowl, go for light and simple dressings, sparingly applied. Heavy, leaden toppings that overwhelm delicate leaves and vibrant flavors are a thing of the past. Now, simple vinaigrettes share the limelight.

So use your imagination, and have fun. A salad is whatever you want it to be.

Salad Tips:

- Explore your local farmers' markets. They offer a wide variety of freshly picked, locally grown vegetables and fruits at reasonable prices. Better yet, plant your own vegetable or herb garden, so delicious salad fixings are no further than your back yard!
- Experiment with different lettuces: peppery arugula and watercress; soft lettuces (also known as butterhead), including the Boston and Bibb varieties; and crisp and slightly bitter endive, escarole, and radicchio are now widely available and add character to your salads. For crunch, use ro-

maine, green or red leaf, oak leaf, or cabbage. I like to use a combination of lettuces for added flavor, texture, and presentation value. You can choose whichever varieties appeal to you and look best at the market.

- Now most supermarkets offer premixed salad varieties, usually labeled gourmet salad mix or *mesclun,* a French word for mixture, either in a self-serve bin or packaged.
- Look for vibrant green leaves for greater vitamin A content.
- Choose greens with crisp leaves. Avoid any that are slimy, wilted, or have an odor.
- Salad greens are perishable. Store greens and vegetables in the refrigerator, and try to use them within three to five days for optimum freshness. Generally, thicker leaves and tighter heads last the longest. For better storage, keep greens in an airtight plastic bag or container.
- Store tomatoes at room temperature to preserve flavor.
- Thoroughly wash lettuce, vegetables, and fruits just before using them. Dirt, bugs, and worms are some of the little nuisances that find their way into fresh produce. Even if you buy "prewashed" packaged veggie or lettuce mixes, it is recommended that you rinse them first.
- To revive wilted greens, soak then in icy water for five minutes.
- Use a salad spinner to remove excess water after washing. This machine efficiently dries greens, keeping them crisp longer. Make sure not to overcrowd the spinner, or it will not be able to properly do its job.
- For easiest eating, tear or cut lettuce and cut vegetables into 1- to 1½ -inch pieces.
- Fresh fruit, dried fruit, cheeses, or toasted nuts or seeds add protein and texture to salads. Experiment with a grapefruit, avocado, and baby lettuce mix, or a combination of pear, walnut, and crumbled blue cheese on arugula.
- Add leftover beans, pasta, chicken, or fish to make your salad a meal in itself. Other great add-ins are olives, arti-

choke hearts, hearts of palm, and croutons. Croutons add extra crunch to your salad. Find your favorite packaged variety, or use leftover bread to make your own. To make croutons, melt 2 tablespoons of butter, add 2 cloves of crushed garlic, and let the mixture sit for 10 minutes. Cut 4 large pieces of French or Italian white bread into 1-inch cubes and toss them with the garlic butter. Spread the bread cubes on a cookie sheet and bake them in a preheated 350-degree oven for 10 to 15 minutes, or until they are golden brown. Let the croutons cool before serving.

- Use a variety of cooked, grilled, or fresh vegetables and fresh herbs in your salad. Mix in fennel, radishes, jicama, steamed haricots verts, or snow peas for added crunch. Lemony chervil, chives, dill, and basil all add interesting flavor.

- There are now many packaged salad and vegetables mixes. Use them for convenience. In a pinch, use fixings from the supermarket salad bar.

- As a general guide, figure about 2 cups of loosely packed greens per person for a side salad, less if there are a lot of vegetables or other additions. Eight loosely packed cups of greens equals about 4 to 7 ounces (depending on the type of lettuce you choose). You'll need about one half cup of salad dressing to coat a salad for four. It is not necessary to use all the dressing the recipe calls for.

- Fixing a salad does not need to be a precise effort. Unlike baking or cooking, it is not essential to use exact measurements. Choose vegetables you enjoy. If you love tomatoes or onions, put in as many as you want! Feel free to exchange onions for scallions or chives. Use cherry, Roma, or beefsteak tomatoes instead of salad tomatoes when they look good.

- Don't overload your salad with heavy dressings. Less dressing saves calories and lets you taste what you are eating.

Make your own dressings and use them sparingly, just enough to coat the salad lightly. Sample different varieties of high quality extra-virgin olive oils and premium vinegars to see which you like best. For a change of pace, experiment with a variety of flavored oils and vinegars. Try lemon, herb, or garlic oils or cider, balsamic, red wine, raspberry, or champagne vinegar; or add your favorite fresh herbs to your dressing for a light and lively flavor. Other dressing intensifiers are mustard (prepared or dried), honey, Worcestershire sauce, poppy seeds, garlic, and dried herbs.

- When making a salad in advance, or if you're bringing it to a party, wait to dress the salad until just before serving.

Chunky Salad

Dressing:

½ cup extra-virgin olive oil
¼ cup balsamic vinegar
1 teaspoon sugar
½ teaspoon salt

Salad:

10 radishes, halved or
    quartered if large
10 mushrooms, halved or
    quartered if large
1 large carrot, cut into 1-inch
    pieces
1 medium red bell pepper,
    seeded and cut into 1-
    inch pieces
1 medium yellow or orange
    bell pepper, seeded and
    cut into 1-inch pieces
1 large celery stalk, cut into
    1-inch pieces
1 medium cucumber, seeded,
    halved, and cut into
    1-inch pieces
1 cup blanched haricot verts
1 cup red or yellow cherry or
    pear tomatoes, halved
    if large

This colorful salad features chunks of raw or quickly blanched vegetables that stand on their own. Cut the vegetables into large pieces so their flavors shine through. The vegetables are the stars of this salad, so just a light oil and vinegar dressing is recommended.

1. Prepare the dressing: In a clean jar, add the oil, vinegar, sugar, and salt and shake well to combine. (You can also mix the dressing in a bowl using a wire whisk). Set aside.

2. Prepare the salad: In a large bowl, combine the radishes, mushrooms, carrots, red peppers, yellow peppers, celery, cucumbers, haricot verts, tomatoes, and enough dressing to coat the vegetables. Toss to combine.

Antipasto

This colorful Italian-inspired salad combines vibrant vegetables with flavorful meats and cheeses. You can toss it with chopped lettuce, or decoratively arrange the toppings on large lettuce leaves. Make sure to seek out full-flavored meats and cheese for optimal enjoyment. This salad is a great way to add protein to an otherwise vegetarian meal and to use up odds and ends in your refrigerator. Make your own Italian herb dressing or use a robust bottled Italian dressing.

1. Prepare the dressing: In a clean jar, add the oil, vinegar, oregano, pepper, and salt and shake well to combine. (You can also mix the dressing in a bowl using a wire whisk). Set aside.
2. Prepare the salad: In a large bowl or on a large platter, combine the lettuce, tomatoes, artichoke hearts, olives, chickpeas, roasted peppers, pepperoncinis, onions, salami, prosciutto, Fontina, and enough dressing to coat the salad. Toss to combine.

Dressing:

½ cup extra-virgin olive oil
¼ cup red wine vinegar
1 teaspoon oregano
½ teaspoon black pepper
¼ teaspoon salt

Salad:

8 cups loosely packed, green or red leaf lettuce
2 large ripe tomatoes, cut into wedges
1 cup drained marinated artichoke hearts
1 cup black Italian olives
1 cup rinsed and drained canned chickpeas
1 cup roasted red peppers or fresh red peppers (optional)
1 cup pepperoncini (optional)
½ cup sliced red onion
¼ pound Genoa salami, thinly sliced
¼ pound prosciutto, cappicola, sopressata, or pepperoni, thinly sliced
¼ pound Fontina, provolone, or Asiago cheese, thinly sliced

Fresh Tomato, Basil, and Mozzarella Salad

Salad:

4 large ripe tomatoes, sliced
½ pound fresh mozzarella cheese, drained and thinly sliced
⅓ cup chopped or torn fresh basil

Dressing:

2 to 3 tablespoons extra-virgin olive oil
1 teaspoon kosher or sea salt
½ teaspoon freshly ground black pepper

This tri-colored salad salutes the colors, flag, and tastes of Italy. It is best made in the height of summer, when in-season tomatoes are bursting with color and flavor and fresh basil is abundant. Fresh mozzarella, formerly only sold in specialty stores, is now found in most large supermarkets. It is packaged with liquid to maintain its moisture and has a distinctively light flavor and texture. Let the flavor of the vegetables and herbs shine through with just a light drizzle of high-quality olive oil, kosher or sea salt, and freshly ground black pepper.

1. Prepare the salad: On a platter, alternate slices of tomato and mozzarella slices to form 3 rows. Sprinkle with the basil.
2. Lightly drizzle the salad with the oil and sprinkle with salt and pepper.

Spinach, Bacon, and Mushroom Salad

This classic salad tops a mound of nutritious spinach with hard-boiled eggs, thinly sliced mushrooms, red onion, and crunchy bacon for a delightful combination of tastes and textures. I like to top this salad with a sweet and spicy honey-mustard dressing, but you can use a simple vinaigrette or a creamy ranch dressing. Whether you choose bagged spinach or bundled spinach, look for tender, small leaves and be sure to rinse them well, as grit clings tightly to these precious greens. For a nice change, substitute cooked pancetta for the bacon or add a sprinkling of goat, Gruyère, or blue cheese.

Dressing:
½ cup extra-virgin olive oil
2 tablespoons cider or red
  wine vinegar
2 tablespoons honey-mustard
1 teaspoon sugar or honey
½ teaspoon salt

Salad:
8 cups loosely packed, spinach
  leaves, stems removed
3 hard-boiled eggs, peeled and
  thinly sliced
2 cups sliced mushrooms
⅓ cup thinly sliced red onions
½ pound bacon, crisply
  cooked and crumbled

1. Prepare the dressing: In a clean jar, add the oil, vinegar, honey-mustard, sugar, and salt and shake well to combine. (You can also mix the dressing in a bowl using a wire whisk). Set aside.
2. Prepare the salad: Place the spinach in a large bowl. Top with the eggs, mushrooms, onions, bacon, and enough dressing to coat the salad. Toss to combine.

Coleslaw

Dressing:

1 large clove garlic
2 tablespoons chopped red
    onions
½ cup Hidden Valley
    buttermilk ranch
    dressing or other ranch
    dressing

Salad:

1 16-ounce package shredded
    coleslaw mix or
    shredded cabbage
2 tablespoons caraway seeds

Coleslaw is a refreshing change from a green salad and is a nice addition to sausage and peppers, fish tacos, or any grilled entrée. This coleslaw is seasoned with a zesty garlic-buttermilk ranch dressing and then sprinkled with caraway seeds. Shred or slice a fifty-fifty mixture of green and red cabbage in your food processor and toss with some shredded carrots for a more colorful version. For tremendous time savings, look for a packaged shredded cabbage and carrot mix in your market's produce section. One note: Coleslaw will give off a lot of moisture and shrink considerably. If you are making the salad ahead, dress it sparingly and add more just before serving, if necessary.

1. Prepare the dressing: In a food processor fitted with a metal chopping blade, with the motor running, add the garlic and purée. Add the onions and ranch dressing and pulse until combined. Set aside.
2. Prepare the salad: In a large bowl, combine the shredded cabbage and enough dressing to coat the salad. Toss to combine. Top with the caraway seeds.

Tomato Salsa

Chunky, homestyle salsa, also known as salsa fresca, *is a mainstay of Mexican-American dining. It features a simple but winning combination of fresh and juicy chopped ripe tomatoes, jalapeño pepper, garlic, cilantro, and onion. It's perfect with the Chile Relleno Phyllo Bake, burritos, tacos, quesadillas, or just with tortilla chips. A word of caution: Make the salsa just before you need it. If you make it too far ahead, it will become watery and will lose some of its distinct flavors.*

2 to 3 large ripe tomatoes, seeded and coarsely chopped
¼ cup chopped red onions
¼ cup chopped fresh cilantro
1 tablespoon fresh lime or lemon juice (optional)
1 teaspoon finely chopped fresh jalapeño peppers
1 teaspoon minced garlic (optional)
½ teaspoon salt
1 to 2 dashes Tabasco, or other hot red pepper sauce (optional)

1. In a large bowl, add the tomatoes, onions, cilantro, lime juice, jalapeños, garlic, salt, and Tabasco and toss to combine.

Caesar Salad

Dressing:

1 clove garlic
½ cup extra-virgin olive oil
¼ cup mayonnaise
2 tablespoons freshly
    squeezed lemon juice
2 teaspoons Dijon mustard
1 teaspoon Worcestershire
    sauce
1 teaspoon anchovy paste,
    or chopped anchovies,
    or salt
1 teaspoon ground black
    pepper

Salad:

8 cups loosely packed romaine
    lettuce
½ cup shaved or grated
    Parmesan cheese
1 cup croutons
4 anchovy fillets (optional)

This classic salad, made with a creamy garlic dressing, is great with more than just Italian entrées. It adds a special touch to any meal it is served with, and becomes a meal in itself in the Chicken Caesar Wrap or Shrimp Caesar Wrap.

1. Prepare the dressing: In a food processor fitted with a metal chopping blade, with the motor running, add the garlic and purée. Add the oil, mayonnaise, lemon juice, mustard, Worcestershire sauce, anchovy paste, and pepper and process to combine. (You can also mix the dressing in a bowl using a wire whisk). Set aside.

2. Prepare the salad: In a large bowl, combine the lettuce and enough dressing to coat the lettuce. Add the cheese, croutons, and anchovies and toss again.

Greek Salad

This wonderful salad is loaded with crunchy cukes, red onions, tomatoes, kalamata olives, and feta cheese and is topped with an herbed-red wine vinaigrette. Try different kinds of feta cheese to find the one you like best. They vary in saltiness, and some are creamier than others. French feta is particularly good.

Dressing:
½ cup extra-virgin olive oil
¼ cup red wine vinegar
1 teaspoon Italian seasoning
1 teaspoon sugar

Salad:
5 cups loosely packed, chopped green or red leaf lettuce
1 cup seeded, chopped cucumbers
1 large ripe tomato, chopped
1 cup kalamata or Greek olives
¼ cup sliced red onions
¼ pound feta cheese, crumbled

1. Prepare the dressing: In a clean jar, add the oil, vinegar, Italian seasoning, and sugar and shake well to combine. (You can also mix the dressing in a bowl using a wire whisk). Set aside.
2. Prepare the salad: In a large bowl, combine the lettuce, cucumbers, tomatoes, olives, onions, feta cheese, and enough dressing to coat the salad. Toss to combine.

Mediterranean Salad

Dressing:

½ cup extra-virgin olive oil
¼ cup balsamic vinegar
1 tablespoon Dijon mustard
1 teaspoon sugar
½ teaspoon salt

Salad:

8 cups loosely packed,
    mesculan or other
    lettuce mix
1 cup seeded and chopped
    cucumbers
1 cup dried cranberries
2 tablespoons finely chopped
    chives (optional)
½ cup pine nuts, lightly
    toasted
¼ pound goat cheese,
    crumbled

This delectable combination pairs sweetened dried cranberries, creamy goat cheese, and toasted, buttery pignoli (also known as pine nuts) with a variety of mixed greens and a light vinaigrette. The combination of tastes, color, and texture will make this salad a favorite for everyday and entertaining. Look for packaged salad mixes that include a variety of baby lettuces, or mix your own using different greens, including arugula and raddicchio, for a more flavorful and colorful salad.

1. Prepare the dressing: In a clean jar, add the oil, vinegar, mustard, sugar, and salt and shake well to combine. (You can also mix the dressing in a bowl using a wire whisk). Set aside.

2. Prepare the salad: In a large bowl, combine the lettuce, cucumbers, cranberries, chives, and enough dressing to coat the salad. Toss to combine. Top with the pine nuts and goat cheese.

Pear, Walnut, Blue Cheese, and Arugula Salad

This unusual salad combines the sweetness of fall's ripe and succulent pears with the crunch of toasted walnuts and the piquancy of blue cheese. Use any lettuce you enjoy to balance the delightfully peppery arugula. For a special touch, make or buy spiced walnuts or pecans. This is a great salad for Thanksgiving or any autumnal dinner.

1. Prepare the dressing: In a clean jar, add the oil, vinegar, mustard, sugar, and salt and shake well to combine. (You can also mix the dressing in a bowl using a wire whisk). Set aside.
2. Prepare the salad: In a large bowl, combine the lettuce, arugula, onions, pears, and enough dressing to coat the salad. Toss to combine. Top with the walnuts and blue cheese.

Dressing:

½ cup extra-virgin olive or walnut oil
¼ cup balsamic vinegar
1 tablespoon Dijon mustard
1 teaspoon sugar
½ teaspoon salt

Salad:

5 cups loosely packed lettuce
3 cups loosely packed arugula
¼ cup thinly sliced red onions
3 ripe pears, peeled, cored, and sliced
1 cup chopped walnuts or pecans, lightly toasted
¼ pound blue cheese, crumbled

8
DESSERTS

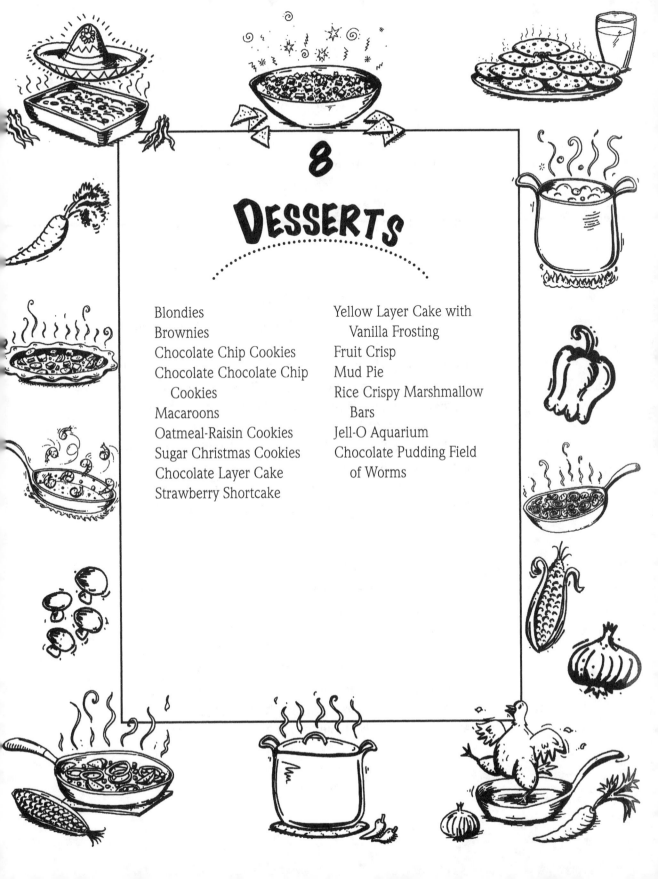

Blondies
Brownies
Chocolate Chip Cookies
Chocolate Chocolate Chip
  Cookies
Macaroons
Oatmeal-Raisin Cookies
Sugar Christmas Cookies
Chocolate Layer Cake
Strawberry Shortcake

Yellow Layer Cake with
  Vanilla Frosting
Fruit Crisp
Mud Pie
Rice Crispy Marshmallow
  Bars
Jell-O Aquarium
Chocolate Pudding Field
  of Worms

I find the desserts my family enjoys the most are the same treats I looked forward to when I was a girl: cookies, brownies, fruit crisps, Jell-O and pudding creations, ice cream pie, and most special of all, birthday layer cakes! These treasures, which bring so much joy, actually require very little effort and time. Most take less than fifteen minutes to prepare and require half an hour or less to bake. Best of all, when it comes time to make dessert, there is no shortage of assistants. With little helpers willing to do tasting and mixing, it's as much an activity as an event.

Cookie Tips:

- Always preheat the oven for at least fifteen minutes before baking.
- Most cookie dough can be easily mixed in a large bowl with a sturdy spoon or your hands. When using an electric mixer or food processor, periodically scrape down the sides and bottom of the bowl for more even blending.
- Baking cookies on baking sheets lined with parchment paper prevents burned bottoms, stops the dough from spreading, and keeps baking sheets from getting dirty. Parchment paper (available at most kitchen supply stores) can be wiped down and reused.
- To prevent excess spreading, refrigerate cookie dough for half an hour before baking.
- After baking, place cookies on a cooling rack to prevent burned cookie bottoms.
- When baking bar cookies, line the baking pan with aluminum foil for easier cleanup. To easily line baking pans, turn the pan upside down and mold a sheet of foil over the outside of the pan, then flip the pan over and drop the foil inside. If the recipe calls for a greased pan, lightly spray or grease the foil. After cooling, gently lift out the foil with the bar cookies.

- Check cookies a couple of minutes before the minimum baking time. It is better to underbake cookies and brownies than to overbake them. Cookies will continue to bake when they are removed from the oven and will harden as they cool.

Cake Tips:

- Always preheat the oven for at least fifteen minutes before baking.
- For optimal results, use ingredients at room temperature, unless directed otherwise. Leave refrigerated items out for one to two hours to achieve the proper temperature.
- An electric mixer does an excellent job of creaming butter and sugar together and aerating the batter. The air incorporated into the batter gives the cake its light and fine-grained texture.
- Although thorough beating is important when creaming butter, sugar, and eggs, mix the dry ingredients just until they combine with the batter. Overmixing dry ingredients will undo much of the aeration achieved through creaming.
- Layer cake pans should be between one-half and two-thirds full. Use any excess batter for cupcakes.
- Don't try to "save time" by increasing the oven temperature for faster results. You'll end up with an overcooked outside and an undercooked inside.
- A cake is done when the top looks dry, a toothpick inserted into the center comes out with no crumbs clinging, and the cake springs back (leaving no depression) when lightly touched in the center. If the cake has started to shrink away from the sides of the pan, it is done. If the other signs are present, do not wait for this or the cake could be slightly dry.
- To remove a cake from its pan, run a sharp knife or frosting spatula around the sides of the pans to prevent sticking.

Then cover the pan with an inverted cooling rack (or your hand) and flip it over. The cake should drop out. To re-invert the cake, so it is right side up, cover it again with a cooling rack (or your hand) and repeat the process. Let the cake finish cooling on the rack.

- Cool cakes completely before frosting them. Freezing a cake for an hour before adding frosting will make it more stable and reduces its crumbs.

Blondies

This bar version of chocolate chip cookies is also known as butterscotch brownies. Because the dough cooks in a pan, it frees you from having to check the oven as frequently as when making trays of individual cookies. For a little change, add 1 cup of chopped walnuts to the batter, or try using a combination of chocolate chips and butterscotch chips.

2½ cups all-purpose flour
2 teaspoons baking powder
½ teaspoon salt
1 cup (2 sticks) butter, melted
1½ cups firmly packed brown
    sugar
2 teaspoons vanilla extract
3 eggs
2 cups semisweet chocolate
    chips

Baking Time: 25 to 30 minutes
Makes: Approximately 36 blondies

1. Preheat the oven to 350 degrees. Lightly grease a 13 × 9 × 2-inch baking pan.
2. In a medium bowl, mix the flour, baking powder, and salt. Set aside.
3. In a large bowl, using a sturdy spoon or an electric mixer, combine the butter, brown sugar, and vanilla.
4. Add the eggs and beat until thoroughly combined.
5. Gradually add the dry ingredients and mix well.
6. Stir in the chocolate chips.
7. Pour the batter into the prepared pan. Smooth the top with a spatula.
8. Bake for 25 to 30 minutes, or until golden and a toothpick inserted in the center comes out almost clean. The blondies should still be slightly moist in the center, but should bounce back when touched.
9. Cool completely on a cooling rack before cutting.

Brownies

1¼ cups all-purpose flour
½ teaspoon baking powder
¼ teaspoon salt
1 cup (2 sticks) butter, melted
2 cups granulated sugar
1 tablespoon vanilla extract
3 eggs
¾ cup unsweetened cocoa
1½ cups semisweet chocolate
    chips

A dense, rich, fudgy brownie is always pretty hard to resist, but this super-chocolatey version is impossible to say no to. They are a snap to make, and any extras store beautifully in the freezer (just waiting to be transformed into brownie à la mode). For an attractive presentation, mix white chocolate chips or chunks with the semisweet chips; or, if you are a nut lover, add 1 cup of walnuts or pecans to the batter and sprinkle another ½ cup on top. The secret for sensational brownies is to slightly underbake them. This gives them their thick, lush texture. If you prefer a more cake-like brownie, bake for an additional 3 to 5 minutes, or until a toothpick inserted in the center comes out dry.

Baking Time: 30 to 35 minutes
Makes: Approximately 36 brownies

1. Preheat the oven to 350 degrees. Lightly grease a 13 × 9 × 2-inch baking pan.
2. In a medium bowl, mix the flour, baking powder, and salt. Set aside.
3. In a large bowl, using a sturdy spoon or an electric mixer, combine the butter, sugar, and vanilla.

4. Add the eggs and beat until well blended.
5. Add the cocoa and beat until thoroughly combined.
6. Gradually add the dry ingredients and mix well.
7. Stir in 1 cup of the chocolate chips.
8. Pour the batter into the prepared pan. Smooth the top with a spatula. Sprinkle the remaining ½ cup of chips on top.
9. Bake for 30 to 35 minutes, or until a toothpick inserted in the center comes out almost clean. The brownies should still be slightly moist in the center, but should bounce back when touched.
10. Cool completely on a cooling rack before cutting.

Chocolate Chip Cookies

2¼ cups all-purpose flour
1 teaspoon baking soda
½ teaspoon salt
1 cup (2 sticks) butter,
    softened
¾ cup granulated sugar
¾ cup firmly packed brown
    sugar
1 teaspoon vanilla extract
2 eggs
2 cups semisweet chocolate
    chips or chocolate
    chunks
1 cup chopped walnuts
    (optional)

This true classic will never go out of style. Today it has been updated to "monster-size"—cookies 4 or 5 inches in diameter, at least two or three times what was originally called for. For giant cookies, use a ¼-cup measure, place the cookies at least 4 inches apart, and add approximately 3 minutes to the baking time. For "gourmet" looking (and tasting) cookies, substitute 12 ounces of chopped chocolate from a high-quality semisweet or bittersweet chocolate bar for the chips.

Baking Time: 8 to 12 minutes
Makes: Approximately 48 2-inch cookies

1. Preheat the oven to 375 degrees.
2. In a medium bowl, mix the flour, baking soda, and salt. Set aside.
3. In a large bowl, using a sturdy spoon or an electric mixer, cream the butter until fluffy and lightened in color.
4. Add the white and brown sugars and beat until well blended.

5. Add the vanilla and eggs. Beat until thoroughly combined.
6. Gradually add the dry ingredients and mix well.
7. Stir in the chocolate chips and walnuts.
8. Drop the dough by rounded tablespoons 2 inches apart onto ungreased baking sheets.
9. Bake for 8 to 12 minutes, or until the cookies are golden and the edges are lightly browned.
10. Let stand for 1 minute. Remove the cookies from the baking sheets to a cooling rack.

Chocolate Chocolate Chip Cookies

2¼ cups all-purpose flour
1 teaspoon baking soda
½ teaspoon salt
¾ cup unsweetened cocoa
1 cup (2 sticks) butter,
    softened
¾ cup granulated sugar
¾ cup firmly packed brown
    sugar
2 teaspoons vanilla extract
2 eggs
2 cups semisweet chocolate
    chips or chocolate
    chunks

For true chocoholics, these cookies offer a double dose of delight—chocolate cookie dough and chocolate chips. A word of caution: Their darker color makes it harder to judge readiness. Be sure to start checking the cookies before the minimum cooking time and watch for burning edges and bottoms. Use insulated baking sheets, or double-stack two sheets to prevent overbaking. To add a little character, I like to combine white chocolate chips or chunks with semisweet chips.

Baking Time: 7 to 12 minutes
Makes: Approximately 48 cookies

1. Preheat the oven to 350 degrees.
2. In a medium bowl, mix the flour, baking soda, salt, and cocoa. Set aside.
3. In a large bowl, using a sturdy spoon or an electric mixer, cream the butter until fluffy and lightened in color.
4. Add the white and brown sugars and beat until well blended.
5. Add the vanilla and eggs. Beat until thoroughly combined.
6. Gradually add the dry ingredients and mix well.
7. Stir in the chocolate chips.

8. Drop the dough by rounded tablespoons 2 inches apart onto ungreased baking sheets.
9. Bake for 7 to 12 minutes, or until set, being careful not to burn. The centers will feel slightly firm to the touch.
10. Let stand for 1 minute. Remove the cookies from the baking sheets to a cooling rack.

Macaroons

⅓ cup all-purpose flour
2¾ cups shredded sweetened coconut (approximately 8 ounces)
⅛ teaspoon salt
⅔ cup sweetened condensed milk (not evaporated milk) (approximately 7 ounces)
1 teaspoon vanilla extract

I have been making these cookies with my son since he was two years old. Needing only five ingredients and no fancy mixing, they are easy enough for him to prepare. But be careful—they are so delicious, they are dangerously easy to eat. Two tips for fool-proof baking: Because macaroon dough tends to be a little sticky, line the baking sheets with parchment paper or greased aluminum foil for easier cleanup. Also, the cookie bottoms have a tendency to bake quickly. Use insulated baking sheets or double-stack baking sheets for better protection, and check the macaroon bottoms during baking. For a special treat, I like to dip my macaroon bottoms into melted dark chocolate after baking.

Baking Time: 13 to 18 minutes
Makes: Approximately 12 macaroons

1. Preheat the oven to 350 degrees. Grease a baking sheet well.
2. In a large bowl, mix the flour, coconut, and salt.
3. Add the condensed milk and vanilla and stir well. The batter will be thick and sticky.
4. Roll the dough into 2-inch balls or drop generous tablespoons onto the baking sheet about 2 inches apart. Bake for 13 to 18 minutes, or until the macaroons are golden and firm to the touch.
5. Remove the cookies from the baking sheet immediately to prevent sticking, and cool on a cooling rack.

Desserts

Oatmeal-Raisin Cookies

Here's another childhood favorite. These aromatic, chewy classics are wonderful on their own, with a large glass of cold milk, or with a steaming cup of hot tea. Use either quick-cooking or old-fashioned oats. Old-fashioned oats make chewier cookies; quick-cooking oats absorb moisture faster and tend to make crisper cookies. Do not use instant oatmeal.

1½ cups all-purpose flour
1 teaspoon baking soda
½ teaspoon salt
1 teaspoon ground cinnamon
½ teaspoon ground nutmeg (optional)
1 cup (2 sticks) butter, softened
1 cup firmly packed brown sugar
½ cup granulated sugar
1 teaspoon vanilla extract
2 eggs
3 cups uncooked oatmeal
1½ cups raisins

Baking Time: 8 to 12 minutes
Makes: Approximately 30 cookies

1. Preheat the oven to 375 degrees.
2. In a medium bowl, mix the flour, baking soda, salt, cinnamon, and nutmeg. Set aside.
3. In a large bowl, using a sturdy spoon or an electric mixer, cream the butter until fluffy and lightened in color.
4. Add both sugars and beat until well blended.
5. Add the vanilla and eggs. Beat until thoroughly combined.
6. Gradually add the dry ingredients and mix well.
7. Gradually add the oatmeal and raisins until combined.
8. Drop the dough by rounded tablespoons 2 inches apart onto ungreased baking sheets.
9. Bake for 8 to 12 minutes, or until the cookies are golden and the edges are lightly browned.
10. Let stand for 1 minute. Remove the cookies from the baking sheets to a cooling rack.

Sugar Christmas Cookies

Cookies:

2½ cups all-purpose flour
¼ teaspoon salt
1 teaspoon baking powder
1 cup (2 sticks) butter,
    softened
1 cup granulated sugar
2 teaspoons vanilla extract
1 egg
Colored sugar, sprinkles, or
    candies (optional)

Icing:

3 cups confectioners' sugar
2 to 3 tablespoons milk

Whether it's a holiday or not, it seems I am always making rolled sugar cookies for one school event or another. My son Alex loves picking out different cutters and then decorating the cookies, especially when candy is involved! While many people have a fear of rolling out cookie dough, once you get the hang of it, it's as easy as can be. Just make sure to follow these three rules and you'll have perfect cookies every time: First, refrigerate the dough until it is no longer sticky but is not so cold that it will crack during rolling. Second, use a light sprinkling of flour when rolling out the dough to prevent sticking. Third, don't roll the cookies too thinly, or they'll be difficult to handle.

Baking Time: 8 to 13 minutes
Makes: Approximately 48 cookies

1. Prepare the cookies: In a medium bowl, mix the flour, salt, and baking powder. Set aside.
2. In a large bowl, using a sturdy spoon or an electric mixer, cream the butter until fluffy and lightened in color.
3. Add the sugar and beat until well blended.
4. Add the vanilla and egg. Beat until thoroughly combined.
5. Gradually add the dry ingredients and mix well.
6. Scrape the dough onto a sheet of plastic wrap. It will be soft and sticky. Press the dough together to form a flat disc between ¼- and ½-inch thick. Wrap tightly

and refrigerate until firm, 1 to 2 hours (or freeze for 30 to 40 minutes).

7. When the cookies are ready to roll out, preheat the oven to 350 degrees. Take out the baking sheets.

8. On a lightly floured surface, with a lightly floured rolling pin, roll out the dough ⅛- to ¼-inch thick, lifting and turning the dough frequently to prevent sticking (add additional flour if necessary to prevent sticking). With flour-dipped cookie cutters or a sharp knife, cut the dough into desired shapes. Carefully transfer the shapes to ungreased baking sheets.

9. Decorate the cookies with colored sugars, sprinkles, or candies. If decorating cookies with icing, bake before frosting.

10. Bake for 8 to 13 minutes, or until the cookies are firm to the touch and the edges are golden.

11. Let the cookies stand for 1 minute. Remove the cookies from the baking sheets to a cooling rack. Cool completely before frosting.

12. Prepare the icing: Combine the confectioners' sugar with 2 tablespoons of milk. Mix until smooth and creamy, but stiff enough that the frosting does not flow from a spoon. If necessary, add additional milk or sugar, ½ teaspoon at a time, to reach the desired consistency. For a lighter glaze, add additional milk, ½ teaspoon at a time, until the mixture flows from a spoon. Spread the icing or glaze with a small spatula or brush. Top with sugar or candy decorations before the glaze dries. If you want to pipe icing on top of a glaze, wait for the glaze to dry first. Allow the decorated cookies to dry completely before storing (about 2 hours).

Chocolate Layer Cake

Cake:

2 cups all-purpose flour
1 teaspoon baking soda
½ teaspoon salt
¾ cup unsweetened cocoa
½ cup (1 stick) butter,
    softened
1½ cups granulated sugar
2 teaspoons vanilla extract
2 eggs
1¼ cups buttermilk

Frosting:

3¾ cups confectioners' sugar
    (1 pound)
½ cup unsweetened cocoa
½ cup (1 stick) butter,
    softened
1 teaspoon vanilla extract
⅓ cup milk (approximately)

> *This is the quintessential layer birthday cake. Rich and chocolatey, but not too sweet, with creamy chocolate frosting. It also makes great cupcakes for school and work parties. For foolproof decorating, the frosting should be soft, pliant, and smooth enough to spread without tearing the cake.*

Baking Time: 25 to 35 minutes
Serves: 12 to 14

1. Prepare the cake: Preheat the oven to 350 degrees. Lightly grease and flour two 9-inch cake pans.
2. In a medium bowl, mix the flour, baking soda, salt, and cocoa. Set aside.
3. In a large bowl, cream the butter, sugar, and vanilla with an electric mixer on medium speed until light and fluffy, about 2 minutes, stopping twice to scrape the bowl and beater(s) with a spatula.
4. Add the eggs, one at a time, beating well after each addition.
5. On low speed, alternate adding one-third of the dry ingredients with half of the buttermilk, mixing for 5 to 10 seconds after each addition. Do not blend each addition in fully before adding the next. When everything has been added, scrape the bowl and beater(s) and mix until blended and smooth (about 5 seconds). Do not overmix.
6. Divide the batter evenly between the prepared pans, and smooth the tops with a spatula. Place the pans on

the middle rack of the oven, leaving 2 inches between the pans and the oven walls.

7. Bake for 25 to 35 minutes, or until a toothpick inserted in the center comes out clean and the cakes spring back when lightly touched. Do not wait for the cakes to pull away from the sides of the pans.

8. Cool the cakes in their pans on a cooling rack for 15 minutes. Loosen the sides with a thin knife and carefully remove the cake layers. Cool completely before frosting.

9. Prepare the frosting: Pour the confectioners' sugar (1 cup at a time) and cocoa into a sifter or wire strainer placed over a medium bowl. Mix until blended.

10. In a large bowl, cream the butter with an electric mixer on medium speed until light and fluffy, about 1 minute.

11. Gradually add half of the dry ingredients and beat well.

12. Add the vanilla and half of the milk. The mixture will be dry and crumbly. Add the rest of the dry ingredients and enough milk for the desired spreading consistency. Beat on high until smooth.

· ·

Variations:

Cupcakes: *Line muffin tins with paper or foil liners. (Liners keep cupcakes moist and make them easier to remove.) Fill tins half to two-thirds full. Bake at 350 degrees for 18 to 23 minutes, or until the tops are firm and a toothpick inserted into a cupcake comes out clean. Cool the cupcakes completely in the tins on a cooling rack. Remove and frost. Makes 24 cupcakes.*

Sheet Cake: *Batter can be baked in a 13 × 9 × 2-inch pan. Bake a sheet cake for 35 to 45 minutes.*

· ·

Strawberry Shortcake

Strawberries:

2 pints strawberries, cleaned,
    hulled, and sliced
⅓ cup granulated sugar
8 to 12 whole strawberries,
    for garnish (optional)

Shortcake:

2 cups all-purpose flour
¼ cup granulated sugar
1 tablespoon baking powder
½ teaspoon salt
½ cup (1 stick) butter, chilled
    and cut into large
    pieces
⅔ cup milk, plus extra for
    glazing
3 tablespoons butter, softened

Whipped cream:

2 cups heavy cream
3 tablespoons confectioners'
    sugar
1 teaspoon vanilla extract

These individual shortcakes are a snap to prepare. Simple biscuits are filled with seasonally sweet strawberries and the always-welcomed whipped cream. But don't limit yourself to just strawberries. Choose from the farmers' markets' finest: blueberries, peaches, and raspberries are all delicious!

Baking Time: 13 to 18 minutes
Serves: 8 to 10

1. Preheat the oven to 450 degrees. Take out a baking sheet.
2. Prepare the strawberries: In a medium bowl, mix the strawberries with the sugar. Set aside.
3. Prepare the shortcakes: In a food processor fitted with a metal chopping blade, add the flour, sugar, baking powder, and salt. Pulse to combine (about 4 pulses).
4. Add the butter and pulse until the mixture resembles coarse crumbs (about 10 pulses).
5. Add the milk and pulse until just combined and evenly moistened (about 4 or 5 pulses). Do not allow the dough to form a ball. (Shortcakes can also be made easily by hand. Combine the dry ingredients in a bowl. Add the butter and work the mixture with your fingertips until it resembles coarse crumbs. Add the milk and stir gently until just combined.)

6. Transfer the dough to a lightly floured surface. Knead, by pushing the dough with the palms of your hands, for about 30 seconds to make the dough less sticky.

7. Pat or gently roll the dough until it is ½-inch thick. Using lightly floured 3-inch round cookie cutters or a knife, cut out the biscuits (scraps can be pressed together for additional biscuits). Transfer the biscuits to an ungreased baking sheet and brush the tops with milk.

8. Bake for 13 to 18 minutes, or until golden and the tops are firm.

9. Cool the shortcakes on a cooling rack for 10 minutes. Split the cakes horizontally into 2 layers and spread the cut sides lightly with butter.

10. Just before serving, prepare the whipped cream: In a large bowl, with an electric mixer on medium-high speed, whip the cream to soft peaks. Add the sugar and vanilla and beat until stiff peaks form. Do not overbeat.

11. Place the bottoms of the shortcakes, cut side up, on a serving plate. Top with the strawberries and whipped cream. Place remaining shortcake on top, cut side down. Top with strawberries and whipped cream. Garnish with whole strawberries.

Yellow Layer Cake with Vanilla Frosting

Cake:

2½ cups cake flour
2 teaspoons baking powder
½ teaspoon salt
¾ cup (1½ sticks) butter, softened
1½ cups granulated sugar
1 teaspoon vanilla extract
3 eggs
1 cup milk

Frosting:

3¾ cups confectioners' sugar (1 pound)
½ cup (1 stick) butter, softened
2 teaspoons vanilla extract
¼ cup milk (approximately)

Celebrating has never been easier! This light and luscious butter cake is perfect for any holiday or event. Chocolate frosting is also good with the cake.

Baking Time: 25 to 35 minutes
Serves: 12 to 14

1. Prepare the cake: Preheat the oven to 350 degrees. Lightly grease and flour two 9-inch cake pans.
2. In a medium bowl, mix the cake flour, baking powder, and salt. Set aside.
3. In a large bowl, cream the butter, sugar, and vanilla with an electric mixer on medium speed until light and fluffy, about 2 minutes, stopping twice to scrape the bowl and beater(s) with a spatula.
4. Add the eggs, one at a time, beating well after each addition.
5. On low speed, alternate adding one-third of the dry ingredients with half of the milk, mixing for 5 to 10 seconds after each addition. Do not blend each addition in fully before adding the next. When everything has been added, scrape the bowl and beater(s), and mix until blended and smooth (about 5 seconds). Do not overmix.
6. Divide the batter evenly between the prepared pans and smooth the tops with a spatula. Place the pans on the middle rack of the oven, leaving 2 inches between the pans and the oven walls.

7. Bake for 25 to 35 minutes, or until lightly golden, a toothpick inserted in the center comes out clean, and the cakes spring back when lightly touched. Do not wait for the cakes to pull away from the sides of the pans.

8. Cool the cakes in their pans on a cooling rack for 15 minutes. Loosen the sides with a thin knife and carefully remove the cake layers. Cool completely before frosting.

9. Prepare the frosting: Pour the confectioners' sugar (1 cup at a time) into a sifter or wire strainer placed over a medium bowl.

10. In a large bowl, cream the butter with an electric mixer on medium speed until light and fluffy, about 1 minute.

11. Gradually add half of the sugar and beat well.

12. Add the vanilla and half of the milk. The mixture will be dry and crumbly. Add the rest of the sugar and enough milk for the desired spreading consistency. Beat on high until smooth.

••••••••••••••••••••

Variations:

Cupcakes: *Line muffin tins with paper or foil liners. (Liners keep cupcakes moist and make them easier to remove.) Fill tins half to two-thirds full. Bake at 350 degrees for 18 to 23 minutes, or until the tops are firm and a toothpick inserted into a cupcake comes out clean. Cool the cupcakes completely in the tins on a cooling rack. Remove and frost. Makes 24 cupcakes.*

Sheet Cake: *Batter can be baked in a 13 × 9 × 2-inch pan. Bake a sheet cake for 35 to 45 minutes.*

••••••••••••••••••••

Fruit Crisp

Fruit Filling:

5 to 6 cups fruit or berries
2 tablespoons fresh lemon
      juice (optional)
2 tablespoons all-purpose flour
½ cup granulated sugar

Topping:

1 cup all-purpose flour
1 cup firmly packed brown
      sugar
½ cup uncooked oatmeal
      (optional)
2 teaspoons ground cinnamon
¼ teaspoon salt
½ cup (1 stick) butter, cut into
      pieces

This delicious fruit dessert is easy to assemble and is a wonderful way to end a meal all year round. For the best taste, choose fruit in season, at the peak of its flavor. In the fall and winter, use apples and pears. In the summer, try a combination of blueberries, strawberries, peaches, and cherries. For a more attractive presentation, bake and serve the crisp in a deep, decorative, ovenproof baking dish.

Baking Time: 35 to 45 minutes
Serves: 6 to 8

1. Preheat the oven to 375 degrees.
2. Prepare the fruit filling: In a 1½- to 2-quart baking dish, mix the fruit, lemon juice, flour, and sugar. Set aside.
3. Prepare the topping: In a food processor fitted with a metal chopping blade, add the flour, brown sugar, oats, cinnamon, and salt. Pulse to mix (about 4 pulses).

4. Add the butter and pulse until the mixture is moistened but crumbly (about 5 to 10 pulses).
5. Sprinkle the topping over the fruit.
6. Bake for 35 to 45 minutes, or until the top is browned and crisp and the filling is bubbling. Check during the second half of baking to make sure the top is not over-browning and that the filling is not bubbling over. Shield the top with foil and/or slip a foil-covered baking sheet under the crisp if necessary.
7. Cool slightly on a cooling rack. Serve warm.

Mud Pie

Cookie Crust:

1½ cups cookie crumbs
(approximately 30
chocolate wafers or
15 Oreos)
¼ cup (½ stick) butter, melted
2 tablespoons sugar

Hot Fudge Sauce:

½ cup heavy cream
2 tablespoons butter, cut in
pieces
2 cups semisweet chocolate
chips (12 ounces)
1 teaspoon vanilla extract

1 quart coffee ice cream (or
other flavor)

Whipped Cream:

1 cup heavy cream
2 tablespoons confectioners'
sugar
½ teaspoon vanilla extract

> This sought-after summertime dessert layers creamy ice cream, gooey fudge, and wonderful whipped cream in a crunchy chocolate-cookie crust. It has everyone's favorite flavors together in each bite. Choose your family's special ice cream, or layer different flavors to please everyone. Allow time for the pie to properly chill.

Baking Time: 5 minutes
Serves: 6 to 8

1. Preheat the oven to 350 degrees.
2. Prepare the cookie crust: Combine the crumbs, butter, and sugar in a food processor or medium bowl. Blend until moistened and smooth. Press the crust evenly into the bottom of a 9-inch pie pan.
3. Bake the crust for 5 minutes. Cool completely on a cooling rack.
4. Prepare the hot fudge sauce: In a saucepan on low heat, warm the cream and butter until just simmering (little bubbles form around edges).
5. Add the chocolate chips and stir until dissolved.
6. Add the vanilla and stir until completely blended. Remove from the heat and cool the sauce completely.

7. Spoon ½ cup of fudge into the crust. Freeze the crust for 30 minutes.
8. Soften the ice cream to spreading consistency. Fill the crust with ice cream, mounding up the center.
9. Freeze the pie for 1 to 2 hours, or until firm.
10. Spread the remaining fudge over the top of the ice cream, covering it completely. Smooth the top. Freeze for 30 minutes, or until serving.
11. Just before serving, prepare the whipped cream: In a large bowl, with an electric mixer on medium-high speed, whip the cream to soft peaks. Add the sugar and vanilla and beat until stiff peaks form. Do not overbeat. Spread the whipped cream on top of the fudge or pipe it decoratively around the edges of the crust.
12. Let the pie soften for 10 minutes for easier slicing.

Rice Crispy Marshmallow Bars

3 tablespoons butter
10 ounces marshmallows
    (approximately 40)
6 cups puffed rice cereal

These chewy rice cereal–marshmallow bars need no baking, so they're perfect for a quickly needed dessert or lunch box snack. For easier cleanup, line your pan with aluminum foil, leaving a 1-inch overhang, before adding the cereal mixture. After cooling, lift the foil and crispy bars out of the pan and peel off the foil. Use fresh marshmallows for best flavor and texture.

Baking Time: None
Makes: Approximately 36 bars

1. Lightly grease a 13 × 9 × 2-inch baking pan.
2. In a medium saucepan, over low heat melt the butter.
3. Add the marshmallows, coat with butter, and stir until melted and smooth. Remove from the heat. (To melt the butter and marshmallows in the microwave, cook them together on high for 2 minutes. Stir to combine and microwave 1 minute more. Stir until smooth.)
4. Add the rice cereal to the marshmallow mixture in 3 batches, stirring to coat it well after each addition.
5. Using a lightly greased spatula, transfer the mixture to the baking pan. Distribute the mixture evenly.
6. Cool the mixture completely in the pan before cutting.

Jell-O Aquarium

I found the idea for this recipe in a parents' magazine and fell in love with it. Gummy fish and worms are added to crystal blue Jell-O to form an edible ocean. If you have an empty goldfish bowl, serve the dessert in it for a truly unusual presentation. If not, use a deep, medium-sized, clear glass bowl for optimum visual impact.

1 6-ounce package Berry Blue Jell-O, or other blue gelatin dessert mix
2 cups boiling water
2 cups cold water
12–16 gummy fish, worms, or other edible aquatic life

Baking Time: None
Serves: 4

1. In a medium glass bowl, pour in the Jell-O mix. Add the boiling water and stir until completely dissolved, at least 2 minutes.
2. Stir in 2 cups cold water.
3. Refrigerate until the Jell-O just begins to set, about 1½ hours. It should still be in a liquid state, but thickening.
4. Using your fingers or a sharp knife, press the gummy fish into the Jell-O, at varying depths, so the fish are swimming at different levels, as if creating a fish tank. Refrigerate for 1½ to 2 hours, or until completely set.

Chocolate Pudding Field of Worms

16 Oreo cookies, or other
    chocolate sandwich
    cookies, crushed
1 5-ounce package Jell-O
    Cook & Serve choco-
    late pudding, or other
    pudding mix
3 cups milk
12 gummy worms

This unappetizing title doesn't give this dessert its due. This kid-friendly treat pairs chocolate pudding with crushed Oreo cookies to simulate a muddy field crawling with candy gummy worms. It's a gruesomely delicious and devastatingly easy dessert.

Baking Time: None
Serves: 4

1. In a 9 × 9-inch or 8 × 8-inch baking pan, layer half of the Oreos, reserving the rest.
2. In a medium saucepan over medium heat, dissolve the pudding mix into the milk.
3. Stir constantly until the mixture comes to a full boil. Remove from the heat.
4. Add the chocolate pudding to the Oreos, cover the surface with plastic wrap, and refrigerate for 1 hour, or until ready to serve.
5. Top with remaining Oreos. Arrange gummy worms as if they are crawling on top of and in the cookie "dirt."

Index

INTERNATIONAL CONVERSION CHART

These are not exact equivalents: they've been slightly rounded to make measuring easier.

LIQUID MEASUREMENTS

American	Imperial	Metric	Australian
2 tablespoons (1 oz.)	1 fl. oz.	30 ml	1 tablespoon
¼ cup (2 oz.)	2 fl. oz.	60 ml	2 tablespoons
⅓ cup (3 oz.)	3 fl. oz.	80 ml	¼ cup
½ cup (4 oz.)	4 fl. oz.	125 ml	⅓ cup
⅔ cup (5 oz.)	5 fl. oz.	165 ml	½ cup
¾ cup (6 oz.)	6 fl. oz.	185 ml	⅔ cup
1 cup (8 oz.)	8 fl. oz.	250 ml	¾ cup

SPOON MEASUREMENTS

American	Metric
¼ teaspoon	1 ml
½ teaspoon	2 ml
1 teaspoon	5 ml
1 tablepoon	15 ml

OVEN TEMPERATURES

Fahrenheit	Centigrade	Gas
250	120	½
300	150	2
325	160	3
350	180	4
375	190	5
400	200	6
450	230	8

WEIGHTS

US/UK	Metric
1 oz.	30 grams (g)
2 oz.	60 g
4 oz. (¼ lb)	125 g
5 oz. (⅓ lb)	155 g
6 oz.	185 g
7 oz.	220 g
8 oz. (½ lb)	250 g
10 oz.	315 g
12 oz. (¾ lb)	375 g
14 oz.	440 g
16 oz. (1 lb)	500 g
2 lbs.	1 kg